Charles Starkweather's Confession to the Murders of Caril Ann Fugate's Mother, Stepfather, and Baby Sister

"The old lady Bartlett said she was going to chop my head off . . . I grabbed the gun from Caril. I just turned around and shot her.

"After I hit the old lady, I just came up with the butt of the gun and hit the little girl. She fell down against the table, and stood there screaming. Caril was yelling at her to shut up."

At that point, Charlie said, Caril warned him that her stepfather was still alive.

"The little girl kept yelling, and I told her to shut up, and I started to walk again, and just turned around and threw the kitchen knife I had at her. They said it hit her in the throat, but I thought it hit her in the chest. I went on into the bedroom. Mr. Bartlett was moving around quite a bit, so I tried to stab him in the throat, but the knife wouldn't go in, and I just hit the top part of it with my hand, and it went in."

WASTE LAND

Books by Michael Newton

Daddy Was the Black Dahlia Killer
Waste Land: The Savage Odyssey of
    Charles Starkweather and Caril Ann Fugate

Published by POCKET BOOKS

waste land

Michael Newton

POCKET BOOKS
New York   London   Toronto   Sydney   Tokyo   Singapore

An *Original* Publication of POCKET BOOKS

POCKET BOOKS, a division of Simon & Schuster Inc.
1230 Avenue of the Americas, New York, NY 10020

Copyright © 1998 by Michael Newton

All rights reserved, including the right to reproduce
this book or portions thereof in any form whatsoever.
For information address Pocket Books, 1230 Avenue
of the Americas, New York, NY 10020

ISBN: 0-671-00198-1

First Pocket Books printing February 1998

10 9 8 7 6 5 4 3 2 1

POCKET and colophon are registered trademarks of
Simon & Schuster Inc.

Cover photos courtesy of AP/Wide World Photos
(top left and right), and © Michael Darter/Photonica (bottom)

Printed in the U.S.A.

*For Don Pendleton, without
whom . . .
God keep.*

Acknowledgments

Many people make a book possible. Special thanks for this one are due to my agent, Nancy Yost, at Barbara Lowenstein Associates; and to my editor, Linda Marrow, at Simon & Schuster. Dave Frasier, at Indiana University in Bloomington, provided critical assistance on the research end, despite a full-time job and busy writing schedule of his own. Thanks, bro'. Here's blood in your eye.

Adolescents tend to be passionate people, and passion is no less real because it is directed toward a hot-rod, a commercialized popular singer, or the leader of a black-jacketed gang.

—Edgar Z. Friedenberg,
The Vanishing Adolescent

As a dimension of man, rebellion actually defines him.

—Robert Lindner,
Must You Conform?

So much of adolescence is an ill-defined dying.
An intolerable waiting,
A longing for another place and time,
Another condition.

—Theodore Roethke,
"I'm Here"

Death is the supreme festival on the road to freedom.

—Dieterich Bonhoeffer,
Letters and Papers from Prison

Contents

CONTENTS

Prologue

Teenage Waste Land

The Fifties.

Looking back, through the distorting lens of memory, It seems to be a golden time. Prosperity. The baby boom. Tract homes and stylish cars. Walt Disney. Buddy Holly. Marilyn Monroe. Ozzie and Harriet. The hula hoop. A little help from Hollywood transforms the postwar decade into *Happy Days*, where everybody rocks—and smiles—around the clock. Their biggest problem is the local malt shop closing down.

Like most myths, the illusion of the Fabulous Fifties has a kernel of truth. You didn't have to live in California to enjoy the sights of Disneyland, once television took the place of radio in American homes, and Fess Parker's "Ballad of Davy Crockett" sold four million copies, its spinoff craze bumping the price of raccoon skins to eight dollars a pound. *McCall's* magazine introduced "togetherness," a concept so popular that it took on the aspect of a social crusade and became the next best thing to a national purpose in the 1950s. Billy Graham put a slick new face on fundamentalism, while Dr. Norman Vincent Peale hawked the power of positive thinking. The "beat generation" bought half a million copies of Jack Kerouac's *On the Road,* despite a warning from Truman Capote that "It isn't writing at all—it's typing." Elvis Presley stormed the *Billboard* charts, followed closely by The Big Bopper and Bill Haley's Comets. The Edsel may have been a $400 million lemon, but at least it was good for a laugh: a model so despised that it was shunned by car thieves. There was even a bright side to nuclear war, as viewed through an ad in the *Pittsburgh Press:* "The bomb's brilliant gleam reminds me of the brilliant gleam Beacon Wax gives to floors. It's a science marvel!"

There was, of course, another side to the America of Richie Cunningham and *I Love Lucy.* Cold War paranoia was a daily fact of life, with *Sputnik* in the heavens, Joe McCarthy in the U.S. Senate, soldiers dying in Korea, and the Rosenbergs en route to the electric chair. In race relations, a "new Negro" demanded social equality, touching off riots from Cicero to Little Rock, church bombings in Alabama, and lynchings in darkest Mississippi. The televised Kefauver hearings turned a spotlight on organized crime, but most Americans were less concerned about the Mafia than the emerging savagery of their own children. The lovable delinquent, à la Henry Winkler's Fonzie, is a figment of the screenwriter's imagination, nowhere to be found in those grim days of leather jackets, sideburns, and switchblades, when J. Edgar Hoover ranked "the juvenile jungle" as a menace second only to international communism.

Charles Starkweather was America's worst nightmare in the early months of 1958, a sneering teenage rebel with a ducktail haircut and a brooding grudge against society that had to be repaid in blood. His very name bespoke adversity and suffering. With fourteen-year-old girlfriend Caril Ann Fugate, Charlie killed eleven persons in a two-month rampage, all but one of them within a grisly week of slaughter that made headlines coast to coast. The victims included Caril's parents and infant sister, a longtime friend of Charlie's family, and seven total strangers. Even worse, the timing and location of the slaughter shook America to its foundations: random murder in the staid

Nebraska heartland, midway through the second term of President Dwight D. Eisenhower. If it could happen in Nebraska, it could happen *anywhere.*

They should have seen him coming, though.

The warning signs were there, not only in the killer's narrow eyes, but all around, in a society that gave "teenagers" a label and distinct identity for the first time in history, dwelling on their "difference" in an endless stream of books, editorials, and lectures. Robert Lindner, a prison psychologist gone straight, explored the issue in *Rebel Without a Cause,* defining his subject as "a religious disobeyer of prevailing codes and standards . . . an agitator without a slogan, a revolutionary without a program . . . incapable of exertions for the sake of others." Two years later, in *Must You Conform?,* Lindner warned that the era's demands for a pliable "mass man" were in danger of mass-producing hair-trigger psychopathic personalities.

And, indeed, it seemed to be a self-fulfilling prophecy, with soaring juvenile crime rates, glue-sniffing and "chicken" runs, zip guns and rumbles. For any slow starters on the road to ruin, a do-it-yourself delinquency kit was as close as the neighborhood theater.

Director Stanley Kramer set the tone in 1953. An article in *Harper's* caught his eye, about a 1947 mini-riot in the town of Hollister, California, where "outlaw" bikers took the streets and briefly ran amok. In Kramer's view— mirrored by "gonzo" journalist Hunter Thompson a decade later—those drunken louts became the last American "individualists," and his celluloid homage, *The Wild One,* made two-wheel hoodlums the symbol of rebellion for a generation. A young Marlon Brando is "Johnny," leading his Black Rebels motorcycle gang into "Wrightsville" and shouting at the world: "A man don't go his own way, he's *nothin'.*" Johnny's dialogue with "nice girl" Cathy could have been a script for 1950s teenage angst.

JOHNNY: On weekends, we just go out and have a ball.
CATHY: What do you do? I mean, do you just ride

around or do you go on some sort of picnic
or something?

JOHNNY: A *picnic*? Man, you are *too square*! I have to
straighten you out. You don't go any one
special place—that's cornball style. You just
go (*snaps his fingers*). A bunch of us get
together after all week and it builds up. The
idea is to have a *ball*. Now, if you're gonna
stay *cool,* you've got to *wail.* You gotta put
something down. You gotta make some *jive.*
Don't you know what I'm talkin' about?

CATHY: Yeah. Yeah, I know what you mean.

JOHNNY: Well, that's all I'm sayin'.

CATHY: My father was going to take me on a fishing
trip to Canada once.

JOHNNY: Yeah?

CATHY: We didn't go.

JOHNNY: Crazy.

When Cathy asks Johnny what he's rebelling against, he
replies with the classic line: "Whaddya got?"

Across America, real-life bikers competed to imitate
Brando's crazy-cool image. Frank Sadilek, president of the
Hell's Angels' San Francisco chapter, drove to Hollywood
and purchased the striped T-shirt worn by Lee Marvin in
The Wild One. Brando's leather cap and jacket were,
presumably, unavailable.

For all his youthful charisma on screen, Nebraska-born
Brando faced stiff competition from another Midwestern
native in the teen-idol department. James Dean was a third-
generation Hoosier whose father could trace his lineage back
to the *Mayflower.* The family moved to California in 1935,
when James was four years old, and his mother died of breast
cancer four years later. Dean struggled in school, reluctant to
acknowledge his poor eyesight, and grew up as a disaffected
loner. In Hollywood, he idolized Brando and Montgomery
Clift, leaving messages with their answering services, so
enraged when they ignored him that he was driven to

"retaliate," calling back and playing "Hound Dog" at full volume, through the telephone. When Clift was told of Dean's obsessive interest in his work, he asked, "Who *is* that fucking creep?" Dean followed Brando to a string of cocktail parties, sometimes dressed as Johnny from *The Wild One*, until Brando took him aside and asked Dean if he "realized he was sick." ("At least his *work* improved," says Brando, looking back.) In letters to his friends, Dean sometimes signed himself "James-Brando-Clift-Dean."

By all accounts, Dean was the odd man out in Tinseltown. A bisexual who registered as gay with his draft board to avoid military service, his sadomasochistic tendencies earned him a reputation as "the human ashtray"—confirmed posthumously by a coroner's report describing a "constellation of keratoid scars" on his torso. Andy Warhol called Dean "the damaged but beautiful soul of our time," but those who knew him personally took a different view. Acting coach Lee Strasberg thought Dean "belonged in the nut-house," while writer-director Elia Kazan found him "revolting" and "a pudding of hatred." When Dennis Hopper asked Dean why he had become an actor, Dean replied, "Because I hate my mother and father. I wanted to get up on stage . . . and I wanted to *show* them."

Dean's rage was palpable, on screen and off. He kept a .45-caliber pistol on the movie lot and earned a reputation for beating his girlfriends while high on a mixture of alcohol, grass, and amphetamines. Leonard Rosenman, a friend of Dean's, recalls that he was "absolutely suicidal with a car," but Jimmy cherished speed. "It's the only time I feel whole," he explained. And while he liked to quote a line from Nicholas Ray's *Knock on Any Door*—"Live fast, die young, and leave a good-looking corpse"—Dean also brandished the prospect of his own annihilation like a weapon, childishly screaming at one lover who abandoned him, "When I die, it'll be your fault!" Lee Strasberg saw the "doomed quality" in Dean and asked if there was anything the young actor respected. Dean replied:

5

That's easy. Death. It's the only thing left to respect. It's the one inevitable, undeniable truth. Everything else can be questioned. But death is truth. In it lies the only mobility for man, and beyond it the only hope.

Back in Nebraska, Charlie Starkweather was listening. He heard Dean, loud and clear.

Dean found his hope on September 30, 1955, four days before his second movie—*Rebel Without a Cause*—opened in theaters nationwide. One studio executive called the fatal car crash a "great career move," but for thousands of teenage fans, Dean had assumed a kind of immortality. A year after the funeral, his studio was still receiving two thousand letters a week, addressed to a dead man. *Picture Post* observed that "America has known many rebellions but none like this. Millions of teenage rebels heading for nowhere, some in hot-rod cars, others on the blare of rock 'n' roll music, some with guns in their hands. And at their head is a dead leader."

Author John Dos Passos saw Dean as one of "the Sinister Adolescents," and his appeal was irresistible. Young Elvis Presley, still more often reviled for singing "black music" than revered as The King, told a reporter, "I know by heart all the dialogue of James Dean's films. I could watch *Rebel* a hundred times over." Another young musician, Robert Zimmerman—later Bob Dylan—emerged from a viewing of *Rebel* to mimic Dean's blue jeans and boots, his slouch and smirk, with a leather jacket added in homage to Brando. In California, teenager Carroll Edward Cole, with one murder behind him and fourteen to go, stood before his mirror by the hour, combing and recombing his hair in Dean's style until the muscles in his arm began to cramp.

And then, there was Charlie Starkweather.

Out in Lincoln, Nebraska, growing up poor on the wrong side of the tracks, he was obsessed with Dean, working overtime to perfect the look that Dean biographer Graham McCann has called "a mixture of moodiness and myopia."

Starkweather's sister says, "He used to pose like James Dean. He'd stand there with a cigarette hanging from out of the front of his mouth. You know, with the lips apart so that his teeth would show." It was more than simple mimicry, however. Charlie almost felt that they were brothers, with a kind of psychic bond that reached beyond the grave. Both handicapped in school by their nearsightedness. Both filled with hatred for a world of mocking peers and cold, unfeeling adults. Dean felt what Charlie felt; he made it obvious on-screen. Was it a mere coincidence that Jimmy's character in *Rebel* had been named "Jim Stark"?

In fact, Dean's whole persona cried out to American youth, defining their generation and their plight. Dennis Hopper called Dean "the first American teenager," while one critic labeled *Rebel Without a Cause* "the touchstone for generational strife in the 1950s." Co-star Sal Mineo explained that "Before James Dean you were either a baby or a man. There was nothing in between." François Truffaut agreed.

> In James Dean, today's youth discovers itself. Less for the reasons usually advanced: violence, sadism, hysteria, cruelty and filth, than for others infinitely more simple and commonplace: modesty of feeling, continual fantasy life, moral purity without relation to everyday morality but all the more rigorous, eternal adolescent love of tests and trials, intoxication, pride and regret at feeling oneself "outside" society, refusal and desire to become integrated and, finally, acceptance—or refusal—of the world as it is.

And what a world it was for young people coming of age in the 1950s. Unparalleled prosperity bloomed in the shadow of nuclear holocaust, with grade-school students drilled in "duck and cover" exercises, as if crawling underneath a desk could save them from The Bomb. China had fallen, and the other Asian dominoes were all at risk. For some teens, living fast and dying young was not a choice, it was the only game in town. What was the harm in getting drunk and running "chicken" races, when their elders might incinerate the world by suppertime?

The madness was not limited to teenagers, of course. In Camden, New Jersey, twenty-eight-year-old Howard Unruh went for a twelve-minute stroll through his neighborhood, packing a 9-millimeter Luger, and killed thirteen victims before he ran out of bullets. "I'm no psycho," the Bible-reading army veteran told police. "I have a good mind." And added: "I'd have killed a thousand if I'd had bullets enough."

Charlie Starkweather knew the feeling.

He could sympathize, as well, with William Cook, a twenty-one-year-old drifter, nicknamed "Bad Eye" for the physical deformity that made him an object of ridicule in school and in the juvenile detention homes where he spent much of his adolescence. Cook tattooed his knuckles with the legend H-A-R-D-L-U-C-K, terrorizing Middle America with a two-week rampage of kidnapping and murder that left six persons dead. Captured in Mexico and returned to the U.S. for trial and ultimately execution, Cook explained his motive to a court-appointed lawyer: "I hate them. I hate their guts—everybody!"

In Lincoln, Charlie Starkweather was building up to an explosion of his own.

Eleven years before another Charlie—Manson—told Americans to watch out for their homicidal children, Starkweather and Caril Ann Fugate drove the message home with blades and bullets, stopping only when their car ran out of gas and they ran out of luck. If Dean and Brando were the poster children for a generation run amok, then Starkweather and Fugate were the word made flesh. Their bloody trek across the heartland represents a turning point as grim and critical as Dallas or Kent State. It taught Americans to look for enemies around the breakfast table, rather than in Moscow or Havana. We have not forgotten Charlie yet, and likely never will.

His grisly handprints were the writing on the wall.

1

The Charnel House

The smell of death is unforgettable, unique. No hunter who has found a rotting carcass in the wild, no law enforcement officer who's worked a murder scene, will ever have a problem picking out that smell a second time. It marks you. Having savored it and traced it to its source, you are among the ones who *know*. And having gained that knowledge, you are never quite the same again.

It was around four-thirty in the afternoon of Monday, January 27, 1958, when Bob Von Busch first sampled death's aroma. He had hardly spoken on the drive to Belmont, Lincoln's "white trash" suburb, and he wasn't talking now. He sat and smoked a cigarette, examining the Bartlett house and wondering why he was suddenly afraid.

The house itself was nothing to be scared of. Just a run-down hovel like its neighbors, five small rooms, with asphalt siding on the outer walls that was supposed to look like brick. There was no plumbing in the house—or in the neighborhood, for that matter. The tenants did their business in a privy, out in back. Von Busch had never seen the house in good condition, when it didn't need some manner of repair. His father-in-law, Marion Bartlett, was a great idea man, but he seldom followed through on any project he began.

Bob turned to Rodney Starkweather and said, "What do you think?"

The young man shrugged and shook his head. "I don't know what to think," he said. "I'm kinda wondering if Charlie went off the deep end, you know? Too many weird things going on. And I ain't never seen Caril lookin' like she did today, so scared and all. I don't know what to make of it."

Bob faced the house again. The family car was sitting right there in the driveway, where it had been for the best part of a week, no sign that it had moved an inch in all that time. How could the Bartletts take off on vacation like the cops were saying, and forget their car?

"I'd feel a whole lot better if we went ahead and checked the house real good," Bob said. "I don't believe the cops looked out in back. They got that old outhouse and chicken coop back there, you know."

"I guess we'd better," Rodney said, reluctance showing on his face.

They left the car together, crossed the scruffy little yard, and stepped up to the front door of the house. There was a yellow piece of paper on the screen door, stirring in the breeze, with childlike writing on it.

Stay a way Every Body is sick with The Flue
                                                    Miss Bartlett

That was something else, Bob thought. If everyone was sick, the way Caril Ann had said, it seemed impossible that they would all be cured at once, without a doctor's help, and take off on a trip to God knows where. More than peculiar; it was downright weird. And who the hell was this "Miss Bartlett," anyway? Bob's mother-in-law was *Mrs*. Bartlett, and Caril Ann used her daddy's last name: Fugate. That left

Betty Jean, but she was under three years old and damn sure couldn't write a note.

Bob knocked and waited. No one answered. When he tried the door, he found it locked.

"Well, shit," he said, "let's see if we can get a window open."

One by one, they tried the windows. Every one of them was latched, the flimsy curtains drawn. Bob felt an urge to smash the glass and reach inside, unlock a window, find out what was going on, but reason stopped him.

"Rodney, bring the car around in back, up through the alley," Bob instructed. "Lemme check the back door, and I'll meet you by the outhouse."

"Right."

Bob walked around the silent house and tried the back door, none too gently. It was no surprise, by now, to find it locked. He heard tires crunching over gravel in the alley, Rodney coming up behind him with the car, and turned to face the outbuildings beyond a sagging clothesline, strung from cruciform supports. The privy and adjacent chicken coop were built from mismatched planks and scraps of lumber, long since weathered gray. The yard between them and the house was strewn with junk, more frozen mud than dry brown grass.

Bob was almost to the privy when Rodney stepped out of the car, sniffing the air. "You smell something?" he asked.

"I smell an outhouse," Bob responded, feeling testy. "What'n hell am I supposed to smell?"

Rodney sniffed again and shook his head. "Don't smell like shit," he answered. "It smells kinda sweet."

"Shut up!" Bob snapped, already reaching for the privy's door. "I'm spooked enough, the way it is."

The door swung open, and he stuck his head inside.

It had begun for Bob Von Busch on Saturday, the twenty-fifth. He had been sitting at the kitchen table, paging through the *Lincoln Star,* when Barbara started in on him again, about her family. It wasn't like Barb's mother to be out of touch so long. A week had passed since Velda Bartlett promised to stop by with photos she had taken of her grandchild—Bob and Barbara's newborn baby—but she never made it, didn't even call. Now Barb was complaining about it again, sitting there with a worried look on her face.

"You know," she said, "I haven't talked to Mom in almost a week."

"So what?" Bob kept the newspaper between them as he spoke. "It's no big deal, right?"

"Maybe not, but all the same she said a week ago that she was gonna bring those pictures by. She just got 'em back and was anxious for us to see them. I took that to mean right away."

Bob sighed and put the paper down. "So, maybe they got busy. Maybe she forgot."

Barb stirred her coffee, frowning to herself. "I don't think so," she said. "That's not something Mom would put off. I feel a bit uneasy, if you want to know the truth."

Bob thought about it. Maybe Barb was right. When Velda told you that she meant to do something, it normally got done. "I'll tell you what," he said. "If it'll put your mind at ease, we can go over there and check it out."

Barb broke into a smile. "Thanks, Bob. I *would* feel better. Why don't you go on and call a cab. I'll get the baby ready."

Half an hour later, Bob was paying off the cabbie in the driveway of the Bartlett house, when Caril Ann opened up the door and started shouting at them from the porch. "Stop, Barb!" she yelled. "Mom, Dad, and the baby are sick. You don't want your baby to catch it."

Barb was startled by her sister's appearance. Caril's face was pale, her hair mussed. She wore a housecoat, looking like she hadn't had a good night's sleep for days.

"I want to see Mom," Barbara called across the yard.

"Just go away!" Caril shouted back at her. "Go away if you know what's best! You need to go away, so Mother won't get hurt."

What does she mean by that? Barb wondered. At the moment, she could think of no response.

Bob called her from the taxi. "What's she talking about?" he asked.

"I don't know," Barb said, "but she's really upset. Maybe we better go."

"Okay," Bob answered with a shrug. "Get in, and we'll go home. We can always come back later."

"I suppose."

Barb climbed into the taxi, with the baby in her arms. She cranked the window down and was about to wave, when Caril came running from the house, across the yard.

"I'm sorry I'm so cranky," she told Barbara, "but I have to be."

"Why's that?"

Caril hesitated, chewing on her lower lip. "I can't say. Just go home and stay there. If you don't, Mom will get hurt."

It looked like she was crying as she turned and ran back toward the house. Barb felt the apprehension gnawing at her, but she couldn't think of anything to do except go home.

And wait.

"There's something fishy going on," Bob muttered on the cab ride home. "I'm calling Rodney when we get back to the house."

Rodney Starkweather was a friend of the family. His brother Charles had been Caril's boyfriend, off and on, for something like a year. The Bartletts didn't like him much, but that had never stopped him from coming by to see Caril Ann. When Rodney told Von Busch that Charles had not been home for several days, Bob smelled a rat.

"Something funny's going on over there," he told Rodney. "I know it."

Together, they drove back to Belmont, parked outside the Bartlett house, and walked up to the porch. Caril answered several moments after Bob knocked on the door.

"I need to pay Velda for doing my laundry," Bob told her.

"If they're sick, the money will come in handy. Can I come in?"

Caril shook her head. "They're sleeping. You can't see them."

Bob was getting angry now. He tried to push his way inside, but Caril Ann threw her weight against the door and blocked his path. "Please don't come in," she said. "My mom's life will be in your hands!"

Bob tried again, but he could not budge Caril, despite the difference in their weight. Her face was twisted, looking desperate, on the verge of tears.

"Please go away," she hissed, "and don't come back 'til Monday."

Bob backed off, reluctantly. "Okay, we'll go," he said, "but I don't like it." Grudgingly, he turned away and walked back to the car.

"What now?" asked Rodney, when they reached the vehicle.

"We're going to the cops," Bob said.

Patrolman Frank Soukup, with two and a half years on the Lincoln Police Department, had been on duty for six hours when he and his partner, Patrolman Donald Kahler, got the radio call at 9:25 P.M. It was an "813"—a code that translates into "call the station." Soukup made the call, and listened with his partner as Captain Joseph Harbaugh ordered them to check out a problem at 924 Belmont Avenue. It sounded like some kind of a domestic beef, one party blocking entry to a residence, while others called for backup from the law. Soukup acknowledged the command and turned his car around.

Five minutes later the two patrolmen arrived at their destination. Pulling up outside the small, ramshackle house, Patrolman Soukup saw the porch light burning, but the house itself was dark, deserted-looking. A feeble street-light showed them no one waiting in the yard or on the street outside.

Soukup confirmed the address and proceeded toward the

house, with Kahler on his heels. Domestics were the worst, they knew, especially when sex and liquor were involved. The two patrolmen were prepared for anything.

There was no answer when he knocked, and Soukup tried again. The house stood silent, windows staring back at them like lifeless eyes. When Soukup tried the door, the knob turned in his hand. He opened it and tried the screen door next, but it refused to budge.

"There must be someone home," he said. "The screen door's locked from the inside."

Before his partner could reply, a sleepy-looking girl appeared in the doorway. She wore a light-colored kimono with a flower print design and looked as if they had awakened her, hair mussed and tangled.

"What?" she asked.

"Lincoln Police Department," Soukup said. "We understand you had some trouble here tonight."

"No trouble," said the girl. "Who told you that?"

"We got a call that some people weren't allowed to enter the house," Soukup said. "Is that true?"

The girl appeared to think about it for a moment, then replied, "Oh, that was my sister, my brother-in-law, and their baby."

"Well, how come they couldn't come in?" Soukup pressed.

"I told them that my mom and dad and little sister have the flu," she said, "especially my sister. Mom said that she didn't want my sister's baby in the house, where she would catch the flu."

It sounded plausible enough to Soukup, but he couldn't let it go. "Is there any kind of trouble between you?" he asked. "Did you have an argument or something?"

"No, we didn't," said the girl. "They left after I told them they couldn't come in."

"What's your name?" Soukup asked her.

"Caril Ann Fugate. My mother's name is Bartlett. She's been married a second time."

"How old are you?"

"Fourteen," she said.

"Well, Caril Ann, it strikes me funny that your brother-in-law would call us out here just because your parents have the flu."

"Oh, we don't get along with him," she said, "and he don't like us very well. He prob'ly called you just because he doesn't like us."

Soukup was studying Caril's face when a small collie pup appeared from somewhere, wagging its tail and jumping up on the leg of his uniform slacks. Its paws were muddy, making a hell of a mess, and Soukup tried to nudge it away, but the puppy returned, insistent in its bid for attention. Finally, Caril Ann unlatched the screen and let the dog inside.

There wasn't much to say beyond that point. Patrolman Soukup could see nothing out of place, no indication of a crime in progress, and he didn't feel like waking up the household to confirm Caril's story. With a simple thanks, he led his partner back to the patrol car, and they drove for several moments, talking it over, finally stopping at a call box on the corner of Tenth Street and Oak. Soukup called the station house and spoke once more with Captain Harbaugh, briefing him on their conversation with Caril Ann. When Soukup asked if they should double back and get the name of the Bartletts' family doctor, Capt. Harbaugh told him to forget about it. They had done their job.

While Officer Soukup was questioning Caril, Bob Von Busch and Rodney Starkweather were watching from Rodney's car, parked farther down the street. They trailed Soukup's black-and-white back to the station and cornered him there, asking what Caril Ann had said. Soukup told them that nothing was wrong at the house, that some people were sick with the flu, and that Bob should just leave them alone for a while.

Bob left the station in disgust, and Rodney drove him home. He was surprised to hear that Charlie Starkweather had telephoned twice in his absence. The first time, he told

Barbara that he had left a .22-caliber rifle, borrowed from
Rodney, at the home of a mutual friend, Harvey Griggs.
Charlie said he was stranded at Tate's Conoco station, out
on Highway 77, and he needed a ride home. Fifteen minutes
later, almost as an afterthought, he had called back to tell
her that the Bartletts had the flu. Charlie had taken them
some groceries, he said, and everybody else should stay
away.

Bob summoned Rodney once again, and they drove out
to visit Harvey Griggs. He had the borrowed .22, all right,
but it was damaged, with the metal butt plate missing. Bob
and Rodney drove the eight miles out to Tate's, but Charlie
wasn't there. More to the point, they were informed that he
had not been in all day. They talked about reporting
Charlie's lie to the police, but finally did nothing, calculat-
ing that the cops would not be interested, either way.

On Sunday morning, Rodney showed the damaged rifle to
his father, asking if they ought to call the cops again, but
Guy Starkweather wanted more evidence before he reported his son to the law. Instead, Guy sent his daughter,
sixteen-year-old Laveta, over to the Bartlett house to have a
look around. Laveta was a friend and confidante of Caril
Ann. Her father hoped that she could find out what was
really happening on Belmont Avenue.

Caril met Laveta at the door and told her tale about the
flu once more. Laveta left, pretending to be satisfied, but she
went back on Sunday evening and confronted Caril Ann.

"You're lying to me," she insisted. "Now, I want to know
what's going on in there."

According to Laveta, Caril Ann hesitated, glanced behind
her, finally whispered through the screen door, "There's
some guy back there with Chuck. He's got a tommy gun. I
think they're going to rob a bank."

Laveta took that startling information home and shared it
with her father. It was serious business, if true, but Guy
Starkweather didn't know if he should believe it or not. By
that time, it was pushing seven o'clock, and there were no

banks open on a Sunday night. He decided to sleep on it, and call the police tomorrow.

Caril Ann's maternal grandmother, sixty-two-year-old Pansy Street, was beside herself with worry by Monday morning. She was used to seeing daughter Velda—Betty, as she called her—on a daily basis, but they had not spoken for nearly a week. Now, she heard from Barbara that the family was ill, refusing to communicate with anyone outside the house. It wasn't Betty's style to leave her mother in the dark that way, when she could just as easily pick up the telephone. Something was wrong, and Pansy meant to check it out herself.

The yellow cab picked Pansy up at 9:00 A.M. and took her to the Bartlett house on Belmont Avenue. She picked her way across the yard, through mud and dirty snow, to reach the porch. The first thing Pansy noticed was the front door standing open several inches. On the screen door, just inside, a crude hand-lettered sign warned everyone to "Stay a way" or risk contamination from the "flue." Ignoring it, she stood and called in through the screen, until she got an answer from Caril Ann.

The girl looked strange to Pansy, pale and agitated, fidgeting as she repeated her account of how the family had taken ill. It wasn't selling, and she seemed to know it, backing off a step and blurting out, "Go home, Grandma. Oh, Granny, go away! Mom's life will be in danger if you don't."

As Caril Ann spoke, she raised one hand and pointed with two fingers toward a corner of the living room that Pansy couldn't see. The old woman was badly frightened, now.

"I want to see Betty," she pleaded. "Please let me see Betty!"

Caril said nothing, standing rock-still in the middle of the room.

Pansy called out again, louder this time, addressing her daughter directly. "Betty, if you can't speak, come to the door! I want to see you!" Answered only by silence, she shouted for her granddaughter. "Betty Jean! Speak to Granny!"

And again, no answer.

Rage was swiftly overcoming Pansy's fear. She reached out for the screen door, found it latched, and shook it angrily. "Caril Ann," she snapped, "you open this door and let me in! I'm coming in this house to see what's wrong with Betty."

Caril stared back at her, stone silent.

"If you don't open this door right now, I'm going into town and get a search warrant. You've got Chuck in there with you, and don't try to tell me he's not!"

Caril turned away, and Pansy shouted after her. "I'll get in here one way or another!"

She stalked back to the waiting cab and directed the driver to the Lincoln police station, fuming all the way. Pansy was fond of Caril Ann, but she was not about to let a teenage girl pull the wool down over her eyes when something was obviously wrong in her daughter's home.

At the station house, a uniformed patrolman tried to calm her down, but Pansy Street would not be pacified. She wanted action, and she pressed her case in no uncertain terms, until Detectives George Hansen and Ben Fischer came to hear her out. Reluctantly, they finally agreed to drive her back to Belmont Avenue and have a word with Caril.

When they arrived, though, there was no one home. The two detectives stood and watched while Pansy hammered on the door, in vain. Despite the note, still mounted on the screen, the house appeared to be deserted.

"Can you try to get in through a window?" Pansy asked.

Detective Fischer frowned at that. "We might," he said, "but we don't have a warrant."

"So?"

"So," he explained, "that means we would be going in illegally. You want to take responsibility?"

The woman did not hesitate. "I will. Go on ahead."

They found an unlocked window on the south side of the house, and Fischer crawled inside. He let the others in, and they began to search the house. No one was home, and there were no signs of a struggle, nothing out of place. In retrospect, Pansy thought the house was *too* neat for a family with three sick people, but she kept the observation to herself. Hansen and Fischer were satisfied, and they had other, more important work to do. They drove Pansy back to her tenement house on Tenth Street, leaving her with a suggestion that she mind her own business in the future.

Alone and feeling helpless, Pansy sat down in her kitchen and began to cry.

In the meantime, Guy Starkweather had decided to have his son picked up. He telephoned police on Monday morning, coincidentally while Pansy Street was at the station house, but they had brushed him off. When he showed up in person, a patrolman sniffed his breath and told him he should give the booze a rest. Again, no one expressed an interest in Laveta's story of the pending bank heist.

Even so, Detectives Fischer and Hansen were dispatched to the Starkweather home after dropping Pansy Street at her flat. They told Guy that his son was nowhere to be found on Belmont Avenue; their notes also record that Starkweather appeared to have been drinking since his visit to the station house. Before they left, a call came in from Barbara Von Busch. She seemed hysterical, insisting that her parents would not leave the house without their car. The officers could not account for quirks of personal behavior, but they tried to calm her down, without success.

A few hours later, Guy Starkweather called the police once again. This time, he wanted to report that Charlie's car had disappeared from Harvey Griggs's house, where it had been in the garage. Police went by the Griggs home and confirmed the car was missing, but they still refused to put a warrant out on Charlie, as his father urged.

So far, they said, there was no evidence that Charlie Starkweather had broken any laws.

Bob Von Busch made another trip to the Lincoln police station on Monday afternoon. He asked for Captain Harbaugh, and they kept him waiting half an hour. He was in a foul mood by the time he entered Harbaugh's office, saw the captain seated at his desk, a pained expression on his face.

"So, what's the problem now, Bob?"

"I want to know if anything's happened yet," he demanded.

"You mean about the Bartletts?" Harbaugh leaned back in his chair and crossed his arms. "We called Marion's job, and they said his nephew or someone called in, said he was sick and wouldn't be in for a while. You know what I think, Bob? I think they went on vacation for a few days and forgot to tell you. Maybe took a trip somewhere and decided to leave Caril Ann home by herself. Then what did she do? Called her boyfriend, this Starkweather kid, to come stay over with her. Obviously, they don't want anyone to know what's going on. What do *you* think?"

"You're wrong," Bob angrily replied. "There's no way Marion would take a trip without his car. It's sitting in the driveway! And he wouldn't leave no fourteen-year-old girl at home alone in Belmont. Caril goes every place they go."

The captain waved one hand in a dismissive gesture. "Bob," he said, "I'm getting tired of this. I'm *telling* you to leave them alone. This isn't the first time you've had trouble with the Bartletts, is it?"

Bob blinked in surprise. "What are you talking about?"

"I mean what I said," Harbaugh told him. "I've seen the reports."

Bob stared at Capt. Harbaugh for a moment, letting it sink in, before it hit him. "You're mistaking me for *Sonny* Von Busch," he said. "He ain't no relation to me."

Harbaugh frowned and shook his head. "I never heard of Sonny Von Busch," he insisted, "just *Bob* Von Busch, and that's you."

Bob saw that it was hopeless; he was talking to himself.

"I gotta go," he said, disgusted. "I can see that you ain't gonna be no help."

Now he was back on Belmont Avenue, and when he thought about what Rodney said, the odor wafting from the outhouse really *didn't* smell too much like shit. He peered in through the open doorway, squinting in the frigid darkness, trying to make sense of what he saw.

It looked like . . .

"Oh, my God!"

Bob lurched back from the privy, slammed the door with a resounding *bang!*

Behind him, Rodney dropped his cigarette. "Christ, Bob, what is it?"

"Velda . . . Betty Jean," Bob gasped. "They're dead! She's halfway down the toilet. Betty's on the seat."

"You're sure?" asked Rodney.

"Sure as hell!" Bob answered. "Let's clear out of here and call the cops back. This is bad, and I think Charlie's in it up to his neck."

Bob had no trouble getting through to Captain Harbaugh this time. When police returned to Belmont Avenue, they found fifty-seven-year-old Marion Bartlett laid out in the chicken coop, his lifeless body wrapped with blood-soaked rags and rolled up in a quilt. Next door, the privy held his wife and daughter. Thirty-six-year-old Velda's body had been wrapped up like her husband's, wedged headfirst into the toilet hole, as if someone had tried to push her through and then had given up when she got stuck. Beside her, on the wooden seat, young Betty Jean was resting in a cardboard box.

Both adult victims had been shot with a small-caliber weapon; Velda Bartlett had also been stabbed several times with a knife. Betty Jean was neither shot nor stabbed. An autopsy would reveal that she died from a fractured skull.

"That shows you how little she was," a sad-faced patrolman remarked to the press. "The poor little thing could fit into a grocery box."

At 5:43 P.M., an all-points bulletin was issued from the Lincoln station house: "Pick up for investigation of murder, Charles R. Starkweather. May live at 3024 N Street, nineteen years old. Also pick up Caril A. Fugate, 924 Belmont. Starkweather will be driving a 1949 Ford, black color, license 2–15628. This is a sedan, no grill, and is painted red where the grill was, and has no hubcaps." The bulletin described Starkweather as five feet five inches tall, 140 pounds, with dark red hair and green eyes, believed to be wearing blue jeans and a black leather jacket. Caril Ann was described as five foot one, 105 pounds, with dark brown hair and blue eyes. She sometimes wore glasses.

Investigators didn't know it yet, but they were about to embark on the Midwest's greatest manhunt since John Dillinger was at large a quarter century earlier, during the Great Depression.

And the killing had only begun.

2

Little Red

Starkweather.

The very name evokes bleak landscapes under leaden clouds, failed crops and wasted fortunes, ruined dreams. And, while it fit one member of the family well enough, in retrospect, it seemed to be a poor description for the clan at large. There was, in fact, no warning whatsoever that the family might produce a monster somewhere down the line.

The first Starkweather journeyed to America in 1640, from the Isle of Man. From that day to this, the name has been respectable, sometimes distinguished, where the family put down roots. A town in North Dakota bears the name, as does a school in Michigan, and several urban streets. There was no history of violence, crime, or mental illness in the family, before young Charlie came along.

The Lincoln Starkweathers were poor and sparsely educated, but their neighbors knew them as hardworking, God-fearing folk. Guy Starkweather, born in 1910, was a carpenter and general-purpose handyman, although a bad back and arthritis limited his prospects. Helen, his wife, was four years younger, a small woman with frizzy red hair and the kind of strength that holds a family together. They produced seven children in all, six boys and one girl. Charles was their third, born at home on November 24, 1938.

It is easy to point fingers and lay blame in the aftermath of tragedy, but there is no appearance of dysfunction in the family that gave us Charlie Starkweather. One neighbor described how the Starkweathers helped their sick neighbors. "They had seen a light go on in a house about midnight," she recalled. "A neighbor woman was ill and had to go to the hospital. Mr. and Mrs. Starkweather went to the house and Mrs. Starkweather accompanied the woman to the hospital. He wanted to go, too, but he said one of them had to stay with the children. They have never left those children alone at all, and I think that's unusual today."

A second neighbor told the press, "We've never heard Mr. Starkweather swear, and when he goes away, the kids all say, 'Good-bye, Dad,' and when he comes home they all run out to meet him."

There were hard times, of course—Helen started waiting tables in 1946, to make ends meet—but nothing extraordinary for the time and place. Years later, in prison, Charlie would speak proudly of his father, reciting Guy's skill at repairing shoes, roofing houses, running a bakery. Guy knew about guns and hunting dogs; he could name all the animals in the zoo and describe where they came from. Charlie loved his mother, too, but in a jailhouse interview with criminologist James Reinhardt, he recalled a sense of insecurity engendered by her worn, tired looks. Helen did not complain about her life, but Reinhardt says that Charlie "used to sit and wonder if someday she might stop being gentle, or if she might suddenly and mysteriously disappear entirely."

Guy Starkweather, for his part, always spoke proudly of Charles to the neighbors. Even looking back, with Charlie on death row, Guy would recall him as a quiet boy who helped around the house by sweeping, dusting, washing dishes, taking out the trash—whatever needed to be done. He seemed to like his chores and did the work efficiently.

His parents thought he was a normal boy, and there was nothing in those early days to prove them wrong. The family was poor, but far from destitute. There were no signs of deprivation or abuse, so common in the early lives of violent criminals. In fact, Charlie himself would later describe his preschool years as a normal—even idyllic—period. By his own account, he spent most of his time playing cowboys and Indians with his brothers, "whopping our way around the house, dodging trees, across the front yard, through long straight rows of corn, around behind the garage." Once, in the midst of play, he fell headfirst against an old washtub and gashed his left eyebrow, requiring two stitches, but the incident was hardly traumatic. "I wasn't the only member of the family that received injuries," he wrote, proceeding to a lengthy description of the afternoon his sister was scalded with a bucket of hot water. "The burn," he went on, "from what I understand, has healed beautifully, and as far as I know does not leave a scar."

In the winter of 1941, the Starkweather family found a new home, on the south side of Lincoln, where Charlie would spend the rest of his formative years. The white, one-story house had five bedrooms, large porches at the front and back, with a full basement. By all accounts, it made a happy home for Guy Starkweather's brood. Charlie would describe the house as "shabby," in his prison writings, but the wooded grounds instantly captured his imagination. "I was raised in this house through most of my childhood," he wrote, "[and] the place looked like a[n] enchanted forest, with its large trees surrounding the house, and at times in the evening when the sun was setting in its tender glory, with its beautiful colors in the western sky, and the birds singing in their melodys [sic] that came softly from the trees—everything was nice and pretty, so peaceful and tranquil—it was as though time itself was standing still. I fell in love with this adventurous land in my earlier days, and the flames still burns [*sic*] deep down inside of me for the love of that enchanted forest."

It was here that Charlie played rough-and-tumble games with his brothers, fortifying the garage against imaginary redskins, riding broomstick horses to one classic showdown after another. Minor injuries aside, he could apparently recall no single moment of unhappiness or lasting pain.

Until the day he started school.

Whatever pleasant memories a person cherishes from early days, the real test comes when he or she is forced to leave the family sanctuary and confront a larger, sometimes hostile world outside. A person is either prepared for that challenge, or he is not.

Charlie Starkweather wasn't.

But, in fairness, we may also say that Lincoln's schools were unprepared for him. Compulsory education was a relatively new concept for Nebraskans in 1944, when Charlie entered kindergarten at the red-brick Saratoga Elementary School. A resounding majority of the state legislature had rejected mandatory schooling in 1871, and as late as 1883 one newspaper dismissed the notion as "a case of legislative delirium tremens." Boys were meant to grow up plowing fields, while girls turned into wives and mothers, learning by example in the home. It was 1891 before Populist lawmakers guaranteed the opportunity of a grade-school education to all young Nebraskans, but facilities and funding were marginal. Outside of Omaha and Lincoln, one-room, single-teacher schools remained the standard teaching format well into the 1950s.

Charlie was looking forward to school that September, later describing himself as "filled with excitement and overwhelming joy" at the prospect of entering kindergarten. Brothers Leonard and Rodney, aged seven and nine, walked him to class that morning, but something went sour in Charlie before he ever reached the schoolhouse.

"Walking along with my brothers to attend my kindergarten class," he later wrote, "all enjoyment and excitement left me and I became very tense and nervous. My brothers

27

did their uppermost to explain that there wasn't nothing to be scare[d] about but even with their hopefull [*sic*] explaining it didn't stop me from trembling as we walked along to school."

At first, as Charlie settled in for class, his apprehension seemed to be misplaced. His teacher, Mrs. Mott, was friendly, and the principal was all smiles when she dropped in to brief the children on basic rules of conduct. Following a ceremony Charles remembered as "the pledge of allegation to the flag," each child was called upon to rise and introduce himself, with a brief recitation of hobbies or summer activities.

"One by one," Charlie wrote, "the kids went before the class to tell of their summer doings and of their hobbies, if they had one. . . . As I sat listening I became more anxious to tell my summer activities. I had no hobbies, but I could tell of good times I had playing with my brothers. . . . I hadn't ever gone swimming, but I had gone to shows with Mom and Dad, and I did go fishing many times with Dad and my brothers. I couldn't hardly wait until it was my turn."

Charlie squirmed in his seat, giddy with anticipation, forced to wait as his classmates were summoned alphabetically. His eagerness evaporated, though, when Mrs. Mott called out his name.

"I felt shy and awkward as I got up from my seat and went before the class," he recalled, "and as I walked past the other girls and boys to get before the class, I heard the girls and boys give off their giggles that started my heart pounding against my chest."

He choked, a windy sobbing noise escaping from his lips in place of words. Embarrassed, blushing to the roots of his red hair, he tried again. The words came, this time, but so softly that the teacher had to ask him to speak louder. For the first time in his life, Charlie discovered that he had a speech impediment, pronouncing "house" as "wouse," and so forth.

"I spoke louder," Charlie wrote, "and as I did my

pronunciation of words got mixed up. And all at once the whole class burst into laughter."

Charlie was losing it. No matter how he tried, the words got tangled up and came out incoherent. Charlie shriveled in the face of mocking laughter, felt himself turn "flaccid, lacking in firmness," as his throat clenched tight. It was a struggle just to breathe, much less continue speaking. Finally, in pity, Mrs. Mott asked him to take his seat.

"There were just a few left to tell their stories," Charlie wrote, "and while they were talking I sat in silence, but swearing to myself. I cursed every person in the class profanely, including Mrs. Mott, and I made a solemn vow, a promise to myself that I'll never stand before another group to make a speech."

From that point on, for the remainder of his school career, Starkweather was convinced the other students "had it in" for him, staring and mocking him, laughing behind his back. Throughout the day, new incidents reminded Charlie of his difference, the seeming fact that he did not belong.

There was a playhouse in one corner of the kindergarten classroom. When Charlie crawled inside to join two of his peers, the other children left. From prison, he would look back on that moment and describe his feelings in a burst of purple prose.

> I sat in silence as my heart was pounding against my breast as it was rising involuntarily in an occasional deep reminiscent sob, that my deformity compelled. My heart became a grimace of hatred, crimson . . . and it seemed as though I could see my heart before my eyes, turning dark black with hate and rage.

At that point, Mrs. Mott appeared, stooping to peer inside the playhouse. Beside her stood the children who had bailed out of the playhouse when he entered. Sneering tattletales.

"Charles," the teacher called to him, "why did you tell these children to get out of the playhouse?"

Charlie had no answer. He was innocent *and* speechless. He could only shrug and squirm.

"Well, you come out of there," said Mrs. Mott.

He crawled out through the little door, the teacher and his classmates looming over him. His heart was pounding as he scrambled to his feet.

"Charles, we don't act like that," the teacher said. "We share and share alike, so don't be telling any of the kids they can't play where they want to. Is that understood?"

Before he could respond, she had him by the arm, steering him back toward his desk. When Mrs. Mott told him to sit down and draw his mother a picture, it was an order, not a suggestion. Charlie glanced around the room and noticed that he was the only student seated at a desk. Others stood around the playhouse, in the sandbox, some were lolling on the floor. He noticed others drawing, at a larger table, and wondered briefly why he had not been allowed to sit with them. "But I knew they wouldn't stay at the tables if I was there, anyway," he recalled, "so I didn't care if I was there or not."

At recess, team leaders were chosen to divide the boys for kickball, a crude form of soccer. As luck would have it, there was an uneven number of boys in the class, and Charlie—the self-described "redheaded, bowlegged kid"—was the odd man out, left standing on the sidelines. As Charlie recalled it, one of the captains was about to select him, albeit reluctantly, when Mrs. Mott intervened, deciding it would be unfair to field unequal teams.

"You can be the substitute, all right, Charles? Would you like that?"

Charlie felt his heart "droop and sadden" in that moment, but he suppressed a sudden urge to turn and flee the playground. Mrs. Mott was waiting for an answer—*everyone* was waiting—so he muttered incoherently and nodded.

"Well," said Mrs. Mott, "you stay along the backstop, near the bench. If anyone gets hurt, you take his place."

No one got hurt that day, as Charlie watched them from the bench. Whenever girls passed by, he heard them giggling and imagined he must be the target of their mirth. As for the boys, there was no doubt about their mockery. They jeered him from the field, one challenging him: "Do you think you can kick with those bowlegs?"

"I felt like cutting loose, kicking them right in the teeth," Charlie wrote, "just to show them that I could kick as well as anybody else."

At one point, three boys stopped in front of Charlie, one imitating his stammer, while another performed a bowlegged waddle, and their companion stood by laughing, fit to burst.

"A black rage swept over me," Charlie recalled, "and the hatred was building itself up inside of me more every second. I got so mad that tears came to my eyes and my knees started to shake. Then one of the boys said, 'Look! He's going to cry!'"

By that time, Charlie was prepared to cry *and* kick, regardless of the consequences to himself, but Mrs. Mott chose that moment to signal the end of recess, calling the children back to class. At the doorway, one of the larger boys crowded in front of Charlie, shooting a quick elbow into his ribs. Huddled over his desk from that point on, he barely heard what Mrs. Mott was saying to the class.

Writing from prison, Starkweather described his feelings on that day. "I said to myself that someday I'd pay them all back, and a[n] overwhelming sense of outrage grew. It roused itself in my mind for a wild thirsting revenge. I wanted . . . revenge upon the world and its human race. My mind and heart became black with hatred as it built up in me. A drawn veil of dilatory cloud seemed to come before my face. The tribute was gratifying. I could not analyze nor recognize my emotions as I broke down into tears."

It is tempting to cut through the melodrama and dismiss

Starkweather's belated self-analysis as an excuse for subsequent behavior—Ted Bundy blaming *Playboy* magazine for thirty-odd sadistic murders—and some of his statements to criminologist Reinhardt appear contradictory. After all the histrionics about "black rages" and "dilatory clouds," he would write: "I didn't get along that day in school with the others. They made me *a little mad,* but more upset than anything." [Emphasis added.]

Still, it is clear that *something* happened in Charlie's mind that first day in school. He recalled weeping on the walk home, arriving red-eyed, as his mother was preparing supper. When she asked about his day, he lied at first, telling her he "had fun," describing his teacher as "pretty" and "nice."

"Well," Helen said, "I'm glad you enjoy school so well. Your brothers don't think much of it."

At that, Charlie broke down and blurted out the truth, relating each indignity in turn. "I hate them kids," he sobbed, "and I'm going to hit one of them, if they don't stop making fun of me."

Helen Starkweather seemed "hurt" by Charlie's outburst, but she gave him a parent's classic reply: "I'll speak to your father about it when he gets home." That night, after supper, Charlie eavesdropped on a telephone conversation, Guy telling someone that he would be late for work the next morning, saying that "he had to explain my dispositions to the school principal."

No record of that conference has survived, if it ever took place, and Charlie, by his own admission, was already beyond help in any case. "My rebellion against the world started that first day in school," he later wrote, "and from that first day . . . I became rebellious. I have stayed in my rebellious mood even to this day. Why did I become rebellious against the world and its human race?—'cause that first day in school I was being made fun at, picked on, laughed at."

Even Charlie seemed to realize that it was a trivial excuse for eleven murders, fourteen years after the fact. "I knew as

I grew older," he wrote, "that it wasn't much of an excuse. But in those younger years of my life I had builded [sic] up a hate that was as hard as iron, and when people tease, make fun of and laugh at a little youngster in hers or his childhood, that little youngster is not going to forget it. I wouldn't deny that I was like a hound prowling for fights, quarreling, and doing wild things and placing everyone among my enemies."

By Charlie's own account, he had his first fight on the second day of kindergarten, thrilling to the sense of release from his pent-up anger and aggression. Even so, the relief was short-lived. His rage and depression always returned when the battle was over, plunging him into another of his "black moods."

When one of those moods came over him, Charlie wrote, "I would just sit in one place and stay motionless in a gloomy manner, and it was obvious that there was no reasoning with me. . . . Boys and girls that I knew didn't bother me when I was in my motionless and gloomy manner, they just let me be and stay in my black mood, and even to this day I have them melancholy moods."

Charlie liked to describe himself as a fearless playground gladiator. When children teased him, he recalled, "I would beat them down, and if I had to I would beat them down again until they knew I wasn't going to take it from them. . . . I fought fast and a little furiously like a maniac in rage and fury, and as I fought [a] sense of outrage grew to striving, to throw, to bend, to hurt, and most of all to beat those who teased me."

As a result of those brawls, Starkweather said, he developed "a reputation for meanness or generosity" among his classmates. Charlie claimed that his "fighting reputation" followed him through school and beyond. He still blamed day one of kindergarten as the root of his trouble, but even as he made the claim, he seemed to recognize its transparency. "I assure you that's not the reason for fighting when I grew up," he conceded, "but the hatred I had builded [sic] up inside of me stayed with me, and it made me hate everybody other than my family . . . a person wouldn't look at me cross-eyed without getting into a fistfight."

Charlie's speech impediment and bowlegs remained the butt of jokes in school, and while he later overcame his lisp to some extent, there was nothing to be done about his legs. "They're just as crooked as before," he wrote from prison. "I never have been able to grow out of them, and if I have to say so myself, I believe a pig could run between them without touching the sides."

Charlie made it through kindergarten, but first grade was even worse. Instead of crying now, when he was teased, Charlie wrote that "I would just get mad and smack them in the mouth, but it seemed like the more I fought those who teased me, the more I was made fun at." It hardly mattered, though, since Charlie recalled that he "began to love fighting, and would walk a mile just to fight someone." He described frequent complaints from the school, each rebuffed by his father with the observation that Charlie would stop fighting when the other students quit harassing him. Indeed, Charlie recalled a brief lull in second grade, but "it didn't last long."

Significantly, Charlie felt more rage toward girls who teased him, than toward boys. Helen Starkweather had taught her sons never to hit a female, regardless of the provocation, since "hitting a lady isn't being a gentleman." He could see nothing ladylike about the girls who called him a "beast," a "brute," or a "redheaded, bowlegged woodpecker," but Charlie swallowed his rage at the "ladies"—or took it out on boys who crossed his path.

Although Charlie was later tested and found to possess "average" intelligence, he drifted through school in the slow-learner track, ranked as "dull-normal," passing grades one through five by the skin of his teeth, held back to repeat the sixth. The academic problems began on day one, and he soon abandoned any real attempt at scholarship. His biggest problem, as with young James Dean, was severe myopia, undetected until he was fifteen years old. By the time Charlie was tested and fitted for glasses, in 1954, his visual acuity was rated at 20/200. In practical terms, he could barely read the giant E on the optometrist's chart from a range of twenty feet; assignments written on the classroom blackboard may as well have been inscribed in Chinese characters, across the dark side of the moon.

If Charlie was blind as a bat in the schoolroom, however, he soon overcame his initial reticence and excelled in athletics. Despite his bowlegs, he was quick and strong, well-coordinated in sports and gymnastics. Charlie was proud when the gym teacher made him an "official assistant," but the whiff of authority went to his head. He had an opportunity to lord it over others, for a change, and he was not about to let it pass. One of Charlie's classmates in those days was Dennis Karnopp, the son of Lancaster County's sheriff, Merle Karnopp. "Dennis was a little overweight then," Sheriff Karnopp remembered. "The day Charlie took over he strutted up to him, poked him in the stomach with his finger, and said, 'We're gonna have to take a little of that off you, fella.'"

Sadly, that marginal success in school was too little and too late for Charlie Starkweather. James Reinhardt offered his professional assessment of Charlie's blighted personality. "On that first day of kindergarten," Reinhardt wrote, "the most important part of the little world that Charles knew went out the window. The Charles he knew went out with it." Stripped of self, acutely conscious of real and imagined insults from his peers, Starkweather yearned to run away and hide, yet "[s]omething inside of him, nameless and uncounted little words, gestures, facial expressions woven into every sensitive nerve fiber, told him not to run away." Instead, he learned to stand his ground, countering pain with an angry rebellion that, in Reinhardt's view, "grew and spread like a poisonous toxin . . . He shaped the outside world into a conniving mess to justify his hate and his insecurity. Hate and fear of himself comprised the dynamic core of his nature. . . . They spread from specific objects to all that limited range of human kind that came within his grasp." The outcome, as described by Charlie, was an endless string of schoolyard brawls, building his reputation as a scrapper who would take no guff from anyone.

Perhaps. Yet Reinhardt's meticulous search of Charlie's school records produced no evidence of the incessant fighting Starkweather described. His sixth-grade teacher remembered Charlie as "very eager to work and to please." Another noted: "Low achievement in general, but on the whole has a good attitude and has never been a disciplinary problem." Yet another found him "much more reachable than many others in my room." The principal at Saratoga Elementary, who would have dealt with any playground brawlers, called Charlie "dependable, helpful; he would do things the teachers assigned him and seemed to be happy to have these assignments, such as unlocking rooms, operating the projector machine, erasing the blackboard." In his biography of Starkweather, Reinhardt was forced to admit that he "could find no evidence in Charles's school record that Charles's citizenship was adjudged 'bad' by any teacher. In fact, his 'citizenship' record was rather consistently above average." In seven years, Charlie was "kept in" for disciplinary reasons on only five occasions. The only referrals in his academic file were those for special testing, based on his "dull" performance in class.

What, then, is the truth of Charlie's years in elementary school? There is no reason to dispute his personal description of the rage he felt inside, the bleak depression he experienced at times, but from the record, it would seem that he concealed his brooding well. His fights, if they occurred at all, were obviously carried on away from school, where adults could not intervene. It is entirely possible that Charlie's memories of daily battles were concocted—or, at least, embellished—in his prison cell, to help him better fit the "teenage rebel" mold that he had chosen for himself.

In any case, there is no doubt that Charlie loved to see himself as a belligerent combatant. "I have seen his face set aglow," Reinhardt said, "by some reference to his 'fighting skill,' or by some sign of his unfailing aim with a gun."

And Charlie *loved* guns.

To some extent, he got that from his father. "My dad never done much talking about my troubles," Charlie recalled. "I used to wonder sometimes about that. He showed me about guns, and was proud of me, I guess, but as I think about it now, it seems that he never did think I'd get grown and have to be important in a different way. I was important maybe if I could listen to him and learn to shoot guns."

In later years, Charlie would lump firearms and hot-rods together as his "ruling passion," but there was never any doubt as to which took first place. "Between the firearms and automobiles," he said, "I'd rather hear the crack of a firearm than have or drive the finest car in the whole wide world."

Charlie enjoyed hunting, although his poor eyesight made squirrels and other small animals difficult targets. He tried hunting with a bow, but despised the drudgery of chasing arrows when he missed a shot. Besides, there was *power* in firearms. They set his ears ringing, extended his reach, made him someone to reckon with.

"Little Red" had come to understood the concept of an equalizer. "I love the smell of guns," he wrote from jail. "I love to take a gun apart and put it together again. The gun gave me a feeling of power that nothing else could match. I remember once thinking that if the devil came at me I would shoot him with a gun."

Through all the early killing, though, there was no evidence of wanton cruelty. Starkweather sometimes let a shot go by, content to sit and watch the animals he hunted. "What I liked best about the outdoors," Charlie said, "was the scenery of the forest and woods." When he did fire, however, he couldn't stop shooting "until the last cartridge was spent," and it irritated him to "miss the head of a living target." More than once, he knelt beside the carcass of some creature he had killed and said, "It didn't hurt much, did it? You know I'm a hunter and hunters have to kill, but a good hunter hits in the head."

At home, he watched his mother working to support the family when his father could not hold a job, and there were times when Charlie feared she might give up, perhaps escape to seek a better life. Sometimes, when Guy spoke harshly to his wife, it puzzled Charlie, since he felt his father "would be lost without her."

Still, he could never find it in his heart to blame Guy for their problems. He remembered good times with his father—"hunting, fishing, going to the zoo." "My dad ain't to blame for nothin' I done," Charlie said. "I just got fed up with havin' nothin' and bein' nobody. Poverty gives you nothin'. People who are poor take what they can get."

And sometimes, if they have the nerve, they take it with a gun.

3

Death Dreams

Charlie Starkweather entered seventh grade at Irving Junior High School, but it was merely a change of scene. The trouble with his eyes had not been diagnosed and Charlie's attitude toward life—he would have said the world's approach to *him*—had only gotten worse. Retention in the sixth grade undoubtedly compounded the effect of isolation from his peers and reinforced his status as the "oddball," an object of curiosity and scorn.

Charlie remembered eighth grade as the year of his worst fights and problems in school, admitting that he started much of the trouble himself, "but not all of it." At one point, he broke his "solemn vow" to avoid public speaking, but as in kindergarten, "laughter broke out" when he rose to address the class.

So much for sociability.

He didn't *always* fight, however. Charlie described one day when he was walking home from school, carrying a watercolor painting he had done in class, when he discovered he was being followed by "a half dozen girls and boys making wisecracks about my bowlegs, red hair, and speech." He walked three more blocks before it dawned on him to take a different route, but when he turned off on his detour, "the wisecracks, imitating, giggles and laughter was still following behind me."

Charlie stopped at the next intersection, waiting for a car to pass, and noted that his group of tormentors had dwindled. Those who remained made up for the shortage of numbers with volume, one in particular leading the now familiar chant of "bowlegged, redheaded woodpecker." Suddenly, the ringleader stepped forward, shoving Charlie off the curb, into the street. He heard a screech of tires on asphalt, saw the driver's eyes "as big as dollars" when the car lurched to a halt, its bumper inches short of impact.

A taunting voice reached out to him. "What happened? Won't those bowlegs hold you up?"

The leader of the pack stepped forward, reaching for the rolled-up painting Charlie held, and jerked it from his grasp. Charlie stood there, trembling, seething, impotent, as they critiqued his work.

"This is a piece of junk," the leader said. "Besides being a bowlegged, redheaded woodpecker, you can't even *draw!*"

The bully ripped his painting in half, encouraged by a chorus of laughter as he tore it into smaller pieces. Charlie clenched his teeth to keep from crying, but the tears streamed down his cheeks, regardless.

"He's going to cry!" one of the girls squealed, delightedly. "He's a crybaby!"

A new chant began. Now it was *"crybaby* bowlegged redheaded woodpecker." Charlie wanted to lash out at them, grab the nearest heavy object and "beat their lousy brains out," but instead he "turned [and] ran as fast as my bowlegs would carry me."

Charlie later blamed his flight on a parental warning not to fight, but such orders had never restrained him before. It may be that the desecration of his artwork was a more traumatic, *personal* attack than any of the insults he had grown accustomed to since kindergarten. Charlie's art was a means of escape and self-expression, praised by his teachers as early as third grade, a source of special pride to his parents. Aside from being unexpected, perpetrated by a gang that had him well outnumbered, the destruction of his painting may have left him feeling doubly violated and unable to defend himself.

Still, whatever others said about his art from time to time, their first and foremost target was his looks. You couldn't help but notice Charlie's size, some three inches shorter than average for other boys his age. He favored cowboy boots, to give himself a lift, but an exaggerated strut only served to emphasize his bowlegs. James Reinhardt found the condition unremarkable, but Charlie's schoolmates liked to joke that he had grown up "straddling a barrel." Looking in the mirror, he was overwhelmed by the image of flaming red hair, angular eyes, and square-cut jaw. Even when his peers weren't razzing him, Charlie imagined them whispering among themselves: "Did you notice that kid's eyes? Get a load of that hair!"

It is impossible to say how much of Charlie's sensitivity derived from real insults, how much was paranoia. In his mind, at least, the vast majority of those around him gawked and giggled, making him the butt of jokes. Whenever laughter reached his ears, he reckoned it must be at his expense. Outside the home and his "enchanted forest" lay a hostile world of enemies.

For ninth grade, Charlie was transferred from Irving to Everett Junior High. The circumstances of the transfer are unclear, and while no records have survived, several classmates recalled that Charlie was "kicked out of Irving," perhaps for fighting. Various sources agree that "it was hoped he could make a better adjustment" at the new school.

Charlie hadn't been on campus long before he tangled with Bob Von Busch, remembered as the toughest boy in school. Bob was a year younger than Charlie, but he was taller and heavier, visibly more mature. He wore his hair in a flat top with "wings," grown long and combed back on the sides. The animosity between two alpha males was automatic, a conditioned reflex. They were bound to have it out, and the result was a slugfest that left both boys battered and exhausted. "For his size," Bob recalled, "Charlie was the roughest guy I ever fought. I'd say neither one of us won that fight—it was more like we both lost it."

And in the process, they became best friends.

Looking back on Charlie in those days, Von Busch described him as a kind of teenage Jekyll and Hyde. "He could be the kindest person you've ever seen," Bob said. "He'd do anything for you, if he liked you. He was a hell of a lot of fun to be around, too. Everything was just one big joke to him. But he had this other side. He could be mean as hell, cruel. If he saw some poor guy on the street who was bigger than he was, better looking, or better dressed, he'd try to take the poor bastard down to his size. But I didn't think too much about it at the time. We were all a little like that, then. We all had a lot of growing up to do."

And part of growing up was girls.

Reports of Charlie's teenage love life are ambiguous, to say the least. In prison, he recalled one "girlfriend" from his days at Everett Junior High, describing her to James Reinhardt as "the nicest girl he had ever known besides his sister," but the nature of their friendship is unclear. Charlie invited her to his home, to "help with his schoolwork."

The girl, for her part, remembered Charlie as "one of the finest boys I've ever known." She says they went to the movies, an occasional church service, and Charlie ran errands for her mother, once sending a get-well card when her mother was ill. "In all the time I knew him," she said, "I never once heard him swear and he never smoked or drank." She recalled that Charlie was rejected by his peers at Everett—"Nobody would accept him"—but his murder rampage was beyond her comprehension. "I can't believe he's done this," she said. "Maybe he's changed a lot in the last four years. Maybe I shouldn't pity him, but I think more people should have given him a chance."

To Reinhardt, Charlie would complain that he always felt

left out while "other kids talked about dates, love affairs, vacations," but his memories were typically contradictory. "Yes, I went out with girls," he wrote. "Some were mild dates with nice Christian girls, but most of the girls I went out with were either the flibberty-gibbet type, that used too much makeup and dressed in expensive clothes, or they were the harlot type, that weren't hard to get a date with, and easy to get along with."

Still, none of the relationships had any substance or potential, as far as Charlie was concerned. "Nobody could ever ask me how I was gettin' along with my girlfriend," he said. "Until I met Caril, I never had the kind [of girl] a kid gets along with. I had a nice girl once, but she got to upsetting my death deal and I had to drop her. . . . Nobody cared about me and my girlfriends, anyhow."

With most peers of either sex, Charlie remained deliberately remote, thus shielding himself from rejection and embarrassment. "I never give nobody much chance to be dirty to me if I didn't have to," he said. "That's one reason I never went into nice places. I bought my clothes in used places. What they thought of me didn't matter. They could look at me, size me up and down, but they couldn't get away with much."

In high school, Charlie's handful of male friends consisted of fellow hot-rodders, and boys whose courage had impressed him in fistfights. Bob Von Busch was first among the chosen few, and they would sometimes double-date, cruising The Strip or driving out to Capitol Beach race track, where Charlie earned a daredevil reputation for his driving in the demolition derby.

"For years, you never saw one of us without the other," Bob recalled. "As long as we stuck together, people pretty much left us alone. He even moved in with me and my old man for a while. That was when he was about sixteen, right after he had a big fight with Guy. After that, he was over at our place more than he was at home."

Bob and Charlie split the cost of a 1941 Ford, making frequent runs to Kansas, where they purchased beer for resale to their friends in Lincoln. Sometimes, they stole cars for joy rides, or to strip for parts that Charlie sold. "We were pretty wild," Bob said, "but mostly we were just out to have a good time."

One night, they spotted a patrol car staked out at the Runza drive-in restaurant and decided to have a few laughs. "You remember the movie *American Graffiti,*" Bob said, "when the kids yanked the rear end out from under the cop car? We did the exact same thing one night—chained the rear axle to the Runza drive-in. When the cop car took off, it moved the whole Runza off its foundation."

Charlie's bravado with cars, stolen or otherwise, helped embellish his reputation in high school, revealing a skill beyond fighting or hunting. Fast cars gave him the heady sensation that "death was close by," and his deft performance at the wheel won him a new—albeit marginal—circle of friends. In prison, Charlie reminisced about the "many times" he spoke before a local hot-rod club, of which he claimed to be the president. He never swerved in "chicken" races, daring anyone to match his reckless courage, but even those dubious victories were later transformed in his mind, reworked into part of the global conspiracy against him. Perhaps, if someone else had backed him down, he might have followed a different path in life. "I go to the chair," he complained, "because my buddies chickened out."

From start to finish, it was always someone else's fault.

If Lincoln's hot-rodders were impressed with Charlie, his high school classmates continued to give him mixed reviews. One boy recalled that Charlie "used to argue an awful lot about little things," suggesting that was "one of the reasons girls couldn't stand him." That aside, he considered Starkweather "was a pretty nice kid but had a terrible temper," further noting that he "sure swaggered on purpose to exaggerate his bowlegs." A girl in Charlie's class remembered that he brought her get-well cards when she was ill; he "was not a bad boy," in her opinion, and she pitied him "because he always seemed to wear mended clothes."

A teacher confirmed Charlie's bad temper, but stopped short of calling it a psychiatric problem. As she observed, "The school psychiatrist was too busy with 'real' personality problems to be bothered with a quick-tempered lad who held his tongue in the classroom and rarely dated a girl. There were others much worse than Charles." A counselor downplayed Charlie's "fighting reputation," noting that "He did not have as many fights as he claimed he had." Another teacher said of Charlie: "He is inclined to be timid, doesn't associate too easily but gets along well enough with boys; not so well with girls. Doesn't like to participate in games with other children, either indoors or out." Yet another found Charlie "especially fond of two of his brothers and fond of his mother. Often speaks of his mother but no so often of his father. Often refers to the attention and care that his mother has given him."

The high school's staff psychologist praised Charlie's "special insight," but noted that "his difficulty was in actually dealing with what he saw, and how to appreciate it. Here he showed inadequacy." At least one teacher found Charlie receptive to friendly criticism, but noted that "the criticism got lost" in his general attitude of suspicion.

While the school counselor minimized Charlie's brawling, it is clear from the statements of various classmates that *some* fighting occurred. One youth described Charlie as "always picking fights," while another recalled that he "went after bigger guys with his fists and knees"—and, sometimes, with a knife. A third admitted that "fights were sometimes set up between Charles and another kid, just for the excitement." Any report that someone had called him a "pinky" or a "punk" was "enough to set him swinging and punching with everything he had." Guy Starkweather himself recalled a football game, in which a rival player called Charlie an "S.O.B." and wound up with seven stitches in his lip after Charlie slammed the ball into his face.

Under the circumstances, it is not surprising that Charlie's contemporaries had difficulty forming a fixed opinion of his personality. Some found him "timid and withdrawn," while others called him "sullen and resentful." He was either a bully prone to "temper tantrums," or a grandstanding show-off who avoided unpleasant situations with a variety of feigned "illnesses, aches, pains and injuries." One teacher called him "cold and feelingless," describing how he loved to nurse a grudge and "fought with the fury of a wild animal."

"Once," a former teacher of Charlie's told James Reinhardt, "I came upon the scene of one of his fights just in time to see his antagonist, a boy somewhat older than Charlie and a little larger, being helped to his feet." The loser's face was a bloody mess, a result of Charlie grinding it into the gravel driveway, but Charlie was perfectly detached, as if "whether the boy lived or died was of no concern to him." The teacher compared him to someone watching a stranger "changing a tire."

For all of the real or imagined turmoil at school, Charlie found at least some measure of release at home with his family. "I went home feelin' all right," he told Reinhardt, "everything was okay, but by morning I was back where I started." Neighbors uniformly missed the signals of distress in Charlie, one pleased to report that "we've always gotten along fine," while another said of the Starkweathers: "They all seem to think a lot of each other. The children sure like the dog and the cats. In fact, they seem to be good to everybody." Charlie was remembered as "a pretty quiet boy," with the exception that "[h]e and his dad both had bad tempers."

For the most part, quiet Charlie on the home front was preoccupied with jumbled dreams and fantasies, described for the world at large in his handwritten autobiography.

> [L]ike almost everybody, I had my dreams of things I wanted. But of all the dreams, fights, and women to me none of them ever seem[ed] to fit in this world. I guess that's what I meant when I said, "I don't know life, or what it was good for," and the reason I didn't know, I just didn't take the time to

find out. When I was younger, I always said to myself that I was going to have the knowledge of what life was good for in this world, but as I grew older, the more I didn't care to find out, and that's the reason why I didn't have time.

By this time my head was spinning, and whirling, the remembrance of happy times and unpleasant events that happen throughout my life came crowding through a foggy mist of recollection. This recollection of events, and many others, were coming back to me, like a[n] after vision of my past life.

It may be that Charlie's single greatest deficiency was his inability to leave the "enchanted forest" of his childhood home and find a place for himself in the real world of everyday people and events. He sought escape from day-to-day reality in solitude, while hunting, or in comic books, the movies, television. Even on death row, he was still wondering "what kind of life I did live in this world," finally concluding that he could never find "a personal world or live in a worthwhile world . . . because I don't know life." He was oppressed by a sense of failure, lamenting that "I haven't ever eaten in a high-class restaurant, never seen the New York Yankees play. . . . [T]here hadn't been a chance for me to have the opportunity, or privilege, for the best things in life."

From the perceived denial of opportunity, Charlie turned increasingly to feelings of distrust and hatred. Detached he may have been, in the aftermath of combat, but a former classmate recalled that Charlie "looked very lonely, as if he wanted something to happen to him."

At age sixteen he quit waiting. He had managed to squeak through ninth grade, but that was the end of the road, as far as Charlie and learning were concerned. He dropped out of school and went to work with brother Rodney, collecting garbage on the Neiderhaus route for thirty-five dollars a week. It was filthy, tedious, backbreaking work, and Charlie soon had his fill, switching to a job at the Western Newspaper Union's warehouse, where he divided his time between baling newsprint and unloading trucks.

As far as Charlie was concerned, it was another dead-end job, the only kind that he was suited for. His schoolyard paranoia followed him into the world of work, revealing enemies in every walk of life.

"At the Newspaper Union," he later said, "the people was always watchin' me. They had me numbered for the bottom. . . . I tried to work as good as anybody; even done things by myself that two of us shoulda done. . . . I used to wonder why 'no goods' I knowed was gettin' praised for doin' what they done. Guess it's 'cause they talked better'n I did, 'cause they had better places to sleep at night."

Manager John Hedge had a very different take on the problem. He pegged Charlie as retarded, later testifying in court that "[s]ometimes you'd have to tell him something two or three times. Of all the employees in the warehouse, he was the dumbest man we had." Worse yet, Charlie often fell asleep on the job—once under a sun lamp he had brought to work, resulting in a painful burn. On the side, he charged auto parts to the company, having the cost deducted from his pay, but Hedge put a stop to the practice when Charlie's bills exceeded his paycheck.

One afternoon, while he was baling paper, the handle on the baling machine slipped out of Charlie's hand and struck him at the corner of his left eye, near the same place he had gashed his eyebrow as a child. The impact knocked him cold, and he was driven to the Lincoln Clinic, where his wound was closed with several stitches. From that day onward, Charlie said, he suffered blinding headaches several times a week, for the remainder of his life. He chewed aspirin constantly, but it provided no relief.

Charlie hated working, but as long as he had a job, he gave his mother fifteen dollars a week toward the household expenses. It was no great fortune, even in 1957, but it helped, and Helen Starkweather appreciated the gesture. More to the point, she was proud of Charlie for *wanting* to help. She had no knowledge, in those days, of his sporadic income from the theft of cars, and honestly believed that he was giving nearly half his paycheck to the family.

Charlie still had cash enough to keep his hot-rod running, though, and to pursue his other hobbies. Aside from racing, he liked "comics with knives" and "shooting movies." Most of all, by 1955 and '56, he liked James Dean.

"I guess you might say James Dean was Charlie's idol," Bob Von Busch explained. "He looked a lot like him, and he acted like him. But Charlie acted like Dean before he had ever heard of the guy. That's why he liked him so much. All of a sudden here was somebody on-screen who was just like he was. Charlie never imitated Dean exactly, but he did get a few ideas from him—little things, mostly, like standing a certain way."

In fact, we know from Charlie's sister that he *was* imitating Dean, rehearsing with mirrors at home, perfecting his stance, the way he held a cigarette between his lips. The smoking was a relatively new addition to his repertoire, beginning since his breakup with the "nice girl," back at Everett Junior High. It helped him with The Look, but he was still no movie star. He had a pug nose, freckles, narrow, slanting eyes beneath thick brows—and those bowlegs. No matter how he squinted at the mirror, he would never see James Dean.

Beer helped, of course.

It was reported that he spent considerable time in one cheap beer joint or another, after work, on weekends. He was not a drunk, per se, but several cold ones helped to lubricate his morbid fantasies. When Charlie had a buzz on, he would feel like facing down the world, but it was sadly temporary. By the time he paid his tab and left for home, the weight of an unfriendly world had settled back onto his shoulders. In the words of one beer hall habitué, "He was an odd sort of kid, but no one believed he could kill. He would sit a long time and stare at something, sometimes at other people. He would leave the place with his head low, his eyes on the floor. His hair was usually uncombed and was matted down around his ears and over his forehead. His short legs carried him out into the dark, empty street."

After a night of drinking, Charlie told James Reinhardt, his mind "worked overtime," replaying the events of his short life, mingling dreams and fantasies with everyday reality until he couldn't tell the difference. Some incidents which had embarrassed him were thus resolved in more heroic fashion, with Charlie beating down the enemies who hated him for no good reason. Even as he won imaginary fights, though, it was never good enough. He "watched" his personality implode and shrivel to a blackened core of self-contempt and hatred for the world outside, leaving "a hull of a body with nothing in it worth keeping alive."

A measure of his immaturity is found in Charlie's absolute refusal to admit that *any* problem in his life could be his fault. If he picked fights with total strangers, they were *asking* for it—by the way they dressed or combed their hair, the way they "looked cross-eyed" at Charlie. If a handful of children teased him in school, he responded by hating "the world and its human race." In Charlie's mind, it was always the other guy.

"Maybe I am to blame for something," he once told Reinhardt, "but I can't remember starting the trouble with anybody. Maybe it started when I was feeding the chickens. I can't find anything I done to make people hate me. . . . If you pull the chain on a toilet, you can't blame it for flushing, can you?"

As Charlie nursed his hatred for mankind, he grew more self-absorbed, his private thoughts increasingly more introverted and bizarre. When he woke in the morning, Charlie often "wasn't sure it was me that's been asleep." Before dressing for work, he would sit on the edge of the bed, listening to his heartbeat and wondering "if it was really a part of him." What would happen if it stopped? On other days, his head "seemed too large for the brain that was in it. . . . It got killed and it lost its direction." There were times when Charlie felt a secret part of himself "rebelling against some other part," but he could make no sense of the feeling. "Anyhow," he told Reinhardt, "by the time I was seventeen I didn't have that feeling no more."

He *did* have nightmares, though. They jolted him awake, and Charlie tried to calm himself by staring at the moonlight streaming through his window. Sometimes, he recalled, it "seemed to be alive," transforming his shabby bedroom into a royal palace, while Charlie wore the flowing robes of a king. "It took me away from the things I hated," he said. "It made me forget."

It didn't always help, though. Some nights, there was terror in the moonlight, panic in the windblown trees outside. Charlie would lie awake and watch the branches thrashing, listening to cars drive past the house. Each sound, no matter how mundane, put his "muscles on edge" and left him paralyzed, convincing Charlie that "this is a wicked, hateful world."

Charlie's dreams and fantasies became increasingly morbid over time, until he began to experience personal visits from Death. In one such dream, the Reaper brought Charlie a casket and ordered him to climb in. When he was settled in the box, the coffin "sailed away with me in it," careening through space until it reached a giant bonfire, whereupon "the coffin sort of melted." Charlie then found himself on a nameless street, surrounded by flames. "But it wasn't hot like I'd always thought hell would be," he reported. "It was more like beautiful flames of gold."

The content of his "Death dreams" varied, soon incorporating accidents that left his body shattered, lifeless. Charlie viewed the dreams as warnings that his "earth time" was coming to an end. "For always," he told Reinhardt, "after one of these dreams I had an accident just like the one in the dream, only it wasn't so bad."

Soon, the image of Death stepped beyond Charlie's dreams, to invade his waking fantasies. Sometimes, the specter announced its arrival with a whistling sound; on other occasions, Charlie would wake from a dream and find Death peering at him through his bedroom window. "All I could see would be the part from the waist up," he told Reinhardt. "It was kind of half human and half bear . . . only it didn't have no neck. It just tapered off from a big chest to a small pointed head. . . . It didn't have no arms and no ears."

Despite the lack of detail, he instantly identified Death as a female, and habitually referred to it as "she." Death never spoke, but Charlie reckoned he could read her thoughts. She wanted him. His time was coming, soon.

Charlie had always pushed his luck in hot-rods, but he started taking even greater chances after Death began to visit him. At times, he thought of swerving off the highway, maybe jumping lanes to meet a truck head-on, but something held him back. "I guess if she had wanted any help," he said, "she woulda told me."

In any case, he had no fear of dying after he began to pal around with Death. The coffin dream convinced him that "[t]he world on the other side couldn't be as bad as this one."

Death was a friend, of sorts, but even she could not escape the blame game Charlie played with everyone who crossed his path. In fact, he told Reinhardt, Death came between him and "the only nice girl I ever went with." They got along together for a while, but then he "had to break her off." As Charlie explained his dilemma, "[S]he made me uneasy sometimes. . . . It seemed like she was coming between me and Death. I worried over it when we were together, and sometimes I'd think about it at night and couldn't sleep."

With no girl to distract him, he could give his morbid fantasies free rein. He imagined himself as the hero of weird and fantastic adventures, always culminating in some kind of bloody showdown with his enemies. Murder fascinated him, and he did not shy away from killing in his daydreams, but he always insisted that he "would not kill anybody just to be killing." Rather, in his fantasies, it was a matter of survival, where "the murder always had to be done."

Of course, in Charlie's mind, the slightest insult—real or

imagined—was enough to justify execution. Those who belittled him were prime targets for murder, since "argument stops" with death, and "[d]ead people are all on the same level." In his daydreams, he could kill and kill without fear of reprisal, yet he still wondered "how many more before Death comes for me."

Despite the comics, "chicken" races, "shooting movies," and his fantasies of murder, Charlie was compelled to face reality at times. His drab life was detestable. No matter how he tried to imitate James Dean, he rapidly grew tired of looking at himself, his shabby thrift-shop clothes. It wasn't bad enough that all his clothes were hand-me-downs: Worse yet, they had been worn by people who despised him, stared at him, and laughed behind his back.

"It was," he told Reinhardt, "like wearing the skin of a dead man."

Only on the hunt, in nature's solitude, could Charlie find some measure of peace. "I am put up with," he wrote, "when I stay away from people and keep my mouth shut." There were times when he imagined living in the woods, in a simple cabin, taking on a hermit's life, but by his middle teens he was already hooked on Death. *She* was his refuge from a world of hate, and Charlie hoped she would not keep him waiting long.

Charlie had banished all feelings of guilt or regret. He no longer wept in rage or embarrassment: "The crying had dried up." His only craving now was for a measure of control over his enemies, a chance to "leave his mark" before he died. Charlie convinced himself that he could live "without loving." He had no wish "to love or to be loved."

And then, he met Caril Ann.

4

Something Worth Killing For

The fateful meeting was arranged by Bob Von Busch, in 1956. He had been dating Barbara Fugate, from the Belmont neighborhood, and Bob kept telling Charlie he should meet Barb's younger sister, Caril Ann. She was barely thirteen, Bob admitted, but she looked five years older, and she had a sassy style that Charlie might appreciate.

Charlie agreed to the meeting and liked what he saw. He asked Caril out, and she accepted. The two couples wound up on a double date at the Nebraska Theater, and the rest, as someone said, is history. From that day forward, Caril Ann would only date one other boy. When Charlie heard about it, he tracked the boy down and threatened to kill him if he "bothered" Caril Ann again. The other boy took Charlie at his word and scratched Caril off his list. Word got around that Charlie and Caril Ann were "going steady."

"After that," Bob told reporter William Allen, "it was the four of us running around together. We went to the movies a lot, the drive-ins mostly. It was all we were old enough to do. But these weren't hot dates at all. It was more like a bunch of kids just piling in the car and looking for a good time. Charlie was pretty young for his age. He wasn't much for making out at all. To tell the truth, I don't think he knew what to do with it. He talked about it a lot, but when it came down to doing anything, I think he just got too excited. And Caril was awfully young, too. She didn't know her way around nearly as well as people thought."

In fact, the memories of young Caril Ann Fugate are almost as strongly divided as those of Charlie Starkweather. Some adults who knew her in those days described her as "spunky," possessed of a certain "elfish charm," but one man's spunk is another's insolence. Caril Ann could be quick-tempered and rebellious, too: One family friend recalled her as a "little snip." Small but well developed for her tender age, she favored a ponytail for her dark brown hair, preferring dungarees and a man's shirt with the sleeves rolled up over dresses. Growing up poor in Belmont, the product of a broken home, she had acquired an attitude that made her seem older, more mature than thirteen. She could swear like a sailor, surprising even Charlie at times, and she had learned to drive a car before most girls gave it a second thought.

It was easy to see why Charlie was smitten. "I never saw a fourteen-year-old girl who knowed so much," he explained from prison. "She could talk like a grown-up woman. She was no kid. It was her being so grown-up, I guess, that made me want to be with her."

And best of all, she liked him back.

Despite the "grown-up" facade, however, Caril Ann was, in her own way, as backward as Charles. Like him, she had failed a grade in elementary school and was branded a slow learner. She had never heard of President Harry Truman, and she didn't know America had been involved in the Korean War. Caril Ann had never traveled out of state; indeed, she had rarely left Lincoln. Omaha, less than sixty miles away, was as foreign to her as the ruins of ancient Rome.

Authors searching for descriptions of Caril Ann, long

after the fact, inevitably fall back on clichés about how absolutely *normal* she appeared. One found her "a typical, colorless, teenaged girl in a normal, nondramatic, midwestern setting," while another pegged her as "a perfect assimilation of the attitudes, fads, and fashions of the times." And both are correct—but only to a point.

The rebellious streak that several neighbors noted and remarked upon ran deeper in Caril Ann than in most other girls her age in Belmont, in the 1950s. It is safe to say that she picked up on something similar in Charlie Starkweather and felt herself attracted to his wild side, the resentment toward society that he was barely keeping under wraps.

The trouble, typically, began at home.

Velda Fugate had divorced Caril's father in 1951 and was remarried to an older man, twenty-two years her senior, with whom she had another child. It's possible that Marion Bartlett was simply too old and set in his ways to "relate" to an adolescent girl. A stern, hardworking man, he believed in an orderly, traditional world, where children did as they were told, *when* they were told, without complaints or "sass."

There is no evidence that Caril Ann was abused at home, but abuse is in the eye of the beholder. Take one feisty teenage girl, subtract a father, and replace him with an older man—a stranger, really—whose ideas of discipline may seem medieval to the child. Toss in a brand-new sister, thus depriving the rebellious child of cherished status as the "baby" of the family. Add several heaping tablespoons of poverty, to nudge the adolescent dreams well out of reach, and clamp a lid on any aspirations for a better life.

The pot was clearly simmering on Belmont Avenue, long before Charlie Starkweather came along and turned up the heat.

Charlie later told James Reinhardt that before he met Caril, the world was "getting more hazy," and he felt himself losing touch with his life. Sometimes he fell asleep at work, or simply sat and daydreamed, drifting in a fantasy realm of his own creation. Once Death came calling, he looked forward to her visits, hoping she would be his "way out."

Caril Ann changed everything. In Charlie's mind, she was the only person on earth who would never leave him. They would spend the rest of their lives together, and Caril Ann would join him on the road "to the next world." Before Caril, he told Reinhardt, "I wasn't too particular about the way I went, 'cause I knowed Death had it all figgered out. Then Caril stirred up somethin' in me . . . [I] guess it was already there, 'cause it came easy and it seemed like it was somethin' I'd been waitin' for."

There was an *urgency* about the new direction in his life, the sense of working on a deadline. Those around him noted Charlie's disengagement from the world, his job, his family. He was burning bridges, and nothing mattered, "so long as [he] had Caril."

"I got divided away from people," he later explained, "but that wasn't because I got in with Caril. It was that way before I knowed Caril."

In his prison conversations with Reinhardt, Charlie admitted to limited sexual contact with girls before Caril Ann, but the criminologist was "not convinced that he lacked sexual maturity." In any case, as Charlie said, Caril "brought everything out." He *wanted* her, and yet the fantasies that filled his waking hours still revolved more around violence and mayhem than sex. When he fantasized about intercourse, it was typically as an expression of power, rather than lust. Caril slipped into his fantasies like the missing piece from a puzzle. She would be his cheerleader, companion, and doting audience. To that extent, at least, she was objectified in Charlie's mind, dehumanized.

But Caril Ann didn't seem to care. She overlooked his speech impediment and runty stature, bowlegs and myopia. His lack of marketable job skills did not faze her. She was not put off by Charlie's temper or "black moods"; if anything, his quirky personality attracted her, convinced Caril Ann that he was a bona fide "rebel without a cause." Instead of adding up his debits and deleting Charlie from her life, she was impressed by his car, his looks, his marksmanship, his "fighting reputation." He was every mother's nightmare, every bobby-soxer's dream.

And he could give her things, despite his skimpy paychecks. Asked about the various possessions found in Caril Ann's room—a phonograph, jewelry, a radio—Charlie told Reinhardt, "If it's there, I gave it to her."

From prison, Charlie would say that he "started a new kind of thinkin'" after he met Caril Ann, but it is more correct to call his thoughts a variation on the old, familiar theme. Since kindergarten, Charlie had felt isolated from the world outside his home and the "enchanted forest" of his youth. Caril Ann did nothing to repair his break with civilized society; instead, she joined him in his self-inflicted exile.

"She meant something that nothing else had ever meant," he told Reinhardt. "I knowed that without her it was going right back to the hated world I was trying to leave. I couldn't go back. I'd rather kill and be killed." In Charlie's mind, his new relationship with Caril was everything, "and it all ended right here. It was something to live for, something to live with. How long? It didn't matter."

They quarreled from time to time, as lovers will, but never over anything of consequence. "I had a way of bringing her around," Charlie said. "She'd do anything I wanted." Where other girls looked down on Charlie, Caril Ann seemed to idolize him. "I quit hatin' myself," he told Reinhardt, "'cause Caril made me quit thinking about my bowlegs. Caril liked my legs. She said the more bowed they were, the better she liked them. She liked my size, too, and she liked to run her fingers through my hair."

It was a new experience for Charlie. Everything about him that provoked derision from his peers delighted Caril Ann. When they were together, he told himself, "Nothin' will ever make me better nor happier than I am now." With Caril in his life, Charlie said, "[i]t was not going home alone, nor being alone any more. It was now I belonged to something."

In the jargon of their era, they had found "togetherness," but it did not extend to anybody else. "We didn't want to spread ourselves out for people to look at," Charlie said. "We wanted to be separated from everybody else. People who looked at us would only laugh. Friends were not for us."

It is impossible to say how much of Charlie's isolationism Caril Ann truly shared. She may have gone along with him to make him happy, or her own estrangement from her broken family may have inclined her toward a world view that was similar to his. They avoided hanging out with "uppity kids from big houses," keeping mostly to themselves when they were not on double dates with Barb and Bob Von Busch.

Caril "made time pass fast" for Charlie. He lost interest in visiting beer joints and playing "chicken." Those around him noted that he calmed perceptibly and seemed less prone to tantrums. If they took him for a new man, however, they were very much mistaken. His feelings for Caril Ann did not translate into any general affection for mankind.

Charlie made a point of telling Reinhardt that Caril "never made me love anybody else. I've heard that when a man loves one girl, he loves everybody a little more. I never tried to love anybody else. I got a kind of thrill out of telling the world to go to hell." In fact, by learning not to hate himself, he had *more* time and energy for hating others. "People didn't bother me no more," Charlie said. "I still hated them, but I had something new. It took away the dread." Perhaps, but he was still uncertain "how I could have wanted to live at all, even with Caril, if I had suddenly quit hating other people, or if suddenly I had found the world worth living in."

The hate was part of Charlie. Letting go of it meant giving up his very life.

Somewhere between the drive-in dates and demolition derbies, Caril Ann was inducted into Charlie's morbid fantasies. His last girlfriend had been discarded for "upsetting his death deal," but Caril seemed to fit right in, whether she knew it or not. "The thought of dying was old to me," Charlie wrote from his cell. "Something to live for, before dying, was new. Something worth killing for had come."

That "something" was Caril.

They may have discussed lashing out at the world, may have plotted a campaign, at least in general terms. No one but Caril Ann will ever know. In any case, as far as Charlie was concerned, they had an understanding. "We'd make people the way we wanted to make them," he told Reinhardt. "They wouldn't love us, but that didn't matter, 'cause we thought enough of each other to last as long as we would last, and after that it didn't matter. Anyhow, the people we got through with *couldn't* hate us."

Not if they were dead.

Caril Ann was finally responsible, however indirectly, for Charlie leaving home. While working at the Newspaper Union, he had devised a plan to get her home from school each day. Charlie would park his Ford close by the school and leave his key beneath the floor mat. Caril would drive it home, illegally, and Charlie would come by to get it later, begging rides from "friends" at work. It was a fine arrangement, for a while—until the afternoon Caril Ann got careless pulling into traffic and collided with a passing car. No one was hurt, and Caril Ann got off easy, forced to write a five-hundred-word essay for the police on the perils of driving without a license. Charlie was not present at the accident, but lawmen slapped him with a ticket for allowing Caril to drive the Ford illegally.

Guy Starkweather was livid. He had taken out a $150 loan to help Charlie purchase the car, and its title was in both their names. He demanded Charlie's promise that Caril Ann would never drive the Ford again. It is a measure of Charlie's infatuation with Caril that he defied his father for the first time, not only refusing to promise, but furthermore staging an incident where two of his younger brothers saw Caril Ann driving the car. The resultant father-son confrontation got physical, with Guy's account the only eyewitness version that remains on record.

"He more or less wanted to go out on his own," Guy later said, "and I forbid him to let Caril drive his car. He slipped, stumbled, and fell back through the window. Charlie slapped me, and I slapped him one back. The windows are low, and he fell into it."

It was the last straw for both. Bob Von Busch remembers Guy shouting at Charlie to get out and never come back. Charlie, for his part, was so enraged that he slammed his fist through one of the Ford's side windows. Bob and Barbara were married by that time, living at Mae Hawley's rooming house on Tenth Street, and Charlie moved in with them for several weeks, until the landlady started dropping none-too-subtle hints that a young married couple didn't need an extra man around the house. She offered him a room across the hall from Bob and Barb, and Charlie was still living there when he began to kill, a few months later.

Guy Starkweather regretted that final scene with Charlie, and while they never really patched things up, he did not go so far as barring Charlie from the house. It took some time, but Charlie started dropping by to visit, maybe grab a bite to eat. The holidays were coming on, but he would not be spending them at home. Everywhere he looked, there were signs that it was time for a change: Brother Rodney and Bob Von Busch were both married men; brother Leonard, the second oldest, had gone off to take a job in Washington state. The family was dwindling, and it looked like Charlie's turn to strike off on his own.

With Caril.

He showed his devotion by spending the bulk of his paycheck on Caril every week. One gift was a gold heart-shaped pendant, with "Caril" engraved on one side and "Chuck" on the other. Caril Ann would be wearing it around her neck the day of her arrest. In mid-October 1957, shortly after leaving home, Charlie drove Caril Ann to the First National Bank of Lincoln, where they opened a joint savings account. It could have been the first step toward a solid life together, but nothing ever seemed to run that way where Charlie was concerned.

Over at the Newspaper Union, John Hedge was on the verge of firing Charlie for his inefficiency and dumb mistakes, but Charlie beat him to the punch and quit his job. His stated reason was that Hedge hired "college boys," made Charlie train them, then promoted them to better-paying jobs, while Charlie lingered at the bottom of the heap. It would have been a fair complaint, if not for Charlie's record on the job, but it was only an excuse.

Caril was the reason Charlie quit his job. He wanted morning work, something that left him free to pick her up from school at 3:00 P.M. Rodney was still employed at Neiderhaus, and Charlie had no difficulty picking up the garbage-hauling trade where he'd left off. Most days, they finished up the route and the attendant cleanup chores in time for him keep his rendezvous with Caril.

The new problem was money. Neiderhaus was paying Charlie forty-two dollars a week, but that wasn't enough to pay his bills *and* lavish gifts on Caril. She came first, in Charlie's mind, and he was soon behind on rent. Mae Hawley started locking him out when he couldn't come up with the money, and Charlie began hanging out at the Crest gas station, on Cornhusker Highway, killing homeless nights with pump jockey Robert McClung.

Months later, in court, McClung would testify about those nights with Charlie, recalling how Starkweather rambled on about cars—rebuilding them and racing at Capitol Beach—when he wasn't bumming sodas or cigarette money. "His conversation didn't always make sense," McClung recalled. "he would talk in circles, and his intelligence seemed limited. He affected me as a person who needed help." Under questioning by prosecutor Elmer Scheele, McClung compared Charlie to a "three-dollar bill," adding: "He is like nothing I have ever seen."

Money aside, the return to hauling garbage was a bitter setback for Charlie. It confirmed the smug opinions of those who had him "numbered for the bottom," reinforcing Charlie's sense of failure in life. He hated the people who left their trash at the curb, yearning for a chance "to throw garbage in somebody's face." Some of the Neiderhaus clients recalled his sullen attitude, but they wisely kept their mouths shut. In Charlie's terms, they "knowed better than to say nothin' to me when [I'm] heavin' their goddamn garbage."

Still, he endured the torment for Caril Ann. "We had to be together," he told Reinhardt. "We had to have money." Lugging garbage to the truck, Charlie filled his mind with images of "how Caril looked last night" or how "her arms and lips felt." Without her, "life was not worth living," but even that feeling of shelter "didn't last long."

If nothing else, at least Caril Ann gave focus to his vision of the future. "One time," Charlie recalled, "I was afraid to die. I used to want to shoot up the world for no reason . . . I was mad at the world. Then Caril made things clear; then everything had a reason. I knowed the end was comin', but it had a reason, too."

And yet, beneath the teenage adulation, Charlie's feelings for Caril remained ambiguous. In custody, he first professed undying love, but later changed his tune. When Reinhardt asked if he had ever *really* loved Caril Ann, Charlie replied: "Not much." She had "laughed at my notion" about a compact with Death, yet she was still willing to accompany Charlie on his last ride. "That was it," he explained. "That was it. A girl to go all the way."

In Charlie's stunted mind, it was like something from a "shooting movie," where the hero and his girl square off against the world, to live or die by their wits and their proficiency with guns. He told Reinhardt that "Havin' Caril with me, doin' the things we was doin' together as the end was comin' on, was different from anything I'd ever had before. It didn't seem real, somehow. Maybe that's why I didn't want to avoid whatever happened. That wouldn't be real, either."

Even so, jailbird Charlie couldn't resist a parting shot at

Caril Ann from death row, suggesting that she had somehow led him to his own destruction, set him up. "I can see her better now," he said. "She knowed more'n I give her credit for knowin'. I can see it now, but I couldn't see it then."

Then, he was busy weaving fantasies about the life they planned to spend together, dropping by the Newspaper Union on his afternoons off, bullshitting with the guys. He told them he and Caril were married, but the story wouldn't fly, since she was underage. "Well, anyway, I'm gonna be a father," Charlie said. "Caril's pregnant." It was yet another lie, but rumors get around, and this one made its way to Belmont Avenue.

Marion Bartlett had never liked Charlie. He was repulsed by the young man's hair, his "sloppy clothes," the fact that Charlie's grand ambition seemed to lie in hauling trash. He didn't care for Charlie's language, the profanity and teenage slang. Most of all, he despised Charlie's arrogance, the look he saw in those slanted eyes when Marion told him to stay away from Caril Ann. He knew that Charlie longed to curse him, maybe even punch him out. Charlie brought out the worst in Caril Ann, her youthful defiance toward Velda, her natural resentment of Marion as the outsider who had stepped into her father's shoes. By dating Charlie, she could "show" them both at once. The more her parents disapproved of Starkweather, the more Caril Ann was drawn to him, compelled to rub him in their faces.

The rumor of Caril's pregnancy was bad enough, but Charlie's proposal of marriage was the last straw. Marion rejected the notion as absurd, reminding Charlie of Caril Ann's tender age and his own pathetic finances. If the youngsters found a way to marry despite his objections, Marion warned, he and Velda would have the marriage annulled, pursue their legal options against Charlie for statutory rape.

Marion was so angry at Charlie, this time, that he could not keep it to himself. Pouring out his heart to relatives, he listed all his grievances against young Starkweather: the hair and clothes, his nasty language, Charlie's evident determination to remain a garbage man. One family member told him not to worry. Given time, the kids would drift apart, as teenage lovers always seemed to do.

"That," Marion said, "is a day I'll be happy to see."

Still, Charlie was persistent. When he raised the specter of marriage a second time, Marion Bartlett was livid, responding with a terse ultimatum. "If you ever mention the subject again," he told Charlie, "you are through seeing Caril Ann for good."

A part of Charlie may have been relieved, for even as he badgered Marion with the proposals, he was skeptical about his future as a husband. Settling down with Caril Ann, he feared, "would be the same thing all over again." He could never hope to build a life for two as a garbage man or in some other dead-end job, "carrying things from one place to another." Charlie acknowledged that "Caril and me never talked about havin' children. I didn't think there would be time for that. Besides, children didn't belong to our kind of thinkin'."

Still, there was a world of difference between giving up on marriage and giving up on *Caril*. She was the only thing on earth with living—or killing—for, and Charlie would not let her slip away. Retreating to his private world of fantasy, Charles seemed to know that he was on the edge. He dared not speak his morbid dreams aloud to anyone but Caril. The larger world would think he was a lunatic, and Charlie made a mental note to shun "the place for crazy people at all costs."

Increasingly, he felt bound to Caril Ann, isolated with her in the midst of a hostile world. "The sullen feeling didn't leave me," Charlie told James Reinhardt, "but it changed. Before I met Caril, my family was all I had. Now, they seemed to be gettin' in my way." Being alone with Caril Ann was like "owning a little world of our own," where nothing could touch them. As for the larger world of men, "[w]e was gonna make it leave us alone . . . [I]f we'da been left alone, we wouldn'ta hurt nobody."

Charlie's familiar lament. It was "the other guy," always "asking for it," every time he turned around. He felt his short life building to a crisis, paranoia taking over to the point that he imagined Marion and Velda Bartlett plotting his death to keep him away from Caril Ann. The solution came to Charlie in a flash: "I must get her away. I'll let her see that I'll kill for her."

How to proceed? He didn't have a clue, but felt that time was running out. "Soon," Charlie thought, "I'll be buried with the dead days. Better to be left to rot on some high hill behind a rock, and be remembered, than to be buried alive in some stinkin' place, and go to bed smelly like a garbage can every night."

In his frustration, Charlie started visiting his favorite dives again. Hanging out at beer joints, Charlie could "forget there, how I was not wanted anywhere else." He thought about his family, sometimes wishing that he could recapture the early days in his "enchanted forest," but his thoughts always returned to Caril Ann. They would "do big things together." He would make her love him all the more, for his skill as an outlaw. It would be just like in the "shooting movies" he adored.

Of course, Charlie told Reinhardt, "I knowed they'd catch me, but what difference did that make? I was through with garbage, emptiness and small fighting that gets you nothing but more hate. . . . A gun can make the people that hate you afraid. A gun can make a girl stand by you."

Suddenly, he didn't mind the old clothes any more. "They cover a man," Charlie said, "and you don't have to be afraid of spoiling them." Even his bowlegs looked better, in the light of his new revelation. "They are my kind of legs," he decided, "just made for me." As for his size, Charlie began to think of himself as "the little killer," asking, "How big was Napoleon?"

The dynamics of his relationship with Caril Ann had come to define Charlie's life. She fit no better with his family than he did with hers, but she *belonged* to him. "Before I met Caril," Charlie wrote from prison, "I wasn't nobody, just a guy with a 'stiff prick' and a little money . . . I knowed [Caril Ann] wouldn't be putting out for some other guy [the] next night."

What kind of future would he have, Charlie asked himself, "throwin' garbage and pickin' up a whore"? Life stretched before him like a barren wasteland. "Forty years?" he wrote. "Too long. Ten years? Too long. Better a week, with the one who loved me for what I was."

In jailhouse interviews and writings, Charlie makes repeated references to "Caril and me decid[ing] what we was going to do." Foreknowledge of the murders would become a crucial issue at Caril's trial, but in the weeks before he killed, there seems no doubt that Charlie *felt* they had an understanding. They were going to live for the moment and "finish together at the same rope." To be with Caril for those brief, shining moments in the spotlight, Charlie was prepared to face the "cold and unpleasant business toward the end of the road."

And the end was coming, Charlie realized. He felt the blood run "hot and cold" in his veins. He saw Caril in his Death dreams, "white and beautiful," supplanting the Grim Reaper as his guide. "Now," he wrote, "everything that mattered was bound up with the girl." Caril Ann's presence in his fantasy world "gave me something that wasn't there before. She put spark and thrill into the killing."

5

First Blood

Cornhusker Highway defines northern Lincoln, winding its irregular way from northeast to southwest, past the State Fairgrounds, skirting the University of Nebraska's Lincoln campus and aiming westbound travelers toward Capitol Beach Lake. In the 1950s, before Interstate 80 divided the state on an east-west axis, Cornhusker Highway saw most of the traffic bound from Omaha to points west, along Highway 6. Sunbaked in summer, plowed and salted in winter, the highway never closed—and neither did the service stations spotted here and there along both sides.

The Crest station, in those days, had cinder block walls and two wide garage doors facing out toward the highway. A triangular canopy stretched from the building to the double row of gas pumps, sheltering customers from rain and snow, though it could not protect them from the biting prairie winds. A large billboard stood to the west of the station, urging drivers IN ALL 48 STATES GET THE BEST! ASK FOR ETHYL! At night, the station's lighted sign was visible for miles, a giant crimson arrow pointing to the price of gasoline: 28.9¢

per gallon. Red pennants fluttered on the station's two light poles.

On the first day of December 1957, the Crest station was decked out for winter and Christmas. A small cardboard sign on one of the gas pumps advertised FRUIT CAKES 98¢, and a special display of Firestone Christmas records occupied one corner of the office, near the window. A box of plastic ice scrapers sat beside the cash register, while a nude pinup calendar decorated one of the walls, still acceptable in those days before mechanics were politically correct.

The station's night man, Robert Colvert, had no time for Miss December in the wee hours of Sunday morning. Business had slacked off at the pumps, thanks in equal part to the hour and the frigid temperature outside, but Colvert still had work to do in the garage, tune-ups and engine repairs that had to be finished bright and early on Monday. Besides, he had a nineteen-year-old wife at home, expecting their first child. It didn't hurt to look, sometimes, but there was only one girl in his life.

At twenty-one, recently discharged from the Navy, Colvert counted himself lucky to have a job he enjoyed. He had only been working at the Crest for two weeks, since he replaced Bob McClung, but he liked it just fine. Colvert already knew most of the college kids who stopped for gas between the football games and forays to the all-night Campus Hut, a diner several hundred yards west of the station. Many of the seniors were Colvert's age, but they still liked to tease him, calling him "Pops" as he filled up their tanks and wiped their windshields. Now and then, Colvert would join them at the Campus Hut for breakfast or a basket of chicken with french fries, toast, and honey.

At five foot six, 150 pounds, Colvert had been nicknamed "Little Bob" by his friends in school, but his stylish pompadour made him look taller, and he carried himself well. The Navy had taught him that. He didn't mind the graveyard shift, because it gave him time to think and work in peace. His wife was fond of saying that their marriage worked so well because they hardly saw each other, but he knew the late-night hours bothered her. She worried about holdups, for one thing, but station manager Leonard Wright had laid down the law on that score, Colvert's first day at work.

"If a guy comes in with a gun," Wright said, "give him everything in the place. Don't be a hero. Don't even *look* like you're going to argue."

That was fine with Colvert, and he readily agreed. So far, in two weeks on the job, his only problem with a customer had been some red-haired kid who tried to buy a teddy bear on credit, then got mouthy when Colvert told him he'd have to pay cash. It was no big deal, and Colvert couldn't have described the punk in any detail, now, a week after the incident.

That Sunday morning, Robert found the time to telephone his wife. He knew she waited up, hoping to hear from him, and didn't seem to mind if he woke her when he called.

"Are you warm enough?" she asked, first thing.

"I'm fine," he told her. "What have you been doing, Hon?"

"I baked a cake, and I've been making lists of baby names," she said. "One if it's a girl, another if it's a boy."

"Read 'em off," Robert said. "I'll help you pick."

She went to get the lists while Robert waited. He was smiling as she started reading off the names.

"For a girl, Eileen, Mary-Lynn, Iris . . ."

A bell rang from the pumps out front, announcing the arrival of another customer.

"I heard," his wife said. "Go ahead. I'll read the rest tomorrow."

" 'Kay. I'll see you in the morning, Hon. I love you."

"Night. I love you, too."

It was the last time she would hear her husband's voice.

Bob Colvert didn't know it, but he had been marked to die before he ever went to work on Saturday, November 30. In fact, he had already lived through one near-miss.

That morning, shortly after 1:00 A.M., a blue '49 Ford had pulled into the station, parking to one side, away from the pumps. The driver was a young man with a ducktail haircut, glasses, and a face that should have been familiar. Colvert couldn't place him, though. The guy asked for a screwdriver, to make some kind of small adjustment on his car, and Colvert loaned him one. He thought nothing about it, got distracted when a carload of college students pulled in to fill up, and by the time he finished jawboning with them, the Ford was gone. He hadn't noticed when it left, but Colvert found the screwdriver sitting on the station's window ledge, beside the door.

It barely qualified as an encounter, and Colvert had forgotten all about the incident by the time he left work, at 7:00 A.M. Still dark in Lincoln, but the frosty daylight would be breaking soon, and he would have to sleep behind closed blinds.

If Bob McClung had been around, he could have briefed his young replacement on the stranger in the Ford. McClung had never learned his name, oddly enough, but they had spent a lot of time together, talking about cars, when Charlie Starkweather was locked out of Mae Hawley's rooming house. He gave McClung the creeps, sometimes, insisting that Bob come outside and *feel* the paint job on his Ford, but there was nothing to suggest that he was dangerous. McClung could not have known about the 12-gauge shotgun Charlie carried in his car that Friday night, when he came by to case the station for a robbery.

Colvert's wife was asleep when he got home on Saturday, and gone when he got up, a little after noon. The note she left told Robert she was going to the doctor, and to do some Christmas shopping. He had showered, shaved, and dressed before she came in with her purchases and started fixing lunch, along with Robert's sandwiches for work that night. There was a small sack on the kitchen table, and it rattled when he picked it up.

"What's this?" he asked.

"The baby's Christmas present."

Opening the bag, he found a little plastic duck with some kind of beads inside that made it rattle in his hand.

"The baby won't be born 'til after New Year's," he reminded her.

"So what? It still deserves a present. I hid yours already."

"Yeah? What is it?" Robert asked.

She made a face. "You think I'd tell?"

" 'Kay, then," he said. *"I* won't tell *you."*

She ate a tuna sandwich while he worked on eggs and sausage, breakfast once removed.

"I'm thinking we should hit the Cornhusker for New Year's Eve," said Colvert. The Cornhusker Hotel was one of Lincoln's gala spots to spend a night out on the town. It featured an outstanding restaurant and bar, live music, and the place was always packed on New Year's Eve.

"In my condition? I don't think so."

"You don't show that much," he told her.

"That's what *you* think. They don't make maternity formals, Hon. I'd rather just stay home, unless we get asked to a private party."

"Well, if you're sure."

"I'm sure."

"What did the doctor say?"

"All normal. Right on schedule."

Colvert must have known that, though. She would have told him right away if anything was wrong.

The temperature was falling by the time he started getting dressed for work, and Colvert knew it would be well below the freezing mark out on the highway. Heading out the door at half past six, he wore Navy fatigues and heavy socks, a pair of thick-soled shoes, a fleece-lined jacket and a cap with earflaps, leather fur-lined gloves. The wind could do its worst; he didn't plan to freeze.

"See you tonight," his wife called to him, as he left, then caught herself. "I mean, tomorrow."

"See you, Hon. I'll call you, if I get a chance."

* * *

Across town, Charlie Starkweather awoke from a fitful sleep, just shy of noon on Saturday. It had been 2:30 A.M. before he got to bed, and he had drifted into gruesome nightmares, waking with another of his too familiar headaches. Aspirin helped a little, washed down with a cup of instant coffee, but the flat was cold, and Charlie shivered as he started getting dressed.

He thought about his dry run at the filling station, Colvert and the money slipping through his fingers, and he cursed the college punks who had prevented him from taking down the score. He could have gone back later, once they left, but Charlie couldn't swear that none of them had seen his car, perhaps his face. They wouldn't *know* him—Charlie didn't hang out with the goddamn stuck-up college crowd—but they could still describe him to the cops, describe his Ford. Hell, maybe one of them had even glimpsed his license plate.

He would go back tonight and do it properly, but he had time to kill.

At least he had the small apartment to himself. Mac Hawley had locked him out again, and he was rooming with Rudy Warren, another hauler from the garbage route, but Rudy had left to visit family in Omaha on Friday afternoon, and he would not be back until some time on Sunday night. They had been arguing a lot, the past few days, since Charlie had gotten fired for "goldbricking" and showed no inclination to go looking for another job.

What was the point? The bosses were against him anyway, no matter where he went. They had him "numbered for the bottom." Charlie couldn't win. The whole damn world was on his back, except for Caril Ann.

But Charlie had a plan in mind to show them all.

He spent a long time at the mirror, practicing The Look and making sure he got his hair just right. When it was perfect, Charlie made a sandwich, turning on the radio and listening to Christmas songs mixed in with rock 'n' roll. Some Elvis. Jimmie Rodgers. "Jingle Bell Rock." Charlie whistled along with Elvis, but he didn't try singing or dancing. Even in a room alone, he knew his limitations.

Some of them, at least.

When Charlie finished eating, he spent the best part of an hour breaking down the shotgun he had "borrowed" from Sonny Von Busch's garage, oiling it until it gleamed, then reassembling the gun with expert hands. He didn't think Bob's cousin would miss the gun for a while—and if he did, so what? No one had been around when Charlie lifted it on Friday afternoon. They couldn't prove a thing.

Two things he knew about a shotgun, from experience and from the "shooting movies" he enjoyed so much: First, no one could survive a close-range blast. And second, since the shotgun was a smooth-bore weapon, it left no ballistics marks on its projectiles for the cops to look at underneath their microscopes.

The 12-gauge would be perfect for the job he had in mind.

When he was finished working on the gun, reloading it, and posing with it in the mirror, Charlie telephoned Caril Ann. Her mother answered, barely civil to him, and he heard the disapproval in her voice as she told Caril, "It's Chuck."

A moment later, Caril Ann's voice came through the earpiece.

"Hi!" She sounded cheerful.

"Can you get away?" asked Charlie.

"Yeah, but Mom says I haveta be home early. We stayed out too late the last time."

Charlie scowled. He could still remember last week's ugly scene, when he took Caril Ann home at midnight in the middle of the week, a school night. Old Man Bartlett had been giving him the bad eye, telling him he ought to find a girl his own age, for a change.

"It's Saturday," he told her, peevishly. "I wanna go to the drive-in, after the races. Tell her we'll be back by eleven."

"Have you got enough money?" Caril asked.

"Five dollars," Charlie told her. "Maybe I can win some at the track."

"Maybe you *won't,*" said Caril Ann, teasing him. "I've got a dollar. Lemme go ask Mom."

He waited on the line, heard muffled voices in the background, Mrs. Bartlett finally giving in. "All right," she said at last. "But be home by eleven, Caril, for sure. Your dad will ground you for good, if you're late again."

Caril came back on the line. "Okay," she said. "When are you coming?"

"Right away."

It was always something of an ordeal, going to the Bartletts'. Charlie didn't like the way Caril's parents looked at him, like he could never pass inspection in their eyes, no matter what he did or said. They had him marked down as a two-bit loser, just like everybody else. The old man wasn't home this time, but Velda Bartlett warned him once again about Caril's curfew.

"Don't you stay out past eleven," she was telling him, "or Mr. Bartlett will be *really* mad."

What else was new?

"We'll be at the drive-in right when the show starts," said Charlie. "I promise we'll be back in time."

It wasn't far from Caril Ann's house, in Belmont, to the race track at Capitol Beach. The old Ford's heater kept them warm, and Charlie fiddled with the radio until he found an Elvis song. With Caril Ann snuggled up beside him, Charlie didn't care what happened next. The world could end that very minute, and he wouldn't mind.

As long as he could get a few licks in against his enemies before it blew.

The race track's parking lot was unpaved dirt, already crowded when they got there. Charlie found a place and led Caril Ann inside, holding her hand. If anyone was staring at him now, he calculated, it was not about his bowlegs or his hair. The sons of bitches would be green with envy, seeing him with Caril.

They separated once inside the fence, Caril looking for a place to sit up in the bleachers, while Charlie made his way onto the track. A battered Chevrolet was waiting for him, lined up with the other cars preparing for the demolition derby. Charlie could have driven in a normal race, but he preferred the demos, smashing into other cars with everything he had and watching as the drivers jolted in their seats. And knowing Caril was up there in the bleachers, watching him, that was the best. The money, if he won some, was a bonus, frosting on the cake.

In fact, he won that afternoon, a twenty-dollar purse. Some of the spectators who knew him would look back on Charlie's driving later, using 20/20 hindsight, and remark on how the demo derby seemed to mesh with his approach to life in general. Smash the other guy, before he has a chance to nail you first.

The victory gave Charlie heart. It stiffened his resolve to make another run at Colvert and the filling station. Hell, it was dumb luck those stuck-up college kids had come along last night. The odds against him being interrupted two nights in a row were . . . well, he reckoned they were too damn long to matter.

Charlie had been counting on a meal of Coke and hot dogs at the track, but with a crisp new twenty in his pocket, he decided they should live it up. He drove Caril Ann to the Wagon Train Steakhouse, getting there well ahead of the main dinner crowd. No reservation, but they didn't need one. If the waitress gave a second glance at Charlie's hand-me-downs, he let it slide.

They settled in a booth and Caril Ann read the menu to him. Charlie found that he was ravenous, elated by his big win at the track, excited by the prospect of his great adventure later on. He ordered a double-thick porterhouse, rare, while Caril Ann went for the filet mignon. They both had french-fried onions, coffee, and pie à la mode for dessert. While Caril Ann sipped her coffee, Charlie got a paper from the wire rack near the door, and checked the movie page.

They settled on *The Enemy Below,* with Robert Mitchum, playing at the Cornhusker Drive-In. Charlie liked war movies, and Robert Mitchum was one of Caril's favorite actors, more a father figure than the kind of star a fourteen-year-old girl would have a crush on. Anyway, the second movie was a Western, lots of gunplay, and the double-feature put them out at half past ten, with time to spare for getting Caril Ann home.

They kissed good-night, and Caril Ann waved as Charlie drove away. Instead of going home directly, Charlie stopped off at a beer joint near the rooming house, to get some liquid courage. It was after midnight, Sunday morning, when he got back to the seedy flat and made his way inside.

Inside the small apartment, Charlie switched the television on and watched part of a murder mystery. He had no sense of irony, but it amused him to be sitting there and watching fictional detectives muddle through a case that Charlie could have solved in seconds flat.

His headache had returned, but that was nothing new. He took some aspirin, washed them down with whiskey—Rudy's bottle of Wild Turkey; screw him if it came up short—and waited for the pain to ebb. It didn't really matter if the headache went away or not. He still had work to do, and nothing was about to stop him this time. By and by, he felt a little better. Good enough, at least, to fetch and load the 12-gauge Remington. He had a box of shells from Greely's Hardware, number six shot, not that pellet size would matter for the work he had in mind. Up close, nobody could survive a shotgun blast, regardless of the load.

He slipped three shells into the weapon's magazine and worked the slide to put one in the chamber. Careful not to touch the trigger now, he practiced sighting—on the television, at the kitchen counters, out the window. Finally, when he was satisfied, he put the safety on and grabbed his jacket from a nearby chair. Besides the shotgun, Charlie took a pair of leather gloves, a canvas money bag that he had picked up on his garbage route, a hunter's cap with ear flaps, and a red bandana. It was half past 2:00 A.M., and there was no one stirring in the house or on the street outside, to see him go.

For weeks before his dry run at the filling station, Charlie's world had narrowed to a kind of tunnel vision, focused totally on Caril Ann and his craving for "some action," to the virtual exclusion of all else. He later told his prosecutors of a vague plan to "get out of town" with Caril Ann, but neither of them had the money they would need to reach escape velocity.

"For a long time," he said, "we made plans to run away, and we had to have money. I thought of robbing a bank, but I knowed there was money in the filling station box, and I decided, several days before I killed Colvert, to get it."

Charlie later told James Reinhardt that he planned the robbery for two weeks in advance, several times sleeping in his car outside the station, so that he could clock the young attendant's movements. There were no security devices in those days, and Charlie knew the station had a safe behind the office counter. He had seen it more than once, when he was hanging out with Bob McClung and talking hot-rods, bumming cigarettes.

There was no need to "case" the job, per se. It was supposed to be a simple in-and-out, no one the wiser. He would wear the red bandana as a mask, like Jesse James, and let the cops go hunting for some transient off the highway, passing through.

As for Bob Colvert, Charlie hedged when Reinhardt asked him if he planned the murder going in. "I meant to get the money," Charlie answered, "but I'd kill him if he knowed who I was, 'cause dead men don't talk." Unsatisfied with the response, Reinhardt rephrased the question: "Would you have shot Colvert anyhow?"

A shrug from Charlie. "I don't know."

That said, we know Charlie was nursing a grudge against Colvert, brooding over Colvert's refusal to sell him the stuffed bear on credit. He had been embarrassed once again, another total stranger ragging on him, making him feel small. He had imagined killing other men for less—a whiff of attitude, a sidelong glance. If Colvert saw through Charlie's lame disguise, it would be his tough luck.

The little woodpecker was finished playing games.

The station looked deserted on his first pass. Charlie drove on for a quarter mile or so, then made a U-turn in the middle of the highway, doubling back. He pulled into the lot, switched off his engine, killed the lights. Determined not to be surprised this time, he left the shotgun on the floorboard of his car, behind the driver's seat, and walked up to the office. Stepping through the door, a welcome blast of heat enveloped him. He looked around the empty office, peering off toward the garage.

"Is anybody here?"

Bob Colvert came in through the side door, wiping stained hands on a greasy rag. "What can I do for you?"

"Gimme a pack of Camels."

"Camels, right."

He paid a quarter for the cigarettes and left the office, walked back to the Ford and drove away. There was nobody else around the place, as far as he could see, but Charlie meant to play it safe. He smoked a cigarette and drove some more before he turned around and headed back.

This time, as he approached the station's office, Charlie could see Colvert talking on the telephone. He hung up just as Charlie reached the door, no smile this time, a look that might have been suspicion on his face.

"Is there a problem?"

"Naw. I'll take a pack of Beechnut."

Colvert stared at Charlie for a moment, finally reaching underneath the counter for the gum.

"Five cents," he said, and took the nickel out of Charlie's hand.

"Hey, thanks again," said Charlie, headed out the door.

Again he drove away, felt Colvert watching him, God-*damn* it! What if he got spooked and called the cops? They could be on their way right now, and Charlie wouldn't know until the red lights started flashing in his rearview mirror. If they caught him with the gun, put two and two together—then, what?

Nothing.

There was no law said he couldn't buy a pack of smokes and accidentally forget about the gum. As for the 12-gauge, it was not illegal to have firearms in a car. He hadn't flashed the gun at anyone, or even carried it inside the station.

He was free and clear.

The more he thought about it, Charlie knew he had to do the job tonight, or not at all. Colvert had shamed him once, over the teddy bear, and he was not about to get another chance.

He drove back to the station, killed his lights before he pulled into the lot this time. It took a moment, tying the bandana snug around his face, then slipping on the cap and gloves. He stuffed the money bag into a pocket, took the shotgun with him as he left the car, and walked up to the office, slipping through the door as quiet as a mouse.

Colvert was back in the garage, so busy working on an Oldsmobile he didn't hear Starkweather creeping up behind him. Only when he felt the shotgun prodding him between his shoulder blades did he glance up and see the masked intruder standing over him.

There was no point in asking what the bandit wanted. Charlie wagged the shotgun's barrel toward the office, Colvert leading as they went to get the cash. Charlie was reaching for the money bag when he glanced through the window, suddenly annoyed by all the lights outside. Suppose someone was driving by and saw them standing there?

"Turn off those lights!" he snapped.

Bob Colvert went to the supply room, flipped the only switch he saw, and watched a couple of the lights go off outside. Still, there were others, shining on the pumps and ice-slick drive.

"You only got two of 'em!" Charlie shouted. "Turn the others off!"

Colvert was trembling now, as he replied, "I don't know where the other switches are."

"You're shittin' me!"

It seemed preposterous, but Charlie thought about it for a moment. Asshole works the night shift, goes home in the dark, maybe they *didn't* tell him how to kill the lights.

"Okay, forget about it. Give me all the money. Fast!"

He tossed the canvas bag to Colvert, watching as his hostage emptied out the cash drawer, adding loose change from his pockets. Anything to satisfy the Big Man with the gun. It was a heady rush.

When Colvert tried to hand the bag back, Charlie shook his head and gestured with the Remington. "I want it all," he said. "Open the safe."

Colvert went pale. "I can't," he said. "I don't know the combination. Honest, mister—if I could, I would! It's not my money."

Charlie felt like killing him right there, but he had worked the whole thing out ahead of time. What was the point of making plans, if you forgot about them in a pinch?

He felt the precious seconds ticking past. "All right," he said at last, "let's go."

"Go where?"

"You're coming with me," Charlie said. "We're going for a little ride."

He followed Colvert to the Ford, around to the passenger's side, eyes flicking nervously in the direction of the highway, back and forth. Before they reached the car, Starkweather realized he couldn't drive and keep his hostage covered with the shotgun, too.

"You're driving," Charlie said. "Get in."

Bob Colvert slid across the front seat, underneath the steering wheel, with Charlie right behind him, steady with the Remington. He passed the keys to Colvert, waited while his captive got the engine running. Charlie told him where to go, a right turn as they left the station, rolling northeast on the highway, being careful not to speed. A left on

Twenty-seventh Street, northbound, and left again when they got to Superior.

"Keep going," Charlie said.

Superior was one of Lincoln's make-out strips, an unpaved road where teenage couples often parked to have some privacy. Unpaved, it could be treacherous in rainy weather, but the ground was frozen now, no risk of bogging down. The hour and the cold ensured that there would be no witnesses.

"Go on past Bloody Mary's," Charlie ordered.

Bloody Mary was the nickname of an old woman who lived near Salt Creek Bridge. Some said her house was haunted, others that she was a witch. Kids sometimes dared each other to park in her driveway, maybe sneak up on the porch and touch the house itself. The risk involved was real enough, and hardly magical, since Bloody Mary kept a shotgun primed with rock salt and was not afraid to use it. Some years later, in the 1960s, she got tired of loading salt and switched to buckshot rounds. A teenage prowler lost his head, and that took all the fun out of the game.

Three quarters of a mile past Bloody Mary's, Charlie saw a railroad crossing in the headlight beams. "Pull over," he commanded. "Stop the car."

Bob Colvert did as he was told.

"What are you gonna do?" he asked.

"Get out," said Charlie. "On your side." The shotgun prodded Colvert's ribs for emphasis.

Officially, the temperature outside the car that night was six below, without allowing for the wind-chill factor. Colvert shivered violently in his fatigues, no gloves or jacket to protect him from the cold. Charlie crawled out behind him, on the driver's side.

We only have Starkweather's version of what happened next. He claimed that Colvert made a wild grab for the shotgun, trying to disarm him, and they scuffled in the middle of the road. "I got into a helluva fight and a shooting gallery," he later told Reinhardt. "He shot himself the first time. He had ahold of the gun from the front, and I cocked it, and we was messing around, and he jerked it, and the thing went off."

Perhaps.

We know the first blast struck Bob Colvert in the upper body, slamming him away from Charlie, off his feet. Charlie was stunned when Colvert struggled to all fours, blood pooling underneath him on the frozen surface of the road. Charlie stepped forward, pumped the shotgun's slide, and fired a second blast at point-blank range into the back of Colvert's head.

The cold wind biting at his scalp and ears told Charlie he had lost his cap. He looked around and spotted it, retrieved it from the ground, and made sure it was clean before he climbed into the Ford. He left Bob Colvert lying in the middle of the road and drove a mile before he thought about the empty shotgun shell he had ejected from his weapon at the murder scene.

Disgusted, cursing bitterly, he turned around and drove back to the point where Colvert's body was sprawled across the road. He found the cartridge after several anxious minutes, put it in his pocket, then retraced his route on Twenty-seventh Street, back to the highway. Cruising past the station, Charlie had to smile at some fool parked beside the gas pumps, waiting for a dead man to come out and fill his tank.

At 5:10 A.M. on Sunday, a police patrol car pulled into the station on Cornhusker Highway and discovered it was unattended, even though the lights were on, the front door left unlocked. The officers searched briefly, found no signs of a struggle in the office or garage, and radioed for someone else to call the station's manager.

By sheer coincidence, Colvert's body had been found nine minutes earlier, at 5:01 A.M. Lancaster County sheriff's deputies were notified, since the discovery was made outside of Lincoln P.D.'s jurisdiction. At a glance, it looked like hit-and-run. One of the deputies alerted newsmen, holding up a long-established bargain with the local media. If they were quick enough, he said, they could get photos of the corpse before the coroner arrived and hauled it off.

One look at Colvert's body told the deputies they had a murder on their hands. A call went out to homicide investigators, and a glance at Colvert's wallet gave the corpse a name. Within the hour, a team of officers and newsmen were at Colvert's home, delivering the news and firing questions at his wife. She had no answers, and they left the small apartment empty-handed, knowing only that there was a brutal predator at large.

Sheriff Karnopp started having trouble with the Colvert murder on day one. As luck would have it, Colvert's body had been found by a security officer from the Nebraska Detective Agency making his nightly rounds. Unfortunately, he was not alone. Two young airmen from Offutt Air Force Base were along for the ride, and one balked at calling the police when they discovered Colvert's body, later claiming that he feared some "personal embarrassment." To help him out, his buddy and the rent-a-cop made the report without him, but their skittish attitude immediately bumped them to the head of the suspect list. Even after the reluctant third party was named, police remained suspicious of the trio, conducting exhaustive interrogations that wasted a week, before they finally passed polygraph tests on December 11.

By that time, Sheriff Karnopp had another red herring on his hands. Ex-convict Philmon Immenschuh, arrested on an unrelated charge in Omaha, confessed to jailers that he was the triggerman in Colvert's murder. He was fuzzy on some details, but the mere admission rated him a trip to Lincoln, where detectives kept their fingers crossed. Another polygraph cleared Immenschuh of any link to Colvert's death, and he reluctantly admitted that the whole confession was a scam. Suffering the aftereffects of a drinking binge, Immenschuh felt the Omaha jailers weren't doing enough to relieve his misery, and he was hoping for more sympathy in Lincoln, if he copped to murder one.

The Colvert case was county business, but detectives from Lincoln P.D. were involved on the fringes from the moment the body was found. Sheriff Karnopp did not officially request their help until December 6, but they were already chasing leads inside the city limits, running interviews and checking out potential witnesses. Lieutenant Eugene Henninger was the police department's specialist in polygraph exams, and he would test eleven different suspects in the case, beginning on December 5.

Weeks later, after Charlie Starkweather was run to earth and caged, investigator Harold G. Robinson, an expert on police procedures, was imported to assess the manhunt and explain apparent lapses in efficiency by local lawmen. His conclusions were so favorable to Karnopp and Lincoln P.D. that some critics called it a whitewash, but his remains the sole professional assessment of the Starkweather investigation, starting with the Colvert case.

"Being confronted with a shocking murder," Robinson wrote in his final report, "and with no witnesses, it is necessary to make a detailed search of the crime scene for physical evidence which might point to the suspect. The files indicate that this was promptly done, and the service station was examined for latent prints. However, in subsequent interviews with Starkweather, [he] has acknowledged that he wore gloves during the time he was in the station."

In fact, detectives went over the Crest station with the proverbial fine-toothed comb, and came up empty. Robert McClung described the red-haired teenager who sometimes hung around the station at night, but he had never cared enough to learn Charlie Starkweather's name. Looking back, McClung didn't think the sheriff's deputies were very interested, but a detective from Lincoln P.D. dropped by several weeks later, following up on the redhead. He talked to Leonard Wright, but the Crest station's manager had never seen Charlie. Wright had a hunch that Bob McClung was probably referring to a frequent customer, Dale ("Pinky") Gardner, but again, the lead went nowhere.

Monday's *Lincoln Journal* carried an appeal from County

Attorney Elmer Scheele, requesting information from any locals who had traveled Cornhusker Highway between midnight and 5:30 A.M. on December 2. What he got, instead, was a telephone call from Mrs. John Kamp, proprietor of a secondhand outlet called the Clothing Resale and Gift Shop. Mrs. Kamp told police that a red-haired young man had come into her shop on Sunday afternoon and purchased $9.55 worth of clothes, paying his bill all in coins. A press report of small change stolen from the service station prompted her to make the call. The young man had been shopping at her store for two years, give or take, but like McClung, she never learned his name. Her description was terse: "[N]ever talked much; usually kept his head down; he was almost always smoking; never smiled; showed no emotional responses; his hair was usually sloppy, and never neatly cut, and he usually wore half-sideburns; he was always alone."

In a later interview, Mrs. Kamp recalled, "I told them all about what he looked like, his red hair and slouch and how short he was, and that I'd recognize him from a photo. The detective took it all down, and then he came back later with some pictures, but none of them were the boy." Five days later, she saw the youth again, while she was waiting for a bus. "I was frightened," she said, "because I thought he might take a swing at me if the police had questioned him." In fact, the redhead ignored her, and Mrs. Kamp did not report the sighting to police, assuming they had already questioned him.

Long after the fact, police dismissed Mrs. Kamp's description of the suspect as useless. According to one department spokesman, "The identification actually given by Mrs. Kamp was of a male, unidentified individual, approximately twenty-five or thirty years of age. She could not give any description of the color of his hair, or the color of his eyes, due to the fact that at the time of his visit he was wearing a hunting cap and thick eyeglasses." This begs the question of his visits to the shop before December 2, but police could not find Charlie in their mug books for the simple reason that he'd never been arrested in his life.

In one respect, at least, Starkweather's expectation for the manhunt was fulfilled: police believed their killer was a transient. Lincoln motels were canvassed, their records examined, and a traffic checkpoint was established on Cornhusker Highway the following Saturday night, December 8, in hopes of turning up a suspect or identifying early-morning travelers who might have seen the crime in progress.

It was all in vain.

With hindsight, we can say that local homicide investigators seemingly did all they could with what they had. Lancaster County sheriff's files reveal that seventy-six persons were interviewed during the course of the Colvert investigation. At least two of them knew Charlie Starkweather by sight, but neither found him interesting enough to learn his name.

Police were searching for the invisible man.

Years later, Sheriff Karnopp remembered the Colvert case as "a difficult one, one of our hardest. But we would have solved it if we'd had the time. I'm convinced of that. Charlie just didn't give us the time."

6

Hang Time

Charlie woke around nine o'clock on Sunday morning, feeling refreshed and pleased with himself. He had some money for a change, and he had killed to get it, thereby proving himself a bona fide outlaw. Just like in the movies.

When he was dressed and had his glasses on, a cup of coffee steaming on the kitchen table, Charlie scanned the morning paper for reports of Colvert's murder. It did not occur to him that even if the body had been found, it would have been too late to make the Sunday paper's deadline. He was disappointed, then suspicious, guessing that police had chosen to withhold the story. Why? To trap him, somehow? Charlie was too slick for that.

He tried the radio, checked several stations, but the Sunday morning offerings were all religious programs, preachers he had never heard of yammering about the plight of his immortal soul. Disgusted, Charlie switched the television on, and still came up with nothing. There was news about the weather, more on *Sputnik* and America's attempt to catch up with the satellite *Explorer,* trouble over school desegregation in the South—but nothing on the most important story of his life.

He shut the TV off and played the radio for background noise, as he began to pack his things. The cash from last night's holdup meant he didn't have to stay with Rudy anymore. He could go back to Hawley's rooming house and catch up on his rent, make up some story for the landlady, to keep her satisfied.

The local news came on when he was almost finished packing. It was sparse on details—Colvert's name and age, the ongoing investigation into his death. Instead of feeling nervous, Charlie was exhilarated, wishing he could play it back when the announcer finished. Posing for the mirror, he imagined all those cops pursuing *him*, without a single clue to help them on their way.

Too cool.

Before he left the small apartment, Charlie telephoned Caril Ann and asked if she would join him at the race track, but her parents turned thumbs down on the idea. They didn't like Caril going out on Sunday night, because of school on Monday morning, and they wouldn't even let her slip the leash that afternoon.

It took the edge off Charlie's morning, but he still had things to do. He went clothes shopping at the secondhand store, even though he could have bought new things, and paid the bill in change. It never crossed his mind that Mrs. Kamp might grow suspicious and report him to police, nor did he count on anonymity to shelter him. "I thought she knowed me," Charlie later told police, when he was safe in jail.

That afternoon, he came in second in the demolition derby, walking off with a ten-dollar prize. He celebrated at a nearby drive-in restaurant—two large cheeseburgers, french fries, with a jumbo Coke—and left the pretty carhop fifty cents to remember him by. When he got back to the apartment, Rudy had returned from Omaha, and Charlie told him he was moving out. He gave Rudy an unexpected twenty-dollar bill and waved away his thanks, explaining that he had been lucky at the track. Rudy was all smiles as he helped load Charlie's suitcase and some loose clothes into the Ford.

Mae Hawley got along with Charlie well enough, much better when he paid his rent, and she was glad to have him back with cash in hand. She asked if he had found another job, and Charlie told her no, but he was looking. In the meantime, he explained, he had withdrawn the money from his bank account. If it occurred to Mrs. Hawley that the banks were closed on weekends, she declined to press the point. That evening, after supper, Charlie watched some TV with the Hawleys and commiserated over young Bob Colvert's fate. They were practically the same age, Charlie noted. How could anyone do such a terrible thing?

The next morning, the *Star* headline read LINCOLNITE SLAIN: THEFT MOTIVE SEEN, with front-page pictures of the body and the filling station. Homicide was rare in Lancaster County, with Colvert's murder only the third for all of 1957. Charlie read the paper over coffee, at a restaurant downtown, then opened a new bank account with a deposit of $100, holding pocket money back.

It was the first time in his life that he had felt like a success. By Monday evening, though, his nerves were jumping, telling him to get rid of the shotgun that was hidden underneath the front seat of his car. In darkness, Charlie drove across the South Street Bridge and tossed the 12-gauge into Salt Creek, close by Neihoff's junkyard, satisfied that he had foiled the cops once more.

Police and sheriff's officers were stymied on the Colvert case as Christmas rolled around. Sheriff Karnopp and Lincoln Police Chief Joe Carroll were disgusted by the brutal murder, apparently committed for less than $200, and it galled them that their men could find no useful clues. Aside from grilling Crest employees and assorted customers, detectives canvassed pawnshops on a theory that their "transient" killer might have bought his weapon locally, or hocked the shotgun prior to leaving town. County Attorney

Scheele was breathing down their necks, prepared to seek the death penalty for any suspects they arrested, but the lawmen were no closer to a bust on New Year's Day than they had been the morning Colvert died.

An old, unwritten rule in homicide investigations states that most murders are solved within forty-eight hours of the crime. Beyond that unofficial deadline, trails grow cold, the killer has more time to rid himself of vital evidence, and possible informants lapse into a silence borne of fear or simple apathy. Of course, in 1958, four-fifths of all reported homicides in the United States were perpetrated by a relative or close acquaintance of the victim. Motives varied—rage or jealousy, adultery or greed, perhaps a drunken fit of violence—but detectives had few problems sorting out the cause and perpetrator of specific crimes. Conviction rates stood comfortably in the 85 to 95 percent range.

When strangers kill, the rules go out the window. Even in a case like Robert Colvert's, with robbery assumed to be the motive, there is no *connection* visible between the killer and his victim, nothing in the way of glaring signs to point detectives on their way to an arrest. Without a witness, fingerprints, or other solid evidence, police are left to theorize and search a suspect pool of thousands—even millions—while they wait for luck or Fate to lend a helping hand. Sometimes it works—the "Son of Sam" was traced through parking tickets; L.A.'s "Skid Row Slasher" dropped his driver's license at the scene of one attack—but what Lincoln's finest quickly learned in 1958 was that most times, luck isn't good enough.

Despite his powerful contempt for the authorities, Charlie was smart enough to hide his tracks. He knew that part of the Crest station's driveway was unpaved, for instance, so he changed his tires, in case the cops got wise and started casting prints. On Friday, December 7, he drove to his parents' home and there removed the old Ford's grill, afterward painting the blue car black. He even mixed a special drying agent with the paint to make it set up faster, in the frosty weather. As the final touch, he used red paint around the gap where he had yanked the grill.

One of his friends asked Charlie why he chose to paint the Ford. "I had to," Charlie told him. "Some guys got drunk the other night and spotted it with different-colored paint."

The shotgun was another problem. He had ditched it in Salt Creek, but now he started having second thoughts. Suppose the cops came by and fished it out? He knew the weapon could be traced to Sonny by its serial number, and even that was too close for comfort. On the evening of December 5, he fetched the gun and cleaned it off. Ironically, that very night, a team of deputies and jail trusties were checking out the creek, with wading boots and garden rakes, but they arrived too late to find the gun. A few days later, it was safely back in the Von Busch garage.

Another step, in Charlie's mind, was to delete himself from anybody's suspect list by "acting natural." It would be out of character, he thought, if he stopped going to the filling station after all those months. Somebody might start asking questions, if he didn't show. Accordingly, on Monday afternoon, December 10, he drove Caril Ann out to the Crest and bought her a stuffed poodle.

No one gave the redhead or his girl a second look.

For all his caution, though, Charlie still reveled in his crime. There is a strong chance that he shared the facts with Caril, at least after the murder, and he was not above joking about the job with his friends. A few days after the murder, Charlie stopped by the Western Newspaper warehouse to kill some time, and one wise guy asked him what he was going to do with the loot from the heist. Starkweather laughed and told the joker, "I got lotsa things to do with it."

Charlie would later tell James Reinhardt that Colvert's killing made him "feel different," and while various acquaintances saw no remarkable change in his attitude or behavior, Charlie had always lived more in his head than he did on the street. The murder was better than hunting, he said. For the first time, he had started to "even the score" with a world he despised. With Colvert, he felt no need to explain or make apologies for killing, as he often had with smaller animals. To some extent, at least, the murder seemed to set him free.

Still, there were problems he would have to deal with down the road.

"After I killed Colvert," Charlie told Reinhardt, "things started changin' faster. Seemed like Caril was always expectin' more and more, and we was havin' trouble with her mom and old man. We had to go away, I told her, where nobody would find us."

He knew they didn't have the money they would need to strike out on their own, but Charlie's first holdup had taught him "that a man could have money without haulin' garbage." He recognized that money "was lyin' around if I'd just pick it up." He knew what it felt like to kill, and "shootin' people was, I guess, a kind of thrill. It brought out somethin'."

But first, last, and always, there was Caril Ann. "Guess my brain just quit on me," Charlie told Reinhardt. "Everything was turned over to my wantin' to be with Caril. . . . To live with Caril and die with Caril. Anyway, I wanted her to see me go down shootin' it out and knowin' it was for her, for us." In the face of such emotions, Charlie's *other* statement, that "We wanted to leave without killin' anybody else," seems unconvincing at the very least.

Fifty days would elapse between Colvert's murder and the Bartlett massacre on Belmont Avenue. Those seven weeks were an impatient, restless time for Charlie, but he covered his mood with a frenzy of holiday activity. And, he was forced to admit, the murder had another beneficial side effect: "For once, I didn't have depression and headaches."

Charlie and Caril spent much of her Christmas vacation from school catching up on new movies, preferring crime dramas and Westerns with guaranteed gunplay on screen. It was cold at the drive-in, but new in-car heaters prevented the windows from fogging while Charlie was watching the action or grappling with Caril. Sometimes, Caril Ann would also visit Charlie at the rooming house, ignoring angry protests from her family. They snacked on junk food, listened to the latest records, and he taught her how to throw a knife. If Caril got tired of practicing with blades, she could sit back and watch while Charlie worked on his quick-draw, facing down the mirror.

"If somebody died every time I drew that gun," he told Reinhardt, "I would've got over a thousand."

Overall, it appeared that Charlie was enjoying the holidays. When loot began to run short, he worked the occasional odd job, but his heart wasn't in it. Work was for suckers and cowards. A *real* man took what he wanted, when he wanted it, and gunned down anyone who tried to stop him.

Mostly, though, when Charlie wasn't out with Caril, he went hunting jackrabbits. The big Nebraska jacks were fast, but Charlie bagged his share, preferring head or neck shots for a quick, clean kill. He hunted often on the farm of August Meyer, an elderly acquaintance. Meyer seemed to like the time they spent together, just talking, after Charlie bagged his limit, and he didn't mind the fact that Charlie left him the fresh-killed rabbits, either. They were always good in stew.

But Charlie wasn't in it for the meat.

Between hunting trips, Charlie went shopping in Lincoln, chipping away at his new bank account, nickle-and-diming himself back into the hole. He spent most of his money on Caril, but she was not the only recipient of his largesse. There were also Christmas presents for his family, a new wool shirt for August Meyer, a bottle of cologne for Mrs. Hawley, a new collar for her little terrier. In any free time that remained, Starkweather kept up with the latest comic books.

In Charlie's mind, the Colvert murder had cemented his relationship with Caril. They were destined for a wild, fast ride together, and the killing would propel them on their way. It is impossible to say how much of Charlie's fantasy Caril shared—or even heard, before their last apocalyptic days of bloodshed—but his take on happy endings might have troubled her. In Charlie's dreams of death, the end came swiftly, with a roar of gunfire. Sometimes, Caril died with him, a latter-day Bonnie to his ducktailed Clyde; in other visions, she was left alive to mourn him, knowing he had done it all for her.

But there was no apparent urgency about their flight, no concrete plan. He meant for them to "go away," and Caril apparently concurred, but they did nothing to effect the break. Starkweather trusted Death to tell him when the time was right.

"And then," he said, "people started getting in our way."

Caril's parents were the worst, but everyone was in on it. The same way they had been in school, on Charlie's garbage route, around the paper company. It was him against the world, but this time he was fighting back.

He meant to show them all.

On New Year's Eve, he took Caril Ann out to dinner at the Capital Table Talk restaurant, followed by a drive-in double feature, Elvis Presley followed by a Western, *Guns Along the Border*. Caril Ann's parents had reluctantly waived curfew for the night, and so they stopped off for another meal, gobbling burgers after midnight at the University Grill. It was approaching 2 A.M. when Charlie took her home.

Starkweather denied any criminal acts between Bob Colvert's murder and his final killing spree with Caril Ann, but there is one more death that some old-timers credit to the bandy-legged redhead. On January 4, 1958, a casual acquaintance of Charlie's, seventeen-year-old Jimmy Law, was shot at his home with a .22-caliber rifle his parents had given to him for Christmas. He died en route to the hospital, and while Law's parents were away from home that fatal night, they reported their son in good spirits, with no signs of depression. In the absence of a suicide note, his death was ruled an accident, but there are still a few skeptics in Lincoln who deride the notion of a simple coincidence.

By mid-January, Charlie had spent the last of his money.

He was behind on his rent again, and Mae Hawley locked him out of his flat. For the next week, he slept in a rented garage with his Ford. The place was unheated, and Charlie came down with a miserable cold that would dog him until he was finally snug in a warm prison cell.

By that time, Charlie had surrendered to his hate once more. Before Mae Hawley locked him out, he would stand in his room and stare at the mirror, hating the sight of himself, "but I just stayed there and looked and hated." After one of his grim mirror sessions, Charlie told Reinhardt, "[S]omebody would look at me, and I wanted to bash in his face." In short order, "the death scenes begin to come out," surprising Charlie with "a kind of relief." Death was a friend, and each passing day drove him "further off" from the world of common men.

"There was no place for me and Caril to go, but away together," Charlie wrote. "There was no way to go but to shoot our way."

And when they went, he vowed that they would leave a trail that "couldn't rub out, like tracks cut in a rock."

7

A Kind of Thrill

Charlie Starkweather made his last, halfhearted effort to find a new job in the days after New Year's, but no one would hire him. It may have been his looks, the way he dressed, or his attitude, but Charlie blamed his former bosses at the garbage-hauling company. They had him on some kind of blacklist, he imagined. Charlie hadn't asked for references when he was fired, but bosses stuck together. Everybody knew that.

It was a conspiracy.

Fresh failure heightened Charlie's anger, boredom, the pervasive loneliness he felt when he was not with Caril Ann. Things would be different, he was certain, if he had a wife. Hell, *anyone* would hire a married man.

The marriage part was tricky, though, since Caril Ann's mom and dad still hated him. "Everything was tightenin' up," he told James Reinhardt, long after the fact. "Her folks was gettin' more threatenin' all the time."

No problem. Charlie could be threatening himself.

Just ask Bob Colvert.

On Monday afternoon, the twentieth of January, Charlie got his courage up and drove to Caril Ann's house on Belmont Avenue. Marion Bartlett was a night watchman at the Watson Brothers Transportation Company, and Charlie knew that he would not have left for work yet. He would have a chance to plead his case once more.

It was a gamble; Charlie knew that going in. Caril's parents had already told him he was finished if he mentioned marriage one more time, but Charlie couldn't help himself. He was in love, but it was more than that. He literally had *no life* without Caril Ann.

The Bartletts weren't exactly thrilled to see him, and the old man scowled when Charlie asked if they could have a private talk. They went into the living room, and Bartlett settled in his favorite chair, while Charlie took the sofa, fidgeting.

"All right, what is it?" Marion demanded.

"Well . . . I want to marry Caril." It sounded incomplete, somehow, so Charlie added, "Right away."

He saw the flush of angry color rise in Bartlett's cheeks. *"Why* right away?"

Caril's family had heard the talk about her being pregnant, some of it traced back to Charles himself, and it was true she had been gaining weight—"getting a little thick around the middle," in Sonny Von Busch's description. It was a sore point with her folks, and Charlie's sudden rush to wedlock set alarm bells jangling in Marion's mind.

The question seemed to startle Charlie, and he missed the old man's undertone completely. "Well," he said, "I think if we're together . . . if I have somebody to take care of . . . uh . . . we'll get along all right. I'll take good care of her."

Bartlett was plainly unconvinced. *"How* are you going to take care of her?" he demanded. "You haven't got a *job.* You haven't even *looked."*

The accusation was a slap in Charlie's face. He felt his pent-up anger rushing to the surface.

"Damn it, I have *too* been looking!"

Marion stood up. He towered over Charlie, fists clenched at his sides, voice taut with fury.

"I don't think you have," he said, "and you've got a hell of a nerve wanting to marry her now. Where would you sleep, in the street?"

"Hey, don't go ape," said Charlie. "I've got money. I can get a place for us."

The jive talk and defiance were too much for Marion to swallow. "Let me say one thing," he told the cocky redhead. "Even if you *had* a job, you couldn't marry her. I've had enough of this. I *told* you not to bring it up again. You're *through*. I never want to see you in this house again, and I don't want you seeing Caril. You hear me? *Never!*"

Charlie snapped, coming back with the only thing he could think of.

"Go to hell, you son of a bitch!"

Marion grabbed him by the collar, hauled him to his feet and over to the door. The next thing Charlie knew, he was outside, cheeks burning from the anger and the cold. He heard the door slam shut behind him.

Jesus, what a mess!

His skull was pounding with a vicious, nauseating headache as he drove back to the cold garage and pulled inside. There was some aspirin in the glove compartment, but it barely took the edge off Charlie's pain. He paced the small enclosure, cursing, pausing now and then to sit and hold his head in trembling hands. The rage, frustration, pain all ran together, made him dizzy, wishing that his head would finally explode and put an end to it.

At last, near 4:00 A.M., exhausted, Charlie fell asleep, but even then he found no relief. His fevered dreams were filled with giant snakes encircling him, their fat coils squeezing tighter, tighter, until Charlie woke up screaming, drenched with sweat.

And he knew exactly what he had to do.

On Tuesday morning, Charlie grudgingly agreed to help his brother on the garbage route, for pocket money. When they finished, he stopped by the Hawley rooming house on Tenth Street, hoping to retrieve a rifle from his room. The door was padlocked, though, and he was cursing, tugging on the lock in blind frustration, when Barb Von Busch stepped out of her apartment, just across the hall.

"What are you doing, Charlie?"

Startled, he stepped back a pace and kept his eyes averted as he spoke. Caril's sister made him nervous these days, after all the trouble he'd been having with her folks.

"Just trying to get into my apartment," he replied. "You know where old man Hawley is?"

"I haven't seen him. Sorry. Let me know if I can help."

"Okay," he muttered, turning from the door. "I'll see ya later."

Frustrated on his first attempt to arm himself, Charlie drove to his brother Rodney's house and borrowed a .22-caliber rifle, explaining that he wanted to go hunting with Caril's stepfather. It was the first thing Charlie thought of, and the strangest lie he could have told, considering the well-known enmity between himself and old man Bartlett. Still, Rodney thought, the story was barely plausible. They could have made the hunting date before their latest falling out, and maybe Chuck was trying to get back in Bartlett's good graces. Whatever, it was none of Rodney's business, and he didn't need the .22 that afternoon, so Charlie took it with him when he left.

It was approaching 1:00 P.M. as he drove back to Belmont Avenue and parked outside Caril's house. Besides the rifle and two boxes of rimfire ammunition, Charlie had some carpet samples he had picked up at the dump. They were in decent shape, and Velda Bartlett had remarked that she would like to have them, if he didn't mind. Thus armed, a gun in one hand and peace offerings in the other, Charlie left his Ford and walked up to the house.

The family's watchdog, a black mongrel called Nig, was chained to a post in the yard. He barked once at Charlie, then came out to meet him, wagging his tail as he got to the end of his chain. At least the mutt was glad to see him, he thought as he walked around in back and started knocking on the kitchen door.

Velda looked angry when she saw him standing there, but made no move to stop him as he stepped into the kitchen. Neither did she seem afraid, since it was not unusual to see Starkweather with a gun.

"I brought those rugs you wanted," Charlie told her, stating the obvious. When she did not reply, he moved into the living room and sat down on the sofa, placing the rugs on the floor.

Velda eyed him for a moment from the kitchen doorway, then moved off toward the bedrooms, beyond his line of sight. There was no sign of Marion, but Charlie heard Caril's little sister, Betty Jean, whining and crying in another room.

"She was a little snot, in my opinion," Charlie later said of Betty Jean. "Caril thought she was a monster. She called her about every name you could think of. She had a lot of reasons. You couldn't make her mind, and she was always getting somebody in trouble. She got me in trouble a few times. She'd go flying in to her old man or mom and say I hit her. One reason Caril didn't like her was she was a stepsister. Marion treated Betty Jean far more [sic] than he ever did Caril. Caril used to gripe about it all the time."

Charlie sat on the couch by himself for a while, fiddling with the rifle's bolt, working it in and out, in and out. Finally, about to jump out of his skin, he rose and walked back through the house, to see what everyone was doing. He saw Marion Bartlett stretched out in one of the bedrooms, apparently asleep. Velda and Betty Jean were in Caril's room, sitting on the bed and listening to the radio Charlie had bought Caril. He stood in the doorway for a moment, feeling awkward, before he found his voice.

"Does Marion still want to go hunting?"

Velda looked at Charlie like he was some kind of idiot, or maybe something weird from outer space. "I don't think so," she told him, bitterly.

"Why not?" he asked, pursuing it for want of something else to say.

"Don't ask *me,*" Velda snapped. "He just doesn't, that's all."

It wasn't playing out the way that he had hoped. He left his gun in Caril Ann's bedroom, propped up against the wall, and walked back to the kitchen, where he sat down in one corner, on a wooden crate. A moment later, Velda found him there. Her face was pale from anger as she spoke.

"You have to leave," she said, "and don't ever come back."

Charlie feigned surprise. "How come?"

"I don't want you to see Caril anymore. You've caused enough trouble here as it is."

"What trouble?" Charlie asked her, playing dumb.

"You know *exactly* what I mean!"

"Do not!" he said. "Why don't you tell me?"

Velda stepped in close and slapped him twice across the face, the sound of flesh on flesh like muffled gunshots in the silent house.

"You got Caril pregnant, and I hate you for it!"

She tried another slap, but Charlie blocked her with his forearm, scrambling to his feet and making for the door. He was intimidated by her sudden fury, too surprised to fight.

"You go to hell!" he shouted as he cleared the back porch, running toward his car.

He needed time to think, calm down and get a grip on the emotions boiling up inside him. Furious and frightened, all at once, he drove around the block to catch his breath and figure out what he should do. The second time around, it came to Charlie that he'd left his brother's rifle in the house. If nothing else, it gave him an excuse for going back.

Charlie was trembling as he parked the Ford and walked back to the Bartletts' kitchen door. He knocked again, and pushed past Velda without speaking, as soon as she opened the door. Two steps inside the kitchen, he found Marion Bartlett blocking his way, face twisted with rage.

"Get the hell out of my house!" Marion shouted, standing

firm. He had at least ten pounds on Charlie, and a lifetime of manual labor had kept him in shape.

"That's fine with me, you son of a bitch!"

Defiantly, he stepped around the old man, moving toward the front door and the street beyond. He left the rifle where it was, aware of Marion behind him all the way. As Charlie crossed the threshold, Bartlett kicked him in the buttocks, hard enough to stagger him.

The pain and shame of it made Charlie clench his fists, but something held him back from swinging at the older man. Perhaps he knew he was outmatched without his gun. In any case, he stalked back to the Ford and drove away.

The time had come for getting even, but he had to watch his step. He drove to Hutson's Grocery, near the house, and went directly to the pay phone. Thumbing through the slim directory, he found a number, memorized it, dropped a dime, and made his call to Watson Brothers. When the switchboard operator answered, Charlie did his best to keep from stammering.

"I'm calling to let you know Marion Bartlett won't be in to work for a couple of days," Charlie said. "He's sick."

"I hope it's nothing serious," the operator said.

"It's not that bad," said Charlie, "but he wanted me to call."

"Well, thank you."

Charlie smiled as he cradled the receiver. He was on a roll.

The Safeway market on North Twenty-seventh Street stood midway between Vine and Holridge, in Belmont, making it a convenient stop for many of the suburb's residents, including Virginia Robson, a switchboard operator for Watson Brothers Transportation Company, who stopped there on Tuesday afternoon. She was using a part of her lunch break to pick up some bread and a few other items, thus saving herself an extra stop at the end of the day.

She was pacing out of the bread aisle when she spotted a familiar figure at the meat counter nearby. She knew

Marion Bartlett casually, from saying "hello" as he wrapped up his night shift. He always seemed friendly enough, and Virginia was pleased to see him now, detouring from her errand momentarily.

"It's nice to see you, Mr. Bartlett."

Marion glanced up from watching the butcher slice thick-cut bologna. A smile cracked his face. "Hi, Virginia," he said. "Looks like we had the same idea."

"I hate to use my lunch hour for shopping," she replied, "but it'll save me later. We go through more groceries than I care to think about."

Marion nodded sympathetically and took his parcel from the butcher. He knew all about the cost of feeding families. "I'd better go," he said. "I need to get some lunch, myself, before I go to work."

"I'll see you later, then."

Virginia returned to Watson Brothers shortly before 2:00 P.M. Her lunchtime stand-in, Vivian Buess, saw her coming and rose from the switchboard, preparing to leave.

"Anything I should know about?" Virginia asked.

"Let's see . . . there was a call from someone who said Marion Bartlett won't be in the next few days. Said he was sick."

Virginia frowned at that.

"What's wrong?"

"That's strange," Virginia said. "I just saw Marion, while I was shopping at the Safeway. He looked fine to me, and never mentioned being sick."

"That *is* strange." Mrs. Buess considered the anomaly for all of fifteen seconds, then said, "Oh, well, I've got work to do. I'll see you later."

"Right."

Virginia wrote a memo to her boss, alerting him that Marion would not be in for work that day. It wasn't her place to describe their meeting at the supermarket, and she didn't want to get the man in trouble, anyway, if he was playing hooky for a day or two. She felt like that herself, sometimes. Still, she could not help wondering who had called on Marion's behalf, until the switchboard started flashing with another wave of calls and drove the problem from her mind.

From Hutson's Grocery, Charlie drove back to the Bartlett house, but this time Velda wouldn't let him in. He sat out in the backyard for a while and played with Nig, until he figured it was coming up on three o'clock, time for him to pick Caril up at school. He walked back to the Ford, but as he slipped it into gear, the old transmission made an angry grinding sound.

Now, what the hell?

He drove a block or so, but didn't like the way the car was acting. It was always some damned thing. The Griggs house was nearby, and Charlie made it that far, parking at the curb in front. He left the Ford and walked back to the Bartlett house. At least he would be waiting when his girl got home.

In fact, he missed her coming in. The first thing Charlie knew of Caril Ann coming home, he later said, was when he heard the sound of angry voices, Caril Ann and her mother yelling back and forth. Starkweather let himself in through the kitchen door, following the noise to Caril Ann's bedroom.

"They was yelling their heads off," he later told police interrogators. "'He was! He wasn't! He was! He wasn't!'"

All that noise about *him*, until Caril Ann stormed into the bathroom and slammed the door behind her, leaving Charlie to face Velda alone. Little Betty Jean was jumping up and down on Caril's bed, squealing in a high-pitched voice.

Velda Bartlett turned on Charlie, livid, fairly hissing at him as she repeated the accusation that Caril Ann was pregnant. Charlie denied it again, but there was no reasoning with Caril Ann's outraged mother.

"She got up and slapped the shit out of me again," Charlie said, "in the head, both sides. I hauled off and hit her one back, in the head. My hand wasn't closed. It knocked her back a couple of steps. She let out a cry, a war cry or somethin', and the old man came flyin' in."

Marion grabbed him by the neck and started dragging Charlie toward the living room, as if to throw him out once more. "I kicked him somewhere," Charlie told detectives, "and he put me down. We started wrestling around in the front room." He was vague about the details later on, believing that the old man may have knocked him down a time or two. "Then he took off for the other room," Charlie said. "I knew what he was heading for, so I thought I'd head for the same thing."

Dashing to Caril's bedroom, Charlie took a cartridge from his pocket and loaded the single-shot .22—just in time, he told police, to meet Marion Bartlett coming back with a claw hammer raised overhead. "I just wheeled around and fired," Charlie said.

His aim was true. The bullet struck Marion in the head, and he collapsed in Caril Ann's bedroom, near the dresser. We have only Charlie's version of what happened next.

In one of several conflicting statements to police, he said that Caril Ann heard the shot and came out of the bathroom, staring at her stepfather's corpse for a moment, before she followed Charlie to the living room. As they got there, Charlie said Velda Bartlett emerged from the kitchen, brandishing a foot-long butcher knife.

"The old lady Bartlett said she was going to chop my head off," Charlie told authorities, "and I loaded the gun again. The old lady started to take a few steps towards me, and Caril jerked the gun away and said she'd blow her to hell. The old lady got mad and knocked her down. I grabbed the gun from Caril. I just turned around and shot her."

Struck in the face, Velda still did not fall.

"She went on by," Starkweather said, "heading for the little girl. She never stopped, and I thought she was going to pick up the girl, but she never, she just turned around and looked at me again, and I hit her with the butt of the gun.

She fell down, but she wasn't quite all the way down, so I hit her again. She just laid there."

Betty Jean was still screaming, her shrill voice grating on his nerves. He couldn't take it anymore.

"After I hit the old lady," Charlie said, "I just came up with the butt of the gun and hit the little girl. She fell down against the table, stood there screaming. Caril was yelling at her to shut up."

At that point, Charlie said, Caril warned him that her stepfather was still alive, moving around in the bedroom. "I picked up the knife that the old lady had and started to walk in there," Charlie said, "in the bedroom. The little girl kept yelling, and I told her to shut up, and I started to walk again, and just turned around and threwe the kitchen knife I had at her. They said it hit her in the throat, but I thought it hit her in the chest. I went on into the bedroom. Mr. Bartlett was moving around quite a bit, so I tried to stab him in the throat, but the knife wouldn't go in, and I just hit the top part of it with my hand, and it went in."

There is, predictably, some difficulty sorting out the whole truth of the Bartlett massacre. None of the victims were around to challenge Charlie's ever-changing story of the lethal brawl, and it is hard—if not impossible—to reconcile some elements of his conflicting statements. Caril, for her part, caught a glimpse of the electric chair and told the world that she was absolutely innocent. She was at school, she says, when Charlie killed her family and hid the bodies, later telling her that they were stashed somewhere, alive and subject to his deadly wrath if she did not comply with Charlie's every whim. Some of Caril Ann's remarks to Barbara and their grandmother, after the fact, would seem to bear out that account. And yet . . .

In the days following his arrest, Starkweather made at least seven confessions in the form of rambling statements, letters, and notes—one scrawled on the wall of his cell. The early statements absolved Caril Ann of any guilt, describing her as a hostage, but he later reversed himself on that point, describing his first few confessions as "hogwash." In the new, improved statements, Charlie said that he had lied initially, protecting Caril, but he had changed his mind. The more detectives heard about Caril's raging arguments with Velda and her stepfather, the more sense Charlie's later statements seemed to make.

Starkweather's first formal confession, to prosecutor Elmer Scheele, sounds almost comical in retrospect. Charlie agreed with Caril Ann's hostage scenario, claiming that he told her he had left her parents and half-sister with an elderly husband-and-wife bank-robbing team. Details are vague, but Charlie made it sound as if the Bartletts had somehow been kidnapped as part of the robbery plan, instead of any plan on Charlie's part to get Caril Ann alone. Even so, by her own admission, Caril "didn't believe him at first. I kept saying, 'I don't believe you.'" What finally convinced her would be anybody's guess. The prosecutor's office later managed to convince twelve jurors that the "hostage" story was a scam, cooked up by Charlie and Caril Ann while they were on the road.

In one of Charlie's later statements, he promoted Caril Ann from the role of witness to an active partner in the murders of her family. In fact, he said, it was Caril Ann who "finished off" her mother with a knife and clubbed her little sister into silence with the rifle butt.

Yet another confession—technically the first—was found in Charlie's pocket at the time he was arrested. It is a curious document, addressed "for the law only," and presented here with spelling and punctuation intact. Charlie admitted writing it himself, but it purports to speak for both him and Caril Ann.

> This is for the cops or law-men who fines us. Caril and i are writing this so that you and ever body will know what has happem. On tue. day 7 days befor you have seen the bodys of ny non, dad and baby sister, there dead because of ne and chuck,

chuck cane down that tue. day happy and full of
joke's but when he cane in nom said for hin to get
out and never come back, chuck look at her, "and
said *why.*" at that ny dad got nad and be gin to hit
hin and was pushing hin all over the room, then
chuck got nad and there was no stoping hin, he had
his gun whit hin cause he and my dad was going
hunting, well chuck pull it and the [drawing of a
bullet] cane out and ny dad drop to the floor, at this
ny non was so nad that she had a [drawing of a knife]
and was going to cut hin she Knot the gun from
chucks hands, chuck just stood there saying he was
sorry he didn't want to do it. i got chuck's gun and
stop my non from killing chuck. betty Jean was
yelling so loud i hit her with the gun about 10 tines
so she would stop chuck had the [drawing of a knife]
so he was about 10 steps fron her, he let it go it stop
some when by her head. ne and chuck just look at
then for about 4 hrs. . . . .

The triple murder on Belmont Avenue was a whole
different ballgame from Charlie's killing of Bob Colvert in
December. That had been a cut-and-dried business transac-
tion, silencing a witness to his first (and somewhat undistin-
guished) robbery. His grudge against young Colvert, from
the teddy bear encounter, was peripheral at best. Charlie
was following the lead of villains he had idolized from
comic books and "shooting movies." He was covering his
tracks.

The Bartlett massacre was something else, entirely. There
was nothing to be gained in killing Caril Ann's parents and
her half-sister except, in Charlie's mind, to win his lady fair.
And if Caril *was* a witness or accomplice to the crimes, then
Charlie had the extra boost of showing off for the one he
loved, impressing her with his gunslinger's art.

It was, as he told Reinhardt in his prison cell, "a kind of
thrill."

The knife he used on old man Bartlett, Charlie told police, was a bone-handled hunting knife with a large Bowie-style blade. He had stabbed Marion several times in the throat, but still wasn't convinced that his victim was dead. Charlie sat on the edge of Caril's bed for a while, standing guard over the corpse, to make sure. When he was satisfied, he went back to the kitchen for a glass of water.

"Caril came in the kitchen," Charlie told police, "and asked what we were going to do with them. I said, 'What do you think we ought to do?'"

In Charlie's tale, Caril did not answer him, but rather walked into the living room and sat down on the couch. He followed moments later, asking, "What's the matter?"

"Nothing," Caril replied.

"We sure got ourselves in a helluva mess," Charlie said.

To which, he claimed Caril answered, "Well, it's what we always wanted."

Charlie reloaded the single-shot .22, in case someone came nosing around, and he switched on the television. "I don't even remember what was on," he told authorities. "I just wanted some noise. It was too quiet."

After watching TV for a while, Charlie says, Caril told him, "We better get them cleaned up."

"Don't worry about it," he answered. "I'll do it myself."

His first step was to wrap the bodies up like mummies, gathering a pile of rugs, rags, bedclothes, and building paper from the shed out back, and cutting down the indoor clotheslines that were strung up in the living room. He started off with Velda, cinched a rope around her knees, then wrapped her in a quilt and a green-fiber rug, before he tied the bundle off.

Betty Jean was still bleeding when Charlie picked her up, so he put her body in the kitchen sink to drain, before he wrapped her in a quilt. There was a cardboard box with garbage in it, standing in the kitchen, and he dumped the garbage out, replacing the refuse with the tiny bundle he had made. Starkweather placed the box on the back porch, and dragged Velda out to join her daughter in the cold. They would be smelling soon, if Charlie put them in the basement, but he had a better place in mind.

His first trip to the outhouse, Charlie carried Betty Jean and placed her on the cold dirt floor. It took some effort, dragging Velda by the heels, but Charlie got her to the privy, hoisted her waist-high, and forced her swaddled head into the toilet opening. She wouldn't fit, so Charlie left her there, half in, half out, and placed the box with Betty Jean's small corpse inside it on the toilet seat.

Back in the house, Charlie spent some time mopping up blood from the floor, using rags, deliberately postponing his wrestling match with Marion Bartlett's corpse. He couldn't put it off forever, though, and when the floors were clean enough to pass inspection, Charlie wrapped the final body in a sheet, tied one of Caril Ann's scarves around the bloody head, then used an army blanket and some heavy building paper to complete the package, binding it with clothesline.

He had done his job too well, for when he tried to drag his bundle through the kitchen door, it wouldn't fit. He had to find a screwdriver and take the screen door off its hinges to accommodate the bulky corpse. That done, he half-dragged, half-carried his burden across the backyard to the chicken coop, where he dumped it against the north wall. For reasons never clear, he finished off the job by taking the screen door and placing it atop the bundled corpse.

It is clear that the three bodies had to be moved, since Charlie and Caril remained in the house for another six days, but the place and method of concealment led to heated speculation by psychologists at Charlie's trial. Why weren't the corpses buried, one professional inquired, if the three murders had been planned out in advance? Why weren't they driven to some more remote location, instead of remaining mere paces away from the house where Charlie and Caril spent the best part of another week?

Anyone who has ever tried to dig a hole—much less a grave—in frozen ground can answer the first question readily enough. It would have been backbreaking work, perhaps impossible for Charlie with the simple tools at hand, and would have lavished too much time on victims he despised. Clint Eastwood said it best, years later, addressing Shirley MacLaine in *Two Mules for Sister Sarah:* "I'll shoot 'em for you, sister, but I'll be damned if I'll sweat over 'em."

As for moving the bodies, what was the point? Charlie did not plan on staying in the Belmont house forever, and his victims were secure as long as he was standing guard, a few yards from their final resting place. If he had dumped them somewhere else, as in the Colvert case, they might have been discovered and identified before he was prepared to hit the road. His choice, in that regard, was no more illogical than the actions of killers like John Gacy, Dennis Nilsen, or Jeffrey Dahmer, who frequently kept their dead victims at home.

There was one aspect of Charlie's disposal technique, however, which provided psychologists with ample grounds for speculation. Stuffing Velda Bartlett's body down the outhouse toilet hole, while Betty Jean was left beside her on the seat, he opened up the gates to theorizing on some kind of childish, anal complex. As Dr. John Steinman later testified for the defense, "Putting them in these types of places is a sort of fantasy children sometimes have—throw them down the toilet, flush them down. And I think all through this there is a desire to be caught and punished."

Maybe so, but at the moment, Charlie showed no evidence of visible remorse. Returning to the house, he found Caril seated in a rocking chair, before the television set. It seemed to him that she had made a clumsy start on cleaning up the mess: He noticed more rags on the floor than had been there when Charlie took her stepfather outside, and Marion's false teeth had suddenly appeared beside the pile of rags. Starkweather finished straightening the furniture around, then sprinkled perfume on the floor to mask the sharp, metallic smell of blood. The missing rug, which he had used to swaddle Velda's body, was replaced with one of those he had recovered from the dump.

A survey of the house provided Charlie with some unexpected bonuses. He found a loaded .410 shotgun and a box of ammunition under Marion and Velda's bed. There was also a .32-caliber revolver in the kitchen, but Charlie searched high and low without finding a single cartridge for the gun.

By that time, it was nearly dark, and Charlie heard his empty stomach growling. Caril was hungry, too, and Charlie walked to Hutson's Grocery, coming back a half hour later with three bottles of Pepsi and a bag of potato chips.

It was Caril Ann's first chance to call for help, if she were truly innocent, but she had let it pass.

When Charles got back, they ate and watched TV until they fell asleep, Caril on the couch, Starkweather lounging in the rocking chair. He woke up in the middle of the night, awakened by a humming sound, and found the local TV station had gone off the air. Its late-night test pattern reminded Charlie of a giant, glaring eye, with rays like moonbeams reaching out to fill the room with ghostly light. He thought about the Death dreams for a moment, finally getting up to switch the television off, and joined Caril on the couch. She muttered sleepily when Charlie wrapped his arms around her, and he told her everything would be all right.

In minutes, they were fast asleep.

8

The Honeymooners

Charlie woke on Wednesday morning to the sound of someone rapping on the door. He tumbled off the couch and grabbed his rifle, double-checking to make sure that it was loaded first, before he shook Caril Ann awake.

"There's someone at the door," he whispered urgently. "Go find out who it is."

Caril rose, still rubbing sleepy eyes, and started for the door, while Charlie backtracked to the bathroom. Hidden from the view of anyone outside, he held his weapon ready. He had proved his willingness to kill. If this was it, the end of everything, he was prepared to face it like a man and go down fighting.

Caril Ann cracked the door and recognized her girlfriend, Bonnie Gardner. Most days, they would walk to school together, but she had forgotten all about it overnight. She wasn't dressed and didn't care. As far as Caril Ann was concerned, her days of "book learning" were over.

"Aren't you ready yet?" asked Bonnie.

"I don't feel good," Caril replied. "I think I've got the flu or something. I'm not going."

"Are you sure?"

"Yeah." Caril was thinking swiftly now. "I don't know how long it'll be before I'm ready to go back, but when I am, I'll call you, 'kay?"

"Okay."

Charlie emerged from hiding once the door was closed and locked. "Good job," he said admiringly, as Caril Ann walked back to the couch.

They needed time, and she had bought them some. With any luck, Caril's pesky friend would not return until she got a call, and that would never happen. Old Man Bartlett's job was taken care of for a while, as well. Starkweather hoped "the flu" would cover them until he was prepared to make his move. And then—

More knocking, this time at the kitchen door. Caril Ann was on her feet as Charlie grabbed his .22 and stepped into the nearest bedroom. He was too far from the kitchen to hear more than muffled voices, but he kept his finger on the trigger, just in case.

An outlaw had to be prepared for anything.

Five minutes later, maybe longer, Caril Ann stepped into the bedroom doorway. "You can come out now," she said.

"Who was it?"

"Just the milkman," she replied. "I got two bottles."

"Good, I'm starving. Let's fry up some eggs and bacon."

Caril had the skillet out, when yet another person came knocking at the back door. Charlie cursed and made a mad dash toward the bedroom, scooping up his rifle on the run. This time, it was the bread man. Caril Ann bought two loaves on credit, filling out their breakfast menu with fresh toast.

It had been hectic, so far, but as Charlie sat down at the kitchen table, he was starting off the best week of his life. "We lived like kings in the house for several days," he later told James Reinhardt. "It was the most wonderful time I ever had."

He felt no guilt for slaughtering the Bartletts, any more than he had felt at killing Robert Colvert. In Starkweather's mind, the slayings had been "self-defense." His years of pent-up rage told Charlie that he had a right to run amok, take what he wanted, when he wanted it. That license covered anything that he could think of—money, guns, new cars, Caril Ann. The world *owed* Charlie something, for the insults he had suffered growing up, and anyone who tried to stop him from collecting on that debt was in for trouble.

For the first time in his short life, Charlie's path was crystal clear. "We had to get far away from the world that made us hate," he told Reinhardt. "We didn't want people in a new place to know us. We was goin' to be strangers to everyone but ourselves."

But even as the thought took shape in Charlie's mind, he knew it was a fantasy. He was beyond the point of no return, a righteous outlaw in the best tradition of the "shooting movies" he adored. "There was nothin'," he said, "for me to go back to."

He knew how bad men ended up—nobody ever *really* beat the law—but it was Charlie's role to run as long and hard as possible, prolong the chase and earn himself a chapter in the record book. He was supposed to make the bastards *work* before they ran him down.

"Sometimes," he said, "I thought about murderin' the whole human race. I never thought much about just killin' individuals. Guess everything changed when I found a girl to stick with me."

With Caril as a witness, the murders transcended revenge. As Charlie told Reinhardt, "Killin' with Caril lookin' on done something to me." It was an addictive rush, and Charlie wanted more.

But not just yet.

Before his final blaze of glory, he would spend a few more days with Caril on Belmont Avenue.

For five days, January 22 through 26, Charlie and Caril Ann remained in the house, living like newlyweds. There was no one to nag and tell them what to do, run Charlie off for some imaginary wrongdoing or ground Caril Ann for breaking stupid rules. Charlie had never known such freedom, even at Mae Hawley's rooming house. Before this, he had always had somebody spying on him, breathing down his neck, making him live *their* way.

No more.

On Wednesday afternoon, he made another hike to Hutson's market, using some of Old Man Bartlett's cash to buy a sack of groceries. He brought back Pepsi, more potato chips, candy and chewing gum, ice cream, sunflower seeds—a sack of party food. It made him laugh to think how Caril Ann's parents would react if they could see her pigging out on all that junk. The fact that they were paying for it made the adolescent banquet that much sweeter.

Caril Ann later claimed that Charlie tied her up each time he left the house, but Starkweather denied it, and police were frankly skeptical. Even reporters working on the case, once Charlie and Caril Ann were named as fugitives, had trouble buying into her account of Charlie holding her at gunpoint every moment they were on the run.

There *was* one incident of bondage, Charlie told police, but it was a pathetic ruse. "We started talking about what the hell we'd do if we ever got caught," he said. "We was trying to make up a story, and it didn't work too well. I thought if we got caught, we'd make up like she was a hostage, you know, and we'd start messing around and make it look like it. Took rope and put it around [her] hands and feet, and untied it, made it look like she was tied up."

It was a silly plan, at best, considering that Charlie left no marks on Caril, and they tidied up the house before they fled, thus wiping out the flimsy "evidence" that she was ever bound. The whole scene may have been a fabrication, something Charlie dreamed up to impress the jailers with his cunning. Either way, it was a dud.

In fact, we have no way of knowing what was on Caril's mind during those days she shared the house with Charlie, heedless of three corpses hidden in the outbuildings nearby.

Because her whole defense was based on pleas of innocence, the claim that Charlie forced her to cooperate, no psychiatric tests of any consequence were ever done on Caril. Her background—with an alcoholic jailbird father, picked up more than once on sex-related charges—raised some questions about Caril's stability, but they were never answered. An insanity plea assumes guilt, and Caril was having none of that.

Extensive questioning by Chief Deputy Dale Fahrnbruch would later disclose most of what happened at 924 Belmont Avenue while Charlie and Caril Ann were playing house. Indeed, their accounts of daily events were nearly identical, with two glaring exceptions. The first discrepancy, of course, was Caril Ann's flat denial of any knowledge that her parents were dead.

The second disagreement had to do with sex.

Dale Fahrnbruch made a point of asking Starkweather how often he and Caril made love while they were staying at the Bartlett house. "Every night and morning," Charlie said, "and twice on Sunday. It might have been five or six times on Sunday, I don't know. Nobody came out Sunday. We was making love all the time, but every time I'd get going the goddamn dog would start barking his head off."

Caril's memory of those events, contained in a 166-page statement that she later refused to sign based on legal advice, was rather different.

"Do you know what a penis is?" Fahrnbruch asked her.

"Yes."

"Did he at any time have his penis out of his trousers?"

"Yes," Caril Ann replied.

"And what was the reason for that?"

"Well," she said, playing dumb, "I don't know what you mean."

"All right. Did he at any time put his penis up to your sexual organs?"

"Yes."

"And did he stick it in very far?"

"No."

"Did he put it in slightly?" Fahrnbruch asked.

"He didn't put it in an inch," Caril said.

"He put it in less than an inch?"

"Yes."

"And what did he say?"

"Then he stopped."

"Now then, Caril, you told me previously that he also put his penis in your rear end, is that right?"

"Yes."

"And were you undressed at that time?"

"Well, not all the way. I still had my nightgown on."

"What sort of nightgown was that?"

"One of them shorties," she answered.

"Now, Caril, when he put his penis in your rear end, did it hurt more or less than when he put his penis in your sexual organs?"

"It hurt less."

"Now, Caril, when you took off your clothes when you had these sexual intercourses, did *you* take them off?"

"Not all the time," she replied.

"Did he take them off some of the time?"

"Yes."

"Had he kissed you before that happened?"

Playing dumb again. "I think so."

"In other words, you had been kissing him, and he was kissing you?"

"Yes."

It was enough to satisfy the prosecution that Caril Ann had been no terrorized hostage in the days she spent with Charlie, at her parents' house. She may have recognized the damage, for she changed her tack, addressing Sheriff Karnopp's wife in earnest tones when Fahrnbruch had been briefly summoned from the room.

"I don't remember what went on in the house," she told Mrs. Karnopp, reversing her very specific stand on recollections of sex with Charlie.

"What do you mean, Caril?" the sheriff's wife asked.

"I don't remember it at all."

"You don't remember it at all?"

"I don't remember it at all," Caril repeated.

"What do you *mean,* you don't remember it at all?"

"I don't remember what went on."

Mrs. Karnopp was visibly flustered. "Can you remember what you told me, when you talked to me?"

"I don't remember."

Caril Ann's amnesia was short-lived, however, vanishing when Fahrnbruch came back into the interrogation room. As he questioned her, Caril drew a detailed portrait of those lazy days on Belmont Avenue. Caril had her pets to feed—two parakeets, old Nig, and the new collie pup, called Kim, that Charlie had bought her at Pet Paradise. When not in the sack, they played lots of gin rummy. ("I don't know if I was any good," Charlie told Fahrnbruch, "but I sure beat *her.*") They ran the TV day and night; *The Thin Man* stuck in Caril Ann's mind, together with an Abbott and Costello movie. Every afternoon, she checked the mailbox, once returning with a special comic book that she had ordered. Caril Ann read it through, then spent the rest of the day cutting out paper dolls.

It wasn't all romance and playtime, though. As Charlie told it, he and Caril Ann also practiced throwing knives and sticking them in walls. They talked about their getaway. He cut the .410's barrel down, so that the shot would spread more rapidly and make the weapon more effective at close range.

His bloody dreams were coming true, and Charlie had a gun to thank for his success, so far. That equalizer made a bandy-legged runt stand tall and brought his enemies to grief. In Charlie's words, "It showed me how easy it is to get people out of the way."

If only his innumerable foes could wait a little longer, he would be a happy man.

Time was a problem, though. By Thursday, uninvited visitors were driving Charlie up the wall. Caril's girlfriend, Bonnie Gardner, was the most persistent, stopping by three mornings in a row, until she finally got the point and stayed away. Then, there was Mrs. William Yordy, one of Caril Ann's neighbors, coming by for eggs. The Bartletts always bought some for her when they got their own, but Caril Ann told the woman that they hadn't purchased any yet that week, and she would have to come back later. Late on Thursday afternoon, Marion's boss stopped by, accompanied by a second man. Caril kept them at a distance, yelling from the porch that Marion was sick and wouldn't be at work for several days.

Each time a new arrival showed up at the house, Starkweather scuttled to the bathroom or one of the bedrooms, huddling in the doorway with a weapon, while Caril sent them on their way. She did it all just right, and never gave a hint that there was any trouble in the house, besides the "flu." They were in mortal danger, hiding out on Belmont Avenue with corpses stashed out back, but Caril seemed perfectly at ease.

Charlie admired her poise and treasured Caril Ann as an audience for his intended exploits. It had been a major stroke of luck, he realized, to find a girl who would accept him as he was, bowlegs and all, without a word of criticism or reproach. He *needed* Caril . . . but was it love?

James Reinhardt asked that question after Charlie was in custody, and Starkweather admitted that he could have given up Caril Ann, at least before the Belmont massacre, if there had only been some way for him to recapture his childhood, return to his "enchanted forest," and escape from reality "with my pretty sister."

But there was no going back, not now. Charlie had started burning bridges years before he shot Bob Colvert. Even after the Colvert murder, there was an outside chance for him to change his ways, leave the detectives checking dead-end leads and slip back into normal life, but "normal" was unbearable for Charlie. It meant slinging garbage, living in a crummy flat and wearing other people's clothes, hearing the snickers when his back was turned, knowing that he was "numbered for the bottom" all his life. The family members who sustained him in his childhood were as strangers now. He had no friends to speak of—no one he could count on in a killing situation, anyway.

Except Caril Ann.

She had already proved herself, and Charlie trusted her

implicitly. He could depend on Caril Ann not to let him down. Whatever happened next, she would be right there, watching his performance with admiring eyes. The perfect audience.

It was the best Charlie could hope for as he started looking toward the last days of his life.

The honeymoon began unraveling in earnest on the afternoon of Saturday, the twenty-fifth. It had been relatively easy scamming tradesmen, neighbors, even old man Bartlett's boss, but relatives were something else. They might expect to see a *person,* even if the object of concern was sick in bed. When Bob and Barb Von Busch came by on Saturday, it was a clear beginning of the end.

And Caril Ann panicked. For the first time, she elaborated on her story of a family sick with flu, advising Barbara that their mother was in danger if she didn't go away. She used the same line later on that night, when Bob came back with Rodney Starkweather. Each time, the danger was unspecified, and no one thought enough of it to mention Caril's remarks to the authorities, but she was clearly showing signs of strain. We have no way of knowing *why* she took that line with Bob and Barbara, whether she was honestly in fear or simply improvising, maybe even playing out a scene she had devised with Charlie's help. He later claimed they had rehearsed the "hostage" ploy, and Caril's outbursts on Saturday could easily have been the first steps in a plan to clear herself of guilt.

In any case, it was dumb luck that her performance did not bring the law down on their heads that very night. It was a little after 9:00 P.M. when Bob Von Busch sat down with Captain Harbaugh at the station house. More than five hours had elapsed since Bob and Barbara left the Bartlett house, a lapse that may have signaled to police that Bob was more pissed off than worried. Who would stall around that long if he had news about a crime in progress?

Even so, the captain sent his uniforms around to check it out. Caril met them at the door and made no mention of a threat to any member of her family, dismissing Bob as one who never "got along" with other members of the family. Harold Robinson's report, drawn from his interviews with officers involved, says that Caril Ann's "deportment was such that it did not arouse any suspicion on the part of the officers. She was poised and did not appear nervous."

Charlie was asleep in Caril Ann's bedroom when the cops arrived that evening. Caril was in the living room, watching television, and Nig's barking led her to the window, where she saw the black-and-white outside. She ran into the bedroom, warning Charlie, then went back to deal with the patrolmen while he slipped into the bathroom with his gun. Moments later, they were gone.

Charlie was worried, thinking fast. He wanted to get rid of Rodney's .22, and so he came up with the plan to leave it at the Griggs house, where his Ford was parked. (Dumb luck, again: Charlie delayed just long enough to miss Bob and his brother, who were staking out the house while Caril Ann talked to the police.) While he was out, he stopped at Hutson's Grocery, using the pay phone to call Barb Von Busch's apartment, telling her where he had left Rodney's rifle, asking for a ride home from Tate's service station. On his return to Belmont Avenue, Starkweather said, Caril told him to call Barb a second time, to warn her to stay away.

Those calls are curious, to say the least, symptomatic of Charlie's disordered, immature thinking. If he wanted to hide the rifle, why announce its location moments later? And why should Barbara care about the gun, in any case? Directing Bob and Rodney to Tate's service station only made them more suspicious, making Charlie out a liar when they learned that he had not been seen around the place all day. His second call compounded the mistake, by placing Charlie at the scene of what would prove to be a triple murder, guaranteeing that he would be fingered as the triggerman.

Or, was that Charlie's plan?

Rodney and Bob retrieved the .22 from Harvey Griggs that night, and Rodney showed the damaged rifle to his father. (Lab technicians later found bloodstains and hair on the gun.) Guy thought about calling the cops, but decided to wait. Bob Von Busch, likewise, had no further contact with Captain Harbaugh, even after he determined that the Bartletts had not seen their family doctor recently. Harold Robinson reports that Bob was "apparently satisfied" with the investigation as it stood on Saturday.

On Sunday morning, Guy Starkweather considered his options. He later spoke of wanting Charlie picked up by police, and said he thought of driving out to August Meyer's place to see if Charlie might be "holed up" there, but he decided not to make the trip and did not mention Meyer to the authorities. Instead, he sent daughter Laveta to the Bartlett house, where she was treated to Caril's story of a family sick with flu. After Laveta left, Caril found a yellow building permit in the house and scrawled a crude quarantine notice on the back, attaching it to the front screen door with bobby pins.

It was 7:00 P.M. when Laveta made her second visit to Belmont Avenue and accused Caril of lying. This time, she came back to Guy with the "bank robber" story, but Guy *still* refrained from calling the authorities. At that point, Harold Robinson seems justified in concluding that "[t]here is . . . reason to question why [Guy] did not go immediately to police headquarters on Sunday night and ask for assistance in getting Charles, knowing through his daughter's report that he was then at 924 Belmont."

Guy was still thinking about that call on Monday morning, when Pansy Street made her appearance at the Bartlett house, demanding to speak with her daughter. Charlie was eating breakfast when Caril's grandmother arrived, and he knew they were in trouble when she threatened to return with a search warrant.

"You could hear that old woman yelling all up and down the block," he later told Deputy Fahrnbruch. "We knew we had to get out fast."

He left the plate of bacon and eggs unfinished, telling Caril to pack. She owned no luggage, so she started tossing things into the carrying case for her phonograph, then decided the case was too bulky and switched to a red swim bag. Aside from the essentials, Caril Ann grabbed a photo album and several loose snapshots: Betty Jean playing with a child's tea set at Christmas; Caril Ann washing clothes with Barbara and their mother; Charlie at the race track, with a crash helmet beneath one arm.

Starkweather tucked the hunting knife and empty .32 into his belt, then wrapped the sawed-off .410 in a blanket. He was ready by the time Caril finished packing. They went out the back and hiked along the alley to the Griggs house. Charlie put his shotgun on the seat, tossed Caril's bag in the back—and then saw the tire that had gone flat sometime since Tuesday.

"Shit!" He turned to Caril. "Wait in the car. This won't take long."

He had a spare, but it was nothing to write home about. The rim was bent, the inner tube exposed, but it would have to do. Charlie was almost finished with the job when Mrs. Griggs pulled up behind him, with her daughter, just returning from the market.

"Everything okay?" she asked him, as she started to unload her bags.

"Just got a flat," Charlie replied. "I'm almost done."

"Okay. I'll see you later, then."

It was approximately 10:00 A.M. when Charlie and Caril Ann pulled into the Crest filling station on Cornhusker Highway. They bought some gas, and Charlie asked about ammunition—another odd slip, since he knew the station didn't carry sporting goods. Attendant Cecil Bowlin waited on his colleague's murderer and made no effort to alert police.

Why should he have?

No one was hunting Charlie—yet.

9

Dead People
Don't Talk

Charlie and Caril Ann knew where they were going when they drove away from Belmont Avenue. Most of his hunting had been done around the town of Bennett, fifteen miles southeast of Lincoln, and much of that on the farm owned by old August Meyer. They had been friends since Charlie was a kid. Meyer wouldn't mind him dropping by with Caril, to kill some time.

But they would have to get there, first.

The bent rim on his spare was causing Charlie's Ford to shimmy as he drove, producing ugly noises, and he knew the ancient tire would not last long. He planned on stopping off at Tate's to get it fixed, but then the damned transmission started acting up again, and Charlie couldn't wait. The nearest help was at Dale's Champion Service, on the corner of seventeenth and Burnham Streets. The station was only one block from the administration building of the Nebraska Highway Patrol, not much farther from the state penitentiary, but Charlie didn't care.

It could be hours yet before the cops got wise.

Owner Dale Smallcomb was on duty with a young assistant, Lee Lamson, when Charlie drove into the service station, nosing his Ford toward one of the service bays. Lamson had gone to school with Starkweather and recognized him instantly, but the girl beside him was a stranger, sitting with a pink bandana wrapped around her head, tied underneath her chin.

The boys made small talk for a moment, nothing special—they had never been close friends—before Charlie stated his business. He wanted the transmission packed, to stop its grinding when he shifted gears. There were no other customers in sight, and Lamson opened up the large door to the service bay, directing Charlie as he drove his Ford over the X-frame hoist. Another minute to adjust the metal arms, and they were set.

Charlie got out and held the door for Caril. "You coming?"

"No," she said, "I think I'll just sit here. Get me a pop?"

"Okay."

Lamson directed Charlie to the pop machine, located in a narrow corridor between the service area and the front office. Charlie came back with two bottles, handing one to Caril before his former schoolmate pressed a button on the wall and the hydraulic lift began to rise. The Ford appeared to levitate, supported by a smooth shaft like a rising periscope. From Charlie's viewpoint, it resembled one of those displays sometimes exhibited at auto dealerships: a life-size car hoisted aloft and visible for miles.

In this case, though, the lift stopped when his Ford was eight feet off the floor. Caril Ann peered down at Charlie, looking like some kind of peasant child from Europe with that pink bandana. Starkweather smiled at her and lit a cigarette, moved toward the broad front windows of the service bay, where he could watch the street. The close proximity of uniforms and the state prison didn't faze him.

He was on his way. He felt invincible.

Caril Ann would later tell Dale Fahrnbruch that she used her time atop the lift to write a note—"Help Police—Don't Ignore"—which she placed in a pocket of her denim jacket, hoping to pass it on later. As Caril told the story, no one ever got the note . . . but neither was it in her pocket when police arrested her two days later, still wearing the same outfit. She did not claim to have thrown the note away; it simply disappeared—another glitch in Caril Ann's "hostage" story that convinced police she had been Charlie's willing sidekick on the murder spree.

Dale Smallcomb later said that he smelled trouble from the moment Charlie pulled into the station. It was nothing he could put his finger on, exactly—Charlie's attitude, as much as anything, but Smallcomb kept a sharp eye on the redhead as he roamed around the service station, used the restroom, came back to the windows, always checking out the street. He wasn't really nervous, Smallcomb thought. More like excited, keyed up over something. Eager to be on his way.

Lamson was finished soon, and brought the Ford back down to earth. Starkweather trailed him to the office, where he wrote the ticket up and gave it to his boss. Smallcomb caught Charlie glaring at him as he asked, "How much?"

"Three pounds at forty cents a pound," said Smallcomb. "That's $1.20."

Charlie's smile had more in common with a sneer. He took his wallet out, asked Smallcomb, "Can you break a twenty?"

Smallcomb frowned, alarm bells going off inside his head. It seemed like too much money for a young punk to be carrying around. There was a chance he had a job, of course, and yet . . .

"No," Smallcomb said, "I don't believe I can."

Before the redhead could respond, another customer walked in, breath smoking in the frosty air, to ask if Smallcomb could change a ten-dollar bill. He was stuck, forced to lie with the young stranger watching him, afraid to let the redhead know that he had cash on hand.

"Sorry," he said, "I don't have it today. You'll have to try somewhere else."

The older customer was clearly puzzled, but he shrugged and turned away without complaint.

It seemed to satisfy the redhead. He replaced his wallet, digging in his other pockets for the proper change. Relief washed over Smallcomb as the Ford pulled out and drove away.

"You know that guy?" he asked Lee Lamson.

"Yeah," the youth replied. "From school. He always seemed a little crazy to me."

"I'm glad he's gone," said Smallcomb. "Seemed like he wanted trouble."

"Maybe so," said Lamson, heading back to work.

It was a hunch, though, nothing more. You couldn't call the cops each time some punk came in the station acting cocky. There was no law Smallcomb knew of against being a jerk.

Too bad.

For whatever reason, Charlie left Dale Smallcomb's station without mentioning the problem with his tire. It may have been a simple oversight, or maybe he was nervous under Smallcomb's scrutiny. Perhaps, once an idea had entered Charlie's head, he simply could not shake it loose. Without an explanation from the source, we're left to speculate in vain about what happened next. One thing is certain, though: The spare with its bent rim had not improved as Charlie headed south on Highway 77, toward the turnoff for Bennett.

Charlie stopped again, this time at Homer Tate's Conoco station, eight miles south of Lincoln, on the west side of the highway. With Brickey's Café next door and the Turnpike Ballroom a short block away, Tate's was a popular stop on the run between Lincoln and points south. Homer Tate had owned the station for more than two decades, coping with any kind of trouble that could roll on wheels. He reckoned he had seen it all.

Starkweather stopped at the northernmost set of gas pumps, closest to Brickey's, and waited for Tate to emerge from the office.

"Need gas?" the station owner asked him.

Charlie nodded. "Fill it up."

As he was moving toward the gas pump, Tate glanced down into the car, and saw a gun butt sticking out from underneath a light blue blanket on the front seat, in between the driver and his girl. Tate shrugged it off, assuming they were on their way to do some quail or pheasant hunting in the open country south of town.

Homer removed the Ford's gas cap, began to fill the tank, and frowned to himself when the nozzle switched off after pumping less than two gallons. The tank was nearly full already, and his sale came to a whopping forty-five cents.

Before he had a chance to brood about it, Charlie was out of the car, removing one of two spare tires he carried on the Ford's back seat.

"I think I got a leak," he told Tate. "Where's the air hose?"

"I'll take care of it," Tate said.

The leak was worse than Charlie thought. No matter how he tried, Tate couldn't get the ancient spare to hold more than twenty-eight pounds PSI. Muttering curses, Charlie asked if it could be repaired. Homer replied in the affirmative, and estimated it would take him ten or fifteen minutes to complete the job.

"Okay," Starkweather said. "I'll move the car while you get started."

As Tate went to work on the spare, he heard the girl ask Starkweather, "Do you want anything to eat?"

"I guess so," Charlie said.

"Well, then, what do you want?" the girl demanded, sounding angry. "I can't read your mind."

"Whatever you want," Charlie told her. "I don't care."

With that, Caril climbed out of the Ford and walked toward Brickey's. Charlie slid into the driver's seat and drove around behind the station, where his car would not be visible to anybody passing by. Tate thought it was a bit peculiar, when he could have simply backed it up to the café, but it was nothing to concern himself about.

Waitress Juanita Bell was halfway through her shift when Caril came in. As she recalled her teenage customer, years later, "I first saw her out at the pumps, coming toward the café. She was walking fast at first, then started to run. She gave a little smile when she came in. She sat on the stool at the end of the counter and ordered four hamburgers to go. I remember she was wearing a blue jacket, pink kerchief, and boots."

Juanita passed Caril's order to the cook, made sure he got it straight, and went back to her other customers.

Next door, Marvin Krueger, one of Homer Tate's employees, had returned from lunch while his boss was patching Charlie's spare. Starkweather walked into the office, giving Krueger quite a turn as Marv saw the revolver in his hand.

"Got any shells for this?" the redhead asked.

Krueger relaxed a little, asking, "What kind is it?"

"It's a .32. Haven't you ever seen one before?"

Marv checked the shelves behind him, found nothing, and finally shouted into the garage. "Hey, Homer! We got any .32 shells?"

No," the answer came back. "We don't carry .32s."

"Guess not," said Krueger.

Charlie made a sour face and stuck the empty pistol back into his belt, where it was covered by his jacket. "Well, then, how about .410s and .22s?"

"We got those," Krueger said. "How many do you want?"

Starkweather thought about it for a moment, finally asking for one box of shotgun shells and three boxes of .22 longs, a total of 175 rounds. Almost as an afterthought, he took a pair of gloves and paid his tab with a five-dollar bill. He was outside, smoking a cigarette, when Homer Tate finished working on his spare, and Charlie put it in the car. That done, he turned toward the café.

"It took about ten minutes to make the hamburgers," Juanita Bell recalled. "Just as they were ready, Charles Starkweather came in and handed [Caril] a ten-dollar bill, which she gave to me. He went to the door, which was between the last booth and the juke box, and waited. After I gave her the change, she walked over and bumped into him. They talked, then she gave him a shove as if she wanted to leave in a hurry. She walked outside and down the sidewalk, looking through the windows at me until she was out of sight. She had watched me like that all the time she had been in the café."

Caril Ann's defenders would later seize on Juanita's account as a description of a young girl in fear for her life. There is, of course, another view, as well. Caril Ann had ten or fifteen minutes on her own, in which she could have passed the disappearing note, explained her plight to someone in the diner, even used the public telephone to call police. The fact that she did none of those things, and appeared to be bossing Charlie around as they left the café, is one more telling argument against her "hostage" plea.

Before they drove a hundred yards, Starkweather later told Dale Fahrnbruch, Caril took a bite from one of the burgers and made a face. "Ugh!" she said. "This tastes like dog food. Let's take them back."

"We're not going back anywhere," he told her.

"Well, we ought to," Charlie quoted her. "We ought to go back and shoot them for serving junk like this."

The public record of Caril Ann's statements includes no answer to this allegation of murderous intent. It may have been a fabrication on Starkweather's part, or Caril Ann may have said it in the way teens—or adults, for that matter—are known to do, without considering the import of her words. Less than an hour later, though, she would, by her own admission, express identical sentiments toward another target.

And he would not escape so easily.

Throughout the drive from Lincoln, Charlie listened to the radio, more interested in news than music for a change. He still believed that Pansy Street would come back with a warrant, as she had threatened to do, and it was only a matter of time before the corpses were discovered back on Belmont Avenue. Starkweather meant to have a decent hiding place by then, if only he could make it through the string of troubles that had plagued him since that morning.

But his luck had not changed yet.

The Meyer farm was two miles east of Bennett. Charlie approached from the north, past the Bennett cemetery, right through town until he saw the Bennett Community Church. It was his landmark, telling him to turn left—eastward—on a two-lane road that served outlying farms. Old August Meyer's mailbox, bullet-riddled by the kind of hunters who were best with stationary targets, marked the entrance to an unpaved driveway that would take them to the old man's white two-story house.

Or, maybe not.

The snow had mostly melted by the time they reached Meyer's turnoff, leaving mud and slush behind. Charlie believed the Ford could make it, even so. He shifted into low and turned into the rutted driveway.

Moments later, they were stuck.

Starkweather tried to rock free of the muck, but he was mired down to the axles. It was hopeless. Cursing bitterly, he slammed a fist against the steering wheel.

Caril Ann's reaction, as described by Charlie to police, was somewhat different. According to Charlie, she said, "We ought to go blast the crap out of that old man."

"How come?" he asked her.

"'Cause he didn't clean his driveway, that's how come!"

"You want to kill him just for that?"

"Why not?" Caril asked.

Dale Fahrnbruch questioned Caril about that conversation later, and her version of events was similar to Charlie's, although she predictably remembered *him* suggesting murder first.

"When we got stuck," she said, "when we were going out there and got stuck, and couldn't get it out, I think he said he could kill him for it, and I said so could I. *And I could. I could, too.* Anyway, I mentioned it. I was mad because it was cold, and I said I could kill him, too." [Emphasis added.]

They had to find him first, though, and the Ford was not about to get them there. It was a bitter walk through slush that nearly sucked their shoes off, cold wind blowing in their faces. Charlie took the sawed-off shotgun from his car and led the way.

Some twenty yards from where the Ford bogged down, they saw the remains of the old District 79 schoolhouse. It had been demolished years before, nothing but the foundation and an old storm cellar, dubbed "the cave" by local kids, remaining. Charlie had visited the ruins many times, on hunting trips to Meyer's farm, flushing ground squirrels from cover, sometimes plinking tin cans with his .22 when he ran short of living targets.

"We can stop here and warm up," he told Caril Ann.

The cellar's domed roof was still covered with dirt, a small ventilation pipe sticking up from the ground. The heavy wooden door was off its hinges but remained in place, hiding a dozen concrete steps that led down to a circular room, some eight feet in diameter. It was dark and dirty, cluttered with windblown trash, dead leaves, and old wooden desks someone had tossed downstairs when they were tearing down the school. Caril didn't like it, but she knew it was too cold for snakes or spiders. They were also sheltered from the wind, and that was something to be thankful for.

They spent an estimated ten or fifteen minutes in the cellar, warming up a little, both still furious about the car. When Charlie told her it was time to go, Caril followed him upstairs and back into the biting wind.

No one can say with any certainty if Charlie's plan to murder August Meyer took shape before he reached the farm. They had been friends since Charlie was a little boy, when Guy first took him hunting on Meyer's land. Charlie had eaten supper there, admired the old man's guns, and borrowed one of them from time to time. At least one source contends that it was Meyer, not Guy, who taught Charlie to shoot. Not long before the Colvert murder, Charlie and Caril Ann had visited the farm to shoot some squirrels. She seemed to get along with Meyer, as well.

Approaching eighty, August Meyer was known to his neighbors as a gentleman and lifelong bachelor who spoke softly, minded his own business, and "wouldn't hurt a flea." The farm was tidy, and he paid his bills on time. In short, he was the kind of neighbor who personified the old cliché: He didn't have an enemy in the world.

Not that he knew of, anyway.

Meyer was not expecting company that Monday afternoon. He was surprised, but probably not worried, when his old dog started barking in the yard. This time, we have the statements of two witnesses, describing what ensued.

Caril's version, first.

"We walked up and the dog started barking," she told police, "and Mr. Meyer came out the back door. I was following Chuck. He was in front of me, walking toward the house. Mr. Meyer came out, and I don't know what he said, and then he walked over to the red barn. It was the first barn, and Chuck said he needed the horses to pull the car out. And Mr. Meyer said . . . I don't know what he said . . . and then he started to go in the door, and I saw Chuck raise the gun and heard a shot."

Predictably, Starkweather told a different story, with the shooting cast as self-defense. In Charlie's version, he and Caril Ann spent several minutes in Meyer's barn to warm themselves, before they finally approached the house. It was only then, he said, that the dog started barking, and August Meyer stepped through the back door, onto the porch.

"I got into a helluva argument with Meyer," Charlie said. "He couldn't understand why I got stuck there. He thought we should have gotten stuck up closer to his house."

In Charlie's story, Meyer went back to get his coat, but he would not allow the teenagers to come inside his house, directing them to a nearby washhouse instead. When Meyer came back out, a moment later, he was shouldering a rifle, squeezing off a shot at Starkweather.

"I felt the bullet go by my head," Charlie told police. The old man allegedly tried to fire again, but his gun jammed, whereupon he turned back toward the house. "Meyer started running back in the house," Charlie said, "and I shot him."

In fact, the sawed-off shotgun blast that shattered Meyer's skull was fired at close to point-blank range, before the pellets had much chance to spread. The distance indicates that Charlie must have chased Meyer toward the house, or possibly surprised him with a close shot from behind.

Why was he killed?

It is incredible that Meyer would have tried to murder Charlie over an issue so trivial as where a car got stuck in mud. Likewise, if the police chronology is accurate, Charlie and Caril arrived at Meyer's farm nearly three hours before the Bartlett corpses were found, almost *four* hours before the first police bulletin identified Charlie and Caril Ann as fugitives.

Thus, we are left with only three feasible scenarios. There is a chance, however slim, that Charlie may have let it slip, somehow, that he was wanted by the law, and Meyer may have tried to make a citizen's arrest. Another possibility, suggested by author William Allen, is that Meyer may have carried a weapon outside when he heard his dog barking at persons unknown, thereby prompting Charlie to react in a fit of violent paranoia.

Or, Starkweather may have meant to kill his old friend all along. As he would later tell James Reinhardt in a jailhouse interview, "Dead people don't talk."

When he shot August Meyer, Charlie told the police, "Caril was around the corner. I told her to come into the house. We went in and I laid down . . . then I came out and dragged him to the outbuilding."

In the privy, some fifty feet from the house, Charlie covered Meyer's body with an old white blanket from the house. Caril dropped the old man's hat beside his body, and Charlie was closing the outhouse door when Meyer's dog approached them, barking angrily. Starkweather shot the dog but failed to kill it, watching as it ran away, across a pasture, toward a brush-lined creek that flowed across the property.

Uncharacteristically for Charlie, the sympathetic hunter, he ignored the wounded animal and led Caril back inside Meyer's house.

"We went in the kitchen," Caril Ann told Dale Fahrn-bruch. "I sat down by the stove there, and then [Charlie] got up and went upstairs. He was looking for a gun. He came down and looked through the downstairs, and I kept looking out the window to see if anyone was coming. Then he came out with the guns, three of them . . . two great big ones, and there was a .22, and then we went into the kitchen. I went in there and sat down. He was looking for some money. Some people gave Mr. Meyer some money, he said. He had about five hundred dollars in the house. Then he said Mr. Meyer had a lot of clothes, brand new clothes he just bought, and he went in the other room, and I went in there, too. He got two pairs of socks and a big jacket and two pairs of white gloves. There should be a pair of white gloves in my black coat. He told me to put on a pair of socks, but I wouldn't."

When Charlie finished changing socks, he continued his search for cash, finally turning up about a hundred dollars in a brown cloth pouch. Back in the kitchen, he found some cookies and Jell-O to eat, but Caril says she refused to share the meager meal.

"He stuck his finger in it and said the Jell-O was good," she told Fahrnbruch. "I kept saying, 'Let's go,' because I was scared." Of what? "I was afraid of Mr. Meyer," she explained, "because he was dead."

After searching the house, Charlie recalled, he took a nap, then went outside with Caril to seek the wounded dog. They followed the pathetic blood trail several hundred feet, until they found their quarry stretched out near the creek.

"I didn't know if he was dead or not," said Charlie, and he made no effort to find out.

The total haul from August Meyer's slaying was a snack, some dry clothes, and about a hundred dollars, plus a new pump-action .22 rifle. Starkweather left behind the "great big" guns Caril had referred to, as they tramped back to the car. He didn't even take a horse along to help him with the car, as he had planned. Instead, he settled for a spade and tried to dig the car out, Caril Ann steering, as he labored for the best part of an hour in the slush. When Charlie got too cold, disgusted with the thankless task, they walked back to the nearby storm cellar and warmed themselves before returning to the car. At last, he used the jack and almost had it, inching backward toward the highway. They were almost there, when Charlie slid the Ford into a ditch. This time, when he tried backing out, the tired transmission gave way, stripping the reverse gear.

Cold, wet, and disgusted, Charlie was prepared to give up on the old Ford, when he saw a pair of headlights coming down the road.

It was after five o'clock, already dark, as farmer Howard Genuchi made his way home from Lincoln. The thirty-five-year-old bachelor had spent his day shopping for spare parts to a combine, stopping for a few beers at the old Star Tavern when he saw that it was too late to begin repairs on the machine that afternoon. Passing the entrance to Meyer's driveway in his 1937 Ford, Genuchi saw a car stuck in the mud and stopped to ask if he could help.

Charlie explained their situation, watching Caril Ann from the car. Genuchi pegged them as a pair of teenage lovers who had picked the wrong place for a winter tryst. No bulletin describing Charlie or his car had yet been broadcast. There was no good reason for Genuchi to suspect the kids were up to anything illegal.

"If you have a rope or something, I can try and pull you out of there," he offered.

Starkweather nodded, moving toward the black Ford's trunk before he hesitated.

"Dammit!"

Charlie didn't have a trunk key, but he used his hunting knife instead. It took a while, but Charlie knew what he was doing. Once the trunk was open, he removed a length of quarter-inch steel cable, walking back to where Genuchi waited on the road.

"This oughta do the trick," Starkweather said.

They linked one car's rear bumper to the other, and

Genuchi towed them clear, Caril steering the black Ford while Charlie stood outside and watched the cable, making sure it didn't slip. When they were safely on the road, uncoupled from Genuchi's car, he walked back to the farmer's vehicle.

"What do I owe you?" Charlie asked.

"Forget it," said Genuchi. "You don't owe me anything."

Starkweather looked confused, maybe embarrassed. "Sure I do," he said, and took two dollars from his wallet.

It was too damned cold to argue. "Suit yourself," Genuchi said, and took the money. Driving off, he had a final glimpse of Charlie in his rearview mirror, climbing back into the other car.

"What are we going to do now?" Caril asked him, sounding peevish.

Charlie thought about it for a minute, staring at the darkened fields on either side. "We might as well go back to Meyer's," he said at last. "Something I wanna check."

Charlie could not explain the urge that took him back to Meyer's house. Maybe it was sanctuary, a convenient place to hide out for the night. In any case, he would not risk the muddy lane a second time.

A quarter mile back down the highway, near a bridge and railroad tracks, he found the entrance to another access road that served Meyer's property. There were gates along the way, and Caril Ann left the car to open them, while Charlie stayed behind the wheel. They stopped within a hundred yards of Meyer's two-story farmhouse, both carrying guns as they left the car and continued on foot. Caril waited, well back from the outhouse, while Charlie edged forward and peered through a window on one side. A moment later, he came running back to join her, breathless.

"Shit! We gotta get out of here!"

"What's wrong?" she asked.

"Somebody's been here," Charlie said. "You know that blanket I put over Meyer? It's gone!"

They ran back to the car, and Charlie turned off on a

narrow side road, telling Caril it was a shortcut to the highway. He was startled and disoriented when they came to a dead end, nothing but corn in front of them.

"Back up and turn around," Caril said.

"I *can't*," he snapped. "This car's got no reverse!"

Starkweather's run to glory had degenerated into a bizarre comedy of errors. When he tried to turn the steering wheel, he found his tires were in a rut. With nothing left to try, he stamped on the accelerator, cutting a wide swath through the frozen field as he circled back toward the highway.

"Boy," he told Dale Fahrnbruch, later, "you shoulda seen the corn fly there, stalks and everything flyin' behind me."

Charlie made it to the highway without bogging down— but where to go from there? If someone had found August Meyer's body, it would not be long before police arrived. Perhaps, if he could lay a phony trail. . . .

Starkweather turned his old Ford north and headed back to Tate's.

According to the state police chronology, it was 5:30 P.M. when the mud-caked Ford pulled into Tate's Conoco station for the second time on January 27. Marv Krueger was weary from the steady stream of customers since lunchtime, and he didn't want to mess around with some kid buying forty-five cents worth of gas, but he still had a job to do.

Charlie wore his version of the James Dean smile as Krueger walked up to the car. "You carry road maps?" he inquired.

"Sure do."

"Okay, I need a Kansas road map and some more shells. A couple of boxes of .22 longs oughta do it."

Krueger didn't like playing carhop, but a sale was a sale. He returned moments later with the map and cartridges— another hundred rounds—and handed them to Charlie through the window on the driver's side. While he was waiting for his money, Krueger noticed Caril Ann, sitting next to Charlie with a rifle and a shotgun in her lap. She had a nervous look about her, and the whole scenario seemed odd somehow.

Why did they need more ammunition after dark?

Krueger was curious enough to pull a note pad from his pocket and jot down the black Ford's license number as it pulled away. Inside the station, he went one step further, telephoning the police to ask if they were interested in two teenagers "acting funny," buying lots of ammunition. Krueger couldn't point to anything illegal they had done, but he felt sure the kids were up to something.

The police department's switchboard operator thanked Marv for the information and hung up. By that time, Charlie and Caril Ann were sought for questioning about a triple murder. The authorities had a description of his car; they knew the license number. Even so, nobody ever called Marv Krueger back.

The Kansas road map was a dodge, as Caril explained it later. "Chuck wanted them to think we were going to Kansas," she told Dale Fahrnbruch.

And it might have worked, if anyone had followed up Marv Krueger's lead. Without that follow-up, however, it was so much wasted effort.

Charlie had the old Ford pointed south, all right, but he had no intention of exploring Kansas.

He was going back to August Meyer's.

A third trip to the old man's farm may seem peculiar, even downright stupid, but Charlie had been thinking since they fled Meyer's farm the second time. The missing blanket didn't prove someone had found the body, after all. The more he thought about it, Charlie managed to convince himself that cold wind blowing underneath the outhouse door could just as easily have pushed the blanket over to one side. He hated feeling like a "chicken," running from an enemy he hadn't even seen.

What was the point in lugging all those guns around, if he allowed himself to be intimidated by a dead man?

Caril was something else. It almost seemed as if a superstitious fear had taken over in her mind. "She thought

[Meyer] was going to get back up and sit there waiting for us," Charlie told Dale Fahrnbruch.

It was laughable, and yet . . .

As they drew closer to the old white farmhouse, Charlie's nerve began to fail. The place was dark and quiet as a graveyard. Never mind the body in the outhouse. What if there were cops spread out around the place, just waiting for their quarry to come back? His favorite comic books and movies talked about felons returning to the scenes of their crimes, and Charlie Starkweather was running true to form.

"Forget this," Charlie said. "We're getting out of here."

He whipped the steering wheel around, stood on the gas pedal . . . and felt his tires sink into soft, wet mud.

The Ford was stuck *again!*

This time, the darkness and frigid wind immediately banished any thought of digging out, a job that would take hours in the freezing cold, if he could pull it off at all. Meyer's house was fairly close, but Caril Ann was afraid of August's corpse, and Charlie wasn't wild about the thought of staying there, himself.

He had a sudden inspiration. They could camp out in the old storm cellar, maybe even light a fire if they were careful with the smoke.

It helped to have a plan, but they were still damned cold as they began the trek back toward the road, taking the guns and spare ammunition along. As they approached the county highway, Charlie spied another pair of headlights coming toward them from the west. Another inspiration came to Charlie on the spot.

He held Meyer's rifle in his left hand, partially concealed behind his back, as he stepped toward the lights and stuck out his thumb.

10

The Cave

Bennett, Nebraska, owes its existence to the Midland Pacific Railroad. Surveyed and platted in 1871, named for railroad officer John Bennett, the town—with a modern population in the neighborhood of four hundred souls—is still too small to register on many highway maps. In 1958, the "downtown" district was a single block of businesses, including the OK Cafe (renowned for its $1.75 "Fried Chicken Night"), a post office, and Jensen's General Store.

Even in 1958, a tour of Jensen's was like slipping back into the good old days of another century. It was Mayberry, once removed, with canned goods on the shelves and an assortment of candies near the register, husky Robert Jensen, Sr., manning the meat counter in a blood-flecked white apron, when he wasn't pushing a broom across the wooden floor. Jensen and his wife, Pauline, were near-lifelong residents of Bennett, and their roots ran deep, as witnessed by the poem he had printed on the back of his sales receipts. It was called "Little Town," and read:

I like to live in a little town
   where the trees meet across the street
Where you wave your hand and say "Hello"
   to everyone you meet . . . .

So I like to live in a little town
   I care no more to roam.

For every home in a little town
   is more than a house, it's home.

The store was a fairly recent endeavor for Jensen, opened in 1950, after he quit his meat-cutting job at the local cold-storage plant. It was a challenge, keeping up with the new "supermarkets" in Lincoln, but Jensen was holding his own with some help from his sons. Robert Jr. was seventeen, a junior in high school, and Dewey had just turned fifteen. The younger Robert—"Bob" to everyone who knew him— had already topped the six-foot mark and weighed 240 pounds. A first-rate student and president of his class, Bob had also played football for a while, but his endurance was hampered by the aftereffects of polio, which had nearly claimed his life at age eleven. Still active in the church at an age when many young people defected, Bob was glad to help around his dad's store after school, as long as there was time left over in the evening for his fiancée.

Carol King was an attractive brunette who lived a half block from the Jensen home. At age sixteen, she shared Bob's interest in the church, sang with him in the choir, and sat beside him during summer Bible classes. At their school, she made good grades while doubling as a majorette and cheerleader. Her father's recent death that autumn made Carol even more grateful for Bob, and they saw each other almost every night.

They made a wholesome couple, in the best 1950s style, as far removed from Charlie and Caril Ann as denizens from outer space. As far as Bob and Carol were concerned, life had its problems, but the same clouds rained on everybody. There was nothing to rebel against, no need to rage against the world, much less to rob and kill. They weren't *completely* square, of course. Despite their obvious devotion to the church, they never came off sounding holier than thou. Bob had a set of loud pipes on his 1950 Ford and kept some "naughty" post cards in his wallet, with a list of obscene sayings attributed to Confucius. When they needed time alone, Bob and Carol sought out the same rural lanes as other young lovers their age. It was a thrill to park like that sometimes, and to at least *consider* "going all the way."

On Monday afternoon, the twenty-seventh, Bob left school and went directly to his father's store, as usual. He helped around the place till closing time, at 6:00 P.M., when Robert Sr. sent him on a final errand, dropping off a half gallon of milk at a customer's house. They met at home for supper, after Robert finished closing up. The Jensen family dined together every night, because it was the way you did things in America, but all of them required their private time, as well. Robert enjoyed a quiet hour in the basement he had recently converted to a den, while Bob preferred to spend his time with Carol.

That night, before he went to pick her up, Bob had a final conversation with his father, neither of them knowing it would be their last. They talked about the price of recapped tires—Bob needed two—and Robert asked his son to pick up some American Legion membership cards from a friend's house while he was out. Bob didn't mind; it would take only ten minutes give or take, and he could take Carol with him.

Better yet.

Carol was fighting a cold that night, but she still jumped at the chance to join Bob on his errands, promising her mother that she would be home by ten o'clock. She dressed in faded jeans, a white sweatshirt, and oxfords, with a scarf and heavy winter coat to keep her warm. Bob showed up in his letterman's jacket, looking for all the world like an extra from *Happy Days*.

They were the all-American couple, blissfully unaware of their impending rendezvous with Death.

Bob stopped to get the Legion cards first thing, then drove to Ernest Hunt's filling station, at the intersection of Highway 34 and Bennett's main drag. He bought three dollars' worth of gas and spoke to Hunt about the recaps, which weren't ready yet. Next week, perhaps.

They still had lots of time before Carol's curfew as they left the service station. Even with her cold, she didn't feel like going home, and Bob was not afraid of germs. He aimed the Ford toward August Meyer's place, one of the better parking spots enjoyed by randy Bennett teens. Considering the weather, it was likely they would have the dark lane to themselves.

The last thing either one of them expected was a pair of muddy hikers on the roadside, packing guns.

It had to be a toss-up in Bob Jensen's mind: To stop, or not to stop? These days, with all the fear of violent crime, a couple of gun-toting teenagers might walk from coast to coast without encountering a single good Samaritan willing to pick them up, but Charlie and Caril Ann had three advantages. The date was January 1958, when random murder by a total stranger was unthinkable. The place, rural Nebraska, where a gun or two was no big deal.

And then, there was the clincher. Young Bob Jensen thought he recognized the redhead, standing with his thumb out and the rifle hanging at his side.

He could have driven past them even so, but it was not the Christian thing to do. Charlie was glad to talk about what happened next.

As he described it, Bob pulled over, rolled his window down, and asked if there was any trouble. Charlie told him that their car was stuck in mud, with the reverse gear stripped. Bob seemed to study Charlie for a moment, putting it together in his mind. He'd seen Charlie around the hot-rod strip.

"You own a Ford, don't you?" he asked.

"Yeah." Charlie felt the paranoia mounting.

"Black? A '49?"

"That's right." He gripped the stolen rifle tightly, wondering if this kid, coming out of nowhere, had been listening to his description on the radio.

"Get in," said Jensen, seemingly oblivious to Charlie's status as a fugitive. "We'll drive you into town."

As Charlie and Caril Ann got in the back, Bob turned and wrapped a hand around the rifle's barrel. "I'll take these, okay?" he said.

"What for?" Charlie demanded. "They ain't loaded."

Caril Ann seemed to take offense at the idea. "We don't just walk around with loaded guns," she said.

Bob glanced at Carol, perhaps a trifle worried now, but let it slide. "Okay," he said. "I don't want anybody getting hurt, that's all."

When Charlie and Caril Ann were settled in the back, Bob turned his car around and started back toward town. Charlie's mind was racing as they drove. Convinced that Jensen recognized him, he would later tell police that he considered surrendering when they got back to Bennett. Not that Charlie felt remorse for what he'd done so far; rather, he decided that he "wasn't going to let them be heroes" by taking him in. Moments later, though, Starkweather changed his mind. Surrender was for pansies. If the lawmen wanted him, they'd have a battle on their hands.

Approaching Bennett, Charlie asked if Bob could take them to a pay phone. Jensen readily agreed, and pulled into a service station that had shut down for the night. The pay phone was inside, unreachable.

"It's all locked up," said Jensen. "We can go to my house. You can call from there."

"Oh, no, we ain't," said Charlie, as he pressed the muzzle of his .22 against Bob's skull. "You just do what I tell you, or somebody will get hurt!"

"What do you want?" asked Jensen.

"Drive us to Lincoln," Charlie answered. "Now!"

Bob pulled out onto Highway 2 and aimed the Ford

northwest, toward Lincoln. They were barely on their way, when Charlie had another bright idea.

"I changed my mind," he said. "Head back to that abandoned school. You know the one I mean?"

"I think so," Jensen said. "How come?"

"Just do what I tell ya."

Bob couldn't let it go at that. "What are you going to do with us?" he asked Charlie.

"Nothin'. We're just gonna leave you there."

"I guess you're gonna take my car?"

"That's right."

The answer almost seemed to help Jensen relax. "Try not to burn it up," he said. "Be careful with the drive shaft when you're going over any bumps."

If we accept Starkweather's version of events, it was Caril Ann's idea to rob the couple. "Have you asked him for his money yet, Charlie?"

"Not yet!" he snapped at her. It was a stupid question, Caril Ann sitting *right there* with him in the car. Still, they could always use the money. "Pass your billfold back here, and be quick about it!" he instructed Jensen.

Bob handed his wallet back to Caril Ann. She opened it, removed four dollar bills, and gave the cash to Starkweather before she passed Bob's empty wallet to Carol King.

"Here, you take it," she said.

Carol had been silent since the ride turned ugly, but she found her voice now, as she took Bob's wallet back. "I want to thank you," she said, "for not being mean to us."

In Charlie's version, Caril glared back at her and snarled, "Shut up!"

"Hey, you won't shoot us, will you?" Jensen asked.

"I will if you don't do what I say," Charlie promised.

"You've got to be kidding." The very thought seemed bizarre to young Robert.

According to Charlie, Caril Ann replied, "If you don't watch it, I'll shoot her and show you if we're kidding or not."

(Caril later denied making any such comment. She also

denied suggesting the robbery, but admitted taking the money from Bob Jensen's wallet and holding a gun on the couple—at Charlie's command. Those acts alone, under Nebraska's felony murder rule, were enough to earn her a life prison term.)

They stopped some twenty paces from the old District 79 storm cellar, Caril Ann waiting in the Ford and listening to music on the radio while Charlie marched his captives toward The Cave. What happened next is known from crime scene photographs and autopsy reports. The *how* and *why* of it remains a point of argument between Starkweather and his prosecutors.

This we know: Bob Jensen was shot six times with August Meyer's pump-action .22, the bullets grouped in a four-inch cluster behind his left ear. His body wound up at the bottom of the concrete stairs, facedown. The prosecution's theory was that Charlie took his time, lined up the shot while Jensen's back was turned, and made a quick, cold-blooded kill. In Charlie's version, it was "self-defense" again, Bob shoving Carol King aside and grabbing for the rifle, losing his balance and starting to fall as Charlie opened fire. In either case, it added up to murder in the course of kidnapping and robbery, but Charlie's version left the killer's self-respect in tact.

In Charlie's first statement to Elmer Scheele, he said that Carol King started screaming after Jensen fell, and Charlie shot her where she stood, to shut her up. That version went along with Caril Ann's claim that she was sitting in the car and heard some shots from the direction of the cellar, but she didn't see the crimes occur.

When Charlie had a chance to think about it, though, he wrote a letter to the prosecutor, changing that part of the story. In the new version, Starkweather said he marched Carol King into the basement, past her boyfriend's huddled corpse, and meant to leave her there, alive. He was about to block the cellar door with some debris, said Charlie, when it came to him that Bob might not be dead. In fact, when Charlie went downstairs, he claimed the wounded boy was sitting upright, but he soon collapsed. Starkweather said he spent another ten or fifteen minutes watching Jensen, counting ragged breaths, until they ceased at last.

Caril Ann, meanwhile, supposedly came over from the car, suspicion bleeding into fury as she pictured Charlie raping Carol King. Starkweather went upstairs to meet her, and they had what he called "bloody talk," before he calmed her down a bit. Carol King was still alive, he said, as they prepared to drive away.

And then, incredibly, the car bogged down.

Charlie told Scheele that he left Caril to guard the sole survivor of their rampage. He was jacking up Bob's Ford, prepared to shove some old boards underneath the tires, when he was startled by a gunshot. Racing to the cellar, Charlie found Carol King dead on the ground, with Caril Ann standing over her. The girl had tried to run, Caril said; she had no choice. Starkweather sent her to the car and ordered her to wait, while he dragged Carol downstairs.

And yet . . .

Bob Jensen's body was discovered in the cellar, fully clothed, blood pooled beneath him on the concrete floor. Carol lay on top of him, her coat pulled up over her head, jeans and panties around her ankles, mud and bloodstains smearing her flesh from waist to mid-thigh. The single shot that killed her had been fired from Carol's right, below the ear. There were drag marks on her back, between the lower rib cage and the sacrum. A postmortem examination for sexual assault was inconclusive, meaning simply that no semen traces were discovered. Several stab wounds marked her groin, one piercing the wall of Carol's cervix to penetrate the rectum. Examination of the wounds eliminated Charlie's hunting knife as the source of Carol's mutilation. The instrument, never found, had a narrow double-edged blade like a stiletto, at least three inches long, no more than three quarters of an inch wide.

Whether she had been raped or not, the knife wounds, by their very nature, constituted sexual assault. Starkweather didn't like discussing that part of the murders in The Cave, presenting several different versions of the incident. At first, he told Lieutenant Eugene Henninger that he had "screwed the shit out of that King girl," but he took a different line with Dale Fahrnbruch.

What had happened in the cellar after Jensen finally stopped breathing? Fahrnbruch asked.

"Temptation," Charlie said.

"What did you do?"

"Well," Charlie said, "I pulled her jeans down, but I didn't screw her."

"What did you do to her?" Fahrnbruch prodded.

"Nothing."

"Charlie, you told the officers different, haven't you?"

"I didn't screw her," Starkweather insisted. "I couldn't get to the point . . . it was colder than hell. I left her lay there and left. I didn't screw her. I'll argue that with you all night, too."

Lieutenant Henninger was present when Charlie recanted his earlier statement, but Charlie stood firm. The only reason he had first confessed to raping King, he told the lawmen now, was to conceal what Caril Ann had done to her.

Fahrnbruch changed his angle of attack, jumping ahead to the point when Charlie returned to Bob's car. "Did Caril leave the car, then?" he asked.

"A couple of times, yes," Charlie said. "She was pissed off, anyway. She called me a dirty bastard and all sorts of things."

"Why did she call you that?" asked Fahrnbruch. "Did you do something in the cave that she might have seen?"

"Well, she might have come up to that cave and thought," Charlie said, "but I wasn't."

"As a matter of fact," Fahrnbruch said, "you asked her for sexual relations?"

"Yes, but I never got them."

"What did she say?"

"I already had mine for the night," Charlie groused. "She probably walked up there and seen me down there. She could have guessed."

"What could she have guessed?" Fahrnbruch asked.

"What I was doing."

"What *did* you do?"

"I didn't do nothing."

Even on death row, Charlie refused to acknowledge the sexual mutilation of Carol King, as if it would somehow diminish his "fighting reputation" and make him less of a "man." In their prison interviews, James Reinhardt picked up on Dale Fahrnbruch's line of questioning, trying to find out what Caril Ann was angry about. "Ask her," Starkweather told the criminologist. "She'd make up somethin'."

After covering the cellar door with cast-off garbage, Charlie and Caril Ann went back to working on the car. They finally put a blanket and some boards beneath the wheels, and managed to escape the sucking mud. According to the state police chronology, it was around ten-thirty when they pulled out of the narrow lane, back onto Highway 2, and started burning up the road toward Lincoln.

Police timed Charlie's departure from The Cave on the basis of two "earwitnesses" living nearby. Farmer Everett Broening had just finished milking his twenty-four cows, returning to the house for a hot cup of coffee, when his dog started barking outside. Broening went back to check it out, but there was nothing out of place that he could see, and the excited watchdog ceased his yapping moments later. It was 9:30 P.M. when Broening reentered the house and glanced at a clock in the kitchen, making his way back to the living room and his favorite easy chair.

It had been a long day, and Broening dozed off in front of the television, awakened by his wife in time to watch the news before he went to bed. He was already dressed in his pajamas at ten-thirty, when the dog began to bark again, demanding his attention. Broening got up, muttering, and made it halfway to the closet for his coat and old galoshes, when he heard a car roar past the house, northbound. Its loud pipes brought his teenage son out of another bedroom down the hall.

"There goes Jensen's car," the boy remarked. He was a friend of Bob's, another car enthusiast, adept at picking out the local hot-rods by their sounds.

The elder Broening frowned at that, wondering if there was anything wrong with young Jensen. "He always blowed the horn when he went by," Broening said later, "and that time he didn't blow it." He would recall the incident on Tuesday afternoon, when word got around that Bob Jensen and Carol King were missing.

Back at the King house, meanwhile, Carol's older brother, Warren, was anxiously checking the time. Carol was late, and she hadn't phoned home, an unprecedented circumstance that troubled Warren and his mother. Carol had school tomorrow, and she had not been feeling well. It wasn't like Bob Jensen to ignore a curfew. Still, they could have had a flat or something, and you couldn't always find a telephone available in Bennett at that hour of the night. Warren decided he would wait a while before he went to Jensen's house, a short walk down the street, to find out what was going on.

It was approaching midnight when he made the trek, and Robert Jensen answered Warren's knock. The kids weren't back yet, and considering the hour, Jensen had begun to worry. Pulling on a coat, he walked back to the King house and got into Warren's car. They drove out to the city limits, watching for Bob's Ford along the way, but they appeared to have the streets all to themselves. The drive became an aimless search, along one narrow country road after another, headlights boring tunnels into the frigid dark. An hour slipped away, and then another. Finally, Jensen suggested that they call the highway patrol, and King agreed.

Warren recalled that it was shortly after two o'clock on Tuesday morning when a female operator listened to his story, took down names and a description of Bob Jensen's car. She told him that an officer would be informed of the report "as soon as possible." According to the state police chronology, another hour and fifteen minutes passed before the missing persons bulletin was broadcast.

Not that the delay made any difference, in the long run. It was already too late.

Charlie would later tell Dale Fahrnbruch that he wanted to surrender after killing Bob and Carol. The pace of bloodletting was wearing Charlie down. Barely a half day on the lam, and he was sick of living as a fugitive. It wasn't so much like his "shooting movies," after all.

Caril Ann was not prepared to give it up so easily, however.

"She kept trying to talk me out of it," Charlie said. "We was going down shooting on the highway. I told her I was going to give myself up, and she said no I wasn't. I said yes I was, and she said no I wasn't."

Fahrnbruch asked him how the argument turned out, and Charlie claimed he felt intimidated by the shotgun Caril Ann carried. "When you got the .410 sitting there," he said, "I wasn't going to do it."

On second thought, Charlie admitted that she didn't really threaten him, but the gun *was* pointing his way, as it lay across Caril's lap. Besides, he told Fahrnbruch, "She said that she wasn't giving herself up and wasn't going to let anything stand in her way. That was good enough for me."

Caril checked the car out on the drive back north, to Lincoln. There was nothing in the glove compartment worth a second glance, but she found several of Bob Jensen's schoolbooks on the floor behind her seat, and tossed them out the window. Later, she would claim the books were thrown out as a "tip" to the police, in hope that she would soon be rescued.

Back in Lincoln, Charlie drove to Belmont on a whim. He felt secure in Jensen's car—the cops were looking for *his* Ford, not Bob's—and he could not resist another visit to the Bartlett house. There was a black-and-white patrol car parked out front, and Charlie kept on going, nervous and excited, all at once. He felt like laughing at the stupid cops. He was *right there,* and still they couldn't see him.

Even so, he knew it was about to hit the fan. Where could they go? He thought of brother Leonard, living in the state of Washington, and started driving west. They got as far as Hastings, better than a hundred miles away, on Highway 6, before Starkweather changed his mind again. He was exhausted, and the stolen car was "running rough." Charlie had doubts that it would take them all the way to Washington. They needed better wheels, and something told him picking up another car would be much easier in Lincoln.

Charlie pulled into an all-night service station, filled the tank, and told Caril Ann, "We're going back."

If she had any arguments against the plan, Caril kept them to herself.

"I wasn't worried," Charlie later said. The cops would never be expecting him to drive in from the west. How could they?

Charlie had been pegged as stupid all his life.

He meant to show the bastards they were wrong.

11

Mad Dog

Bob Jensen and Carol King had been officially listed as missing persons for seven hours when Leo Schwenke gave police their first break in the case. A fifty-year-old truck driver employed by Nebraska's State Highway Department, Schwenke lived in Lincoln and worked from the state shops at Sixth and South Streets, just across from Gooch's Mills. The past few days, he had been hauling loads of asphalt to the junction of Highways 2 and 43, some sixteen miles away, a half mile east of Bennett. It was cold out, but the veteran of fourteen years on bleak Nebraska highway jobs enjoyed the winter landscape. In winter, quail and pheasant sheltered in the stubbled fields of corn. Schwenke liked to spot them from his truck and come back on his days off with a shotgun, for some sport.

That Tuesday morning, close to 10:15, Schwenke was eleven miles due west of Bennett when a flash of color on the roadside caught his eye. It was unusual enough for him to stop and take a closer look—no hurry with the asphalt he was hauling, anyway. Once he had parked the truck, he counted three books lying on the shoulder of the highway.

Books?

Schwenke climbed down from the dump truck's cab, retrieved the volumes, examining their titles. They were schoolbooks, he discovered—English, history, and math. A label on the inside cover of the math book marked it as PROPERTY OF THE BENNETT PUBLIC SCHOOLS. A piece of folded paper wedged between the pages like a bookmark proved to be a math test, marked in red at several points where it had been corrected by a teacher. Schwenke squinted at the name handwritten in the paper's upper right-hand corner.

Robert Jensen.

It was weird, he thought, for some kid to discard his books that way, along the road. The more he thought about it, Schwenke told himself that there was something badly out of place about the whole damned thing. He'd never heard of Robert Jensen, didn't know that he had been reported missing with his girlfriend seven hours earlier. Still, Leo was the kind of man who couldn't leave a mystery alone.

He made his mind up to inform the State Patrol of what he'd found.

Schwenke drove on and dumped his load of asphalt, returning empty. It was coming up on eleven o'clock when he parked outside the State Patrol headquarters, on Cornhusker Highway, and carried the schoolbooks inside. After another ten or fifteen minutes of waiting, Schwenke told his story to Patrolman John O'Neal. The officer agreed that it was odd for textbooks to be tossed out on the road, that way. As for the owner, there was something . . .

Jensen. Jensen. Why did that name sound familiar?

Thanking Leo Schwenke for his time, O'Neal assured the helpful citizen that he would check it out himself, as soon as possible.

The unofficial search for Bob and Carol had resumed as soon as daylight broke across the cold Nebraska plains, with

Robert Sr. telephoning everyone he knew to ask for help. One of the searchers was Merle Boldt, who owned the Bennett Champlain station. Teamed with good friend Dennis Nelson, Boldt had spent the morning prowling back roads, south and east of town, but they had come up empty.

By 11:45 A.M., the frozen dirt roads had begun to thaw enough that Boldt decided he should drive back into Bennett, to retrieve his pickup truck with four-wheel drive. Experience had taught him that the rural tracks were treacherous. The last thing Boldt and Nelson needed was to get bogged down in muck and have to hike for miles to find a telephone.

Boldt made it home, switched vehicles, and dropped his partner at the nearby Standard station. Nelson was supposed to be at work by noon, and Boldt would carry on the search alone, until he had run out of back roads to explore.

The first he came to, less than two miles east of Bennett, was a narrow lane that led to August Meyer's farmhouse. Boldt knew Meyer by sight, but they were not close friends. Still, he could not imagine Meyer objecting if he checked the private road for any sign of Bob and Carol.

Boldt hadn't traveled far before he spied a car off to his left, perhaps a hundred yards away. It was a black Ford, 1949, mired to the axles in the middle of a field. Not young Bob Jensen's car . . . but then, whose could it be?

Boldt thought about continuing to Meyer's house, but he didn't feel he knew the old man well enough to just drop in that way. Instead, he doubled back and drove to Hubert Beecham's farm, not far away. Beecham was working on a truck, beside his barn, when Boldt pulled up and hailed him from the pickup.

Boldt explained what he was doing, what he'd seen, and Beecham readily agreed to join him on the short drive back to Meyer's place. As a friend and longtime neighbor, it would be no problem if he showed up unexpectedly at August's door. They could inquire about the car, find out if Meyer had seen the missing kids, and then be on their way.

Returning to Meyer's lane, Boldt stopped his pickup

twenty paces from the Ford and closed the gap on foot. It came as a relief to find that there was no one in the car, but that relief evaporated as Boldt read the license number: 2-15268.

It clicked, then: the reports he had been hearing on the radio, since yesterday. Three people dead in Lincoln, one of them a little girl. Police were looking for a boy named Charles Starkweather and his girlfriend, riding in the very car that Boldt had found.

He ran back to the pickup, trembling as he slid behind the wheel. "Christ, Hubert! It's the car the cops are looking for, from Lincoln! You know, the Starkweather car!"

"God almighty!" Beecham's face went pale. "What should we do?"

"We're going back to town and call the State Patrol, that's what," said Boldt. "They've been out looking for this car all night."

It was a short run back to Bennett, but it seemed to take forever, even with the pickup truck's accelerator mashed down to the floor. Boldt checked the rearview mirror frequently, relieved each time he saw the two-lane blacktop empty at his back.

Let's keep it that way, Jesus.

He was fairly certain they would be all right, if they could just get back to town alive.

As Boldt and Beecham sped toward Bennett, westbound, Patrolman John O'Neal was headed in the opposite direction, driving east on Highway 2, from Lincoln. He had read the missing persons sheet on Bob Jensen and Carol King, and he was worried that there might be some connection with the Bartlett homicides in Lincoln. Granted, it was still a long shot, but his ten years on the job had honed O'Neal's gut instinct to the point where he could sometimes *feel* the bad news coming, without any solid evidence to back it up.

He stopped off at the Standard station and received directions to the Jensen residence. Bob's dad was talking to a neighbor on the front porch when O'Neal drove up and parked his cruiser in the driveway. Moments later, he had confirmation that the books retrieved by Leo Schwenke were Bob's. Robert was briefing the patrolman on the progress of their search so far, when John O'Neal was summoned by an urgent message on his two-way radio. A man named Boldt was waiting for him at the Champlain service station, claiming he had information about Charlie Starkweather and Caril Ann Fugate.

Trooper O'Neal excused himself and drove to Boldt's station, where he was informed of the discovery near August Meyer's farm. He didn't know the way, himself, so Merle Boldt led the cruiser back to Charlie's car. O'Neal approached the Ford on foot, with gun in hand, and verified its license number from the Lincoln all-points bulletin. A quick search turned up keys in the ignition, road maps, and a half-eaten hamburger abandoned on the front seat. An envelope from the Internal Revenue Service bore Charlie's name, with his Tenth Street address. Three spare tires were piled on the back seat, with .22-caliber cartridges littering the floorboard. O'Neal tried the trunk lid, but he couldn't get it open. Giving up, he walked back to his car and radioed the news to headquarters.

By 1:30 P.M., twenty-five officers from the Nebraska State Patrol, Lancaster County Sheriff's Department, and the Lincoln P.D. had converged on Meyer's farm, along with thirty-odd farmers from the Bennett neighborhood, all packing guns. News teams arrived from Lincoln while the raiders waited for their tear gas to arrive, and word came in that TV crews were on their way from Omaha. It was assumed that Charlie and Caril Ann were hiding out at Meyer's place. Nobody planned to miss the show.

By the time the tear gas arrived, the farmhouse was surrounded. Assistant Police Chief Eugene Masters, from Lincoln, stood behind an elm tree with a loud hailer and warned the silent house, "We know you're in there. We'll give you five minutes to come out with your hands up."

When the deadline passed without an answer from the house, Merle Karnopp led a flying squad of deputies to seek a better vantage point. Tear gas was pumped in through the nearest windows, spreading quickly through the rooms of August Meyer's home.

Still no response.

It was apparent to the officers by now that Charlie and Caril Ann had somehow wriggled through the net. While they were waiting for the gas to dissipate, they checked the outbuildings. State Trooper Gary Tesch found August Meyer in the washhouse, bringing Charlie's body count to four.

One of the witnesses to that discovery was neighbor Everett Broening, who had heard Bob Jensen's Ford pass by his house the night before. He went home in a daze and tried to do some work in his garage, but he could not erase the mental image of Meyer's bloody corpse. Worse yet, he thought about the missing teenagers and what it meant for Jensen's car to have been in the neighborhood last night, with mad-dog killers on the prowl.

Broening decided that he had to do something, even if it meant searching for the lost kids on his own. His wife objected, but he took his .30-30 Winchester along for company and started driving south, toward the remains of old District 79. Along the way, he checked the roadside, scanning snowy ditches, finding nothing out of place.

Arriving at the old school ruins, Broening took his rifle with him, careful to be quiet as he paced off the perimeter. For all he knew, a pair of desperate fugitives was hiding in The Cave, prepared to open fire if they suspected he was sneaking up on them. To Broening's eye, it seemed that there was something out of place about the ruins. Something.

Finally, he had it. On his last trip to the site, the cellar door had been lying off to one side of the opening; now it was back in place, with rubbish scattered over it in an apparent effort at concealment. Broening knew that couldn't be an accident. The *good* news was that Charlie Starkweather could not have piled the trash that way, if he was down there in the cellar.

Satisfied that he was not about to meet a deadly ambush, Broening stepped up to the cellar door and started clearing trash away. A moment later, he was startled to observe a pool of blood, congealed before the cellar doorway. Dreading whatever awaited him within, he dragged the heavy door aside and let it drop.

The concrete steps below were smeared with blood, as if it had been spilled in buckets, smeared around with mops. Down at the bottom of the steps, a half-nude girl lay facedown on the cellar floor, her jeans and panties snagged around her ankles. More blood on her legs and buttocks, rusty brown by now. The farmer hesitated, swallowed hard to keep from vomiting, and took a few steps down the stairs, to get a closer look.

If this was Carol King, then where . . .

He saw a second pair of legs protruding from beneath the female's prostrate form. A man's legs, from the look of them. The shoes resembled oxfords.

Broening bolted from the cellar, reeling toward his car. The .30-30 in his hand was dead weight now. The only thing that he could think of was alerting the police at August Meyer's farm. They had to see what he had found and track down the monsters who had done it before they killed again.

According to the State Police chronology, the bodies of Carol King and Robert Jensen were found about 3:00 P.M. on Tuesday, thirty minutes after August Meyer was discovered in his outhouse. Within an hour, a hundred officers were fanning out from Bennett, searching empty fields, their number swelled by farmers who had purchased every last round of ammunition at the Bennett hardware store. Locals who did not join the hunt stayed home and checked their guns, alert for any sign of strangers on their property.

The search went on in Lincoln, too, although it seemed impossible that Charlie and Caril Ann would linger there. Some manhunters believed that Caril was dead, after they glimpsed Carol King's remains. Her mutilations seemed to be the work of a demented sex fiend. How could anyone believe a fourteen-year-old girl would stick with Charlie after that? Despite such questions, Elmer Scheele filed charges of first-degree murder against both fugitives, and new descriptions were released, to help the hunt along.

Starkweather: Five feet five inches tall, 150 pounds. Scar over right eye. Green eyes. Dark red hair cut short on top, long on sides and back. Bowlegged and pigeon-toed, swaggers when he walks. Believed wearing blue jeans and black leather motorcycle jacket, black boots or cowboy boots. Sometimes has a speech impediment, trouble pronouncing W's and R's.

Caril Fugate: Five feet one inch tall, 105 pounds. Looks about eighteen. Blue eyes. Dark brown hair usually worn in a ponytail. Sometimes wears glasses, possibly wearing ring with red setting. Dressed in jeans and blouse or sweater, may be wearing a medium blue parka. Might have on white baton boots or gray suede loafers.

By late afternoon, the *Lincoln Journal* had found a snapshot of Charlie and Caril Ann together, seated close together on a love seat, smiling for the camera. There was nothing out of place about Caril's look, from bobby socks to beaming grin, but Charlie had his head cocked to one side, his mouth curled in a tight-lipped smile, brows arched almost demonically above predatory eyes, reflecting bright pinpoints of light from the flashbulb. Staring out at frightened strangers from the front page of the *Journal*, Charlie was enough to make their blood run cold.

It was a little after 4:00 P.M. when Rodney Starkweather found Bob Von Busch and told him Guy had just received a call from Charlie. He had telephoned to say that he and Caril were out of Lincoln, but he planned on coming back

163

that night, to murder Bob. They would be coming from the west, on Highway 6, he said. If Bob knew what was good for him, he would be gone when Charlie got to town.

Nobody ever got around to asking Charlie if he made that call. As Bob told author William Allen, decades later, "There's no way to prove if Guy was telling the truth or not. Looking back, I can see how he might have made it up, but I never even questioned it, at the time."

Instead of being frightened, Bob was furious. With Rodney at his side, he drove out to the viaduct where Highway 6—the road to Hastings—entered Lincoln and became O Street. Their plan, as Bob explained it later, was to meet with Charlie, try to talk with him, then overpower him and tie him up for the police. They waited in the freezing cold for several hours, well past nightfall, but their quarry didn't show.

Reflecting on his action, later, Bob told William Allen, "We figured we didn't have that much to lose, I guess. Anyway, it was two against one. We didn't think he would start shooting right away—he would want to talk first, and when he did, we were going to jump him."

Considering the fact that Charlie had already killed six people that they knew of, including one lifelong friend and three members of Caril Ann's immediate family, it was no doubt fortunate for Bob and Rodney that the call turned out to be a hoax.

Their blood would not be spilled that night, but Charlie wasn't far away, and he had already improved his score.

Bennett, Nebraska, was an armed camp by sundown on Tuesday, drawing morbid curiosity seekers who placed themselves at risk by simply passing through the neighborhood that night, when everyone was jumpy, most of them with weapons close at hand. Patrolmen tried to keep the gawkers moving, out on Highway 43, while homicide investigators gathered at the King and Jensen homes, confirming what they knew already. Bob and Carol were dead, the girl a victim of what television newscasters were calling an "unnatural assault." The FCC's production code left viewers to supply the details from their own imaginations, wondering what she had suffered, casting Charlie as the kind of "mad dog" who would violate a female victim, even after death.

It was a cold night out for salesmen and delivery boys, that Tuesday. Albert Patterson was bound for Lincoln, from his home in Fargo, North Dakota, when his car broke down five miles from Bennett, shortly past eleven-thirty. He was looking for a telephone when he approached the rural home of Harold and Alma Albertson. Neighbor Ralph Porter, along with his wife and daughter, had dropped by to visit and to watch the grim news on TV, and a gallon jug of bourbon was making the rounds, while each man kept one hand near his shotgun. Patterson made it as far as the gate, when a watchdog announced his arrival, and frightened voices started shouting for him to "Get out of here, or you're dead!" A moment later, guns were blazing in the night, and while the stranded traveler was able to identify himself before the tipsy gunmen found their mark, it had been touch and go.

By sunrise, state police and local officers were ready to resume their search. The APB on Charlie and Caril Ann had widened to include Wyoming, Kansas, and North and South Dakota. Roadblocks were established, watching for Bob Jensen's Ford, but it was nowhere to be found.

By noon on Wednesday, lawmen in Nebraska feared that Charlie had eluded them once more. It was nearly a day and a half since he had stolen young Bob Jensen's Ford. If he and Caril were driving all that time, straight through, they could be anywhere.

The hunters didn't know it yet, but they were due to catch a break. Instead of running for his life, Charlie had gone to ground in Lincoln, at the very epicenter of the hunt. The good news was, they hadn't lost him yet. Their quarry was within their grasp.

The bad news: He had slaughtered three more victims in a bid to buy himself some time.

12

"I Knowed It Couldn't Last Long"

Charlie and Caril Ann were already back in Lincoln by the time Bob Jensen and Carol King were officially reported missing, at 3:15 A.M. on Tuesday, January 28. Starkweather killed some time driving around the ritzy Country Club section of town, in the southeastern quadrant, and finally parked near the corner of Twenty-fourth and Van Dorn. They spent the night there, bundled up in their jackets, and slept fitfully until daybreak.

Critics later had a field day with the fact that Lincoln's two most-wanted fugitives could literally camp out on the street for hours in a stolen car without attracting some attention from police. Harold Robinson, in his dissection of the manhunt, pointed out that it was no great feat of cunning to elude police between the hours of 3:00 and 8:00 A.M. In fact, he later wrote, Lincoln P.D. had only three cars on the street during that time, while Sheriff Karnopp had *one* car "on countywide patrol." There is no evidence that Charlie knew the details of police patrol procedure, but the scarcity of uniforms in Lincoln through those predawn hours demonstrates that no one thought the teenage fugitives would hang around.

Sunrise comes late in winter on the plains. It was already after 7:00 A.M. when Charlie and Caril Ann roused themselves and started cruising, looking for a place to hide. Starkweather knew the neighborhood from picking up the rich folks' trash and shoveling sidewalks in the wintertime for pocket money, in the days before he found his calling as an outlaw. Now he was convinced that he could beat the manhunt if he simply holed up through the daylight hours in the last place nosy cops would look. That night, with new wheels under them, they could head west again, and this time, they would make it all the way.

It was a kick for Charlie, driving past those stately mansions, house-hunting with Caril Ann. The best that Lincoln had to offer could be his, upon demand. He had the hardware and the will to use it. He had proved himself to everyone who had him "numbered for the bottom" all those years.

There was an argument between the lovers, later, over who picked out the home they would invade. Charlie told Elmer Scheele that Caril Ann chose the mansion on South Twenty-fourth Street; she denied it. Either way, the choice was made.

The white two-story house belonged to wealthy businessman and lawyer C. Lauer Ward. A native son made good, Ward had graduated from the University of Nebraska before going on to study at Harvard and the University of Chicago. A millionaire at forty-seven, he served as president of both Capital Steel and the Capital Bridge Company, as a director of Provident Savings and Loan Association, Norden Laboratories, and the National Bank of Commerce, while filling a seat on the board of trustees for Bankers Life of Nebraska. Ward was also a member of the Lincoln Country Club, the University Club, and the Lincoln Rotary Club. His influence extended into politics through a personal friendship with Governor Victor Anderson.

In short, he was everything Charlie was not.

Ward's wife, Clara, was almost equally prestigious in the insular community they occupied. A college graduate herself, she served as vice president of the Nebraska Alumni Association—that organization's highest available rank for a woman. With her husband, she was active in community and church affairs. Their fourteen-year-old son was off at a private school in Connecticut, but Clara had help around the house, in the person of housekeeper Lillian Fencl, who had served the family for twenty-six of her fifty-one years. Two dogs completed the family: a Chesapeake Bay retriever named Queenie, and a pampered black poodle called Suzy.

Charlie had never hauled trash for the Wards, but he had shoveled snow along their street within the past few weeks, and he despised them sight unseen, over the fact that they had prospered while his own life went to hell.

The Wards' driveway circled around behind the house to a two-car garage, with a separate entrance at the back that allowed the residents to come and go, unobserved by their neighbors. Charlie pulled into that driveway in Bob Jensen's Ford sometime between 8:00 and 8:30 A.M. He left Caril in the car, took the stolen rifle with him, and walked up to the back door of the house. Starkweather's hunting knife was tucked into his boot.

Lillian Fencl may have seen Charlie drive up and get out of the car. If so, the gun he carried at his side did not prevent her from opening the door to Charlie's knock. Starkweather shoved his way inside and closed the door behind him, ready with the .22 as Queenie started barking in alarm. He ordered Lillian to take the dog downstairs, but she was nearly deaf and apparently misunderstood, removing Queenie to a nearby bathroom, rather than the basement. Either way, it didn't matter to Charlie, as long as the sixty-pound retriever was safely tucked away.

He started asking questions: Was there anybody else at home? Did they keep money in the house? The frightened housekeeper just stared at him, then pointed to one ear and shook her head. There was a pencil and a notepad near the telephone. Starkweather tried again, his near illiteracy slowing down communications to a crawl.

The first note was simple: *Sit down and shut up.*

Lillian settled in a kitchen chair and waited while the redhead scrawled a question: *Is there anyone else in the house?*

Lillian told him that Mrs. Ward was upstairs, and that she would be coming down to breakfast soon. In fact, the housekeeper had been starting to cook when Charlie's knock interrupted her.

Go on and finish it, he wrote, and sat down at the kitchen table, with the rifle in his lap.

Clara Ward was startled to see him, a few moments later, when she came downstairs. "What's going on here?" she asked Charlie. "Who are you?"

"Shut up and sit down!" he demanded.

A copy of the *Lincoln Star* lay on the table with its headline showing: BELMONT FAMILY SLAIN. A smaller subhead added, DAUGHTER, BOYFRIEND SOUGHT FOR QUESTIONING. It is impossible for us to know what went through Clara's mind as she sat down, but simply seeing Charlie with his rifle was enough to strike fear in her heart.

Perhaps Starkweather caught her glancing at the newspaper. In any case, if we believe his later statement to police, he tried to put his hostages at ease. "Don't worry," he told Mrs. Ward, "we're not going to hurt you. We'll just wait here 'til it's dark, then tie you up and leave."

She didn't know who "we" meant yet, with Caril still sitting in the car outside. It hardly mattered, anyway. "All right," she told her captor. "You can trust us. You don't have to point the gun at us or anything."

The mention of his weapon sparked a thought in Charlie's mind. "Do you have any guns around the house?" he asked.

Charlie recalled that Clara thought about it for a moment, finally responding in the negative. Her husband had a BB gun upstairs, she said, for shooting gophers in the yard, but nothing else.

Relaxing, Charlie stepped back to the kitchen door and waved for Caril to come inside. She brought the shotgun with her, and his leather jacket, pockets stuffed with ammunition.

Just in case.

Caril Ann looked weary when she came into the kitchen. Clara Ward gave her a cup of coffee, and Caril took it with her as she scouted out the ground floor of the house. She wound up in the library and lay down on the couch, to catch up on her sleep, while Charlie invited himself to breakfast. He wanted pancakes, then decided waffles sounded better, wolfing down six before he had his fill.

There was a close call in the midst of Charlie's pigging out, when a delivery truck from Lincoln's Skyline Dairy pulled into the driveway, parking right beside Bob Jensen's Ford. Starkweather kept the women covered while the driver left his merchandise and drove away, but it was troubling that the milkman might have recognized Bob's car from broadcasts on the radio. An hour passed without police arriving, though, and then another. Charlie finally decided he was safe.

While they were clearing off the breakfast dishes, Clara Ward told Charlie that she had a date for coffee at a friend's house, later in the morning. Charlie ordered her to call and cancel, saying she was ill. That done, the lady of the house asked Starkweather if she and Lillian might do some housework, just to kill the time. He didn't mind, as long as no one used the telephone or went outside, and Charlie watched them for a while before he went into the library, woke Caril, and ordered her to guard the women while he took a nap.

On waking, Charlie found that Clara and the maid were still engaged in ironing, waxing furniture, the usual. He saw no reason to object when Clara asked if she could go upstairs and change her shoes to a more comfortable pair.

"Don't take all day," he warned her, as she moved in the direction of the stairs.

It was around this time, said Charlie, that he sat down

with Caril Ann to write their letter, addressed "for the law only," that was later found in Charlie's pocket.

"Who wrote the letter?" Fahrnbruch asked him later, at the county jail.

"I did," said Charlie.

"Who was present?"

"Caril."

"Did you figure out the language all by yourself?"

That seemed to confuse Charlie. "What do you mean?"

"Did anybody tell you the things to put into the letter?"

Charlie shrugged. "She was just talking, and I was just writing it down. She was just saying it, and I was writing it down."

"You wrote down what she said?" asked Fahrnbruch.

"Yes."

"Did you sign both of the names?"

"Yes," Charlie answered. "She wouldn't sign it, and got sore, so I signed it for both. It was in my jacket in Wyoming when we got picked up. Look, we didn't think we was going to be taken alive. That's why it was written. We had a few others, too. Notes."

No other notes were found, and Fahrnbruch asked, "Why did you throw them out the window?"

Charlie frowned. "I said I was going to throw that one out. I thought I did, but I didn't. I don't know, we just threw them out the window."

"What did you write it for?" Fahrnbruch pressed.

"I just told you, we didn't think we'd be taken alive."

Caril Ann denied any part in writing the note, but she admitted clipping photos out of the afternoon paper, at Clara Ward's house. Her courtroom testimony, under questioning by Elmer Scheele, did nothing to persuade the jury of her innocence.

"Now, Caril," Scheele asked, "while you were in the house there, did you look at any newspapers?"

"Yes," she said, then seemed to contradict herself. "I didn't look at it. There was a newspaper there. The newspaper came, and he had it and cut out some pictures."

"And did *you* cut out any pictures?"

"Well, he cut part of them out," she said, "and I cut the rest of them out."

"What pictures did you cut out?" Scheele asked.

"The pictures of him and I."

"You cut that one out?"

"I helped cut that one out," Caril amended. "He cut partway, and I cut the rest."

"And is that picture—what kind of picture was that, Caril? Can you describe that?"

"It was Chuck and I sitting on a chair," she said, "and he had his cowboy boots on, and I had my regular shoes on."

"Did you cut out some other pictures, Caril?"

"I don't know whether he cut them out or I cut them out."

"What pictures were those?"

"Of my sister and mother and dad," she replied.

"And those pictures were in that paper, also?"

"I think so."

"In any event, either you or he cut them out, is that right?"

Smelling the trap. "I think he cut them out."

"Were they in there when you cut out the picture of you and Chuck?"

"I don't know," Caril replied. "I didn't get to see the paper. He wouldn't let me see it."

"You cut out the other picture, didn't you?"

"Yes."

"Were those, the pictures of your mother and dad and little sister, in the paper when you cut out the big picture?"

"No, they weren't in the paper," Caril said. "I didn't see them."

"Either you or he cut them out?"

"Yes."

Scheele driving home the point. "Do you know which one?"

"I think he cut them out," Caril said, "or I think I cut them out."

It was much ado about newspaper clippings, but Scheele made his point. If Caril had seen the newspaper on January 28 and clipped out photos of her murdered relatives—or even if she merely saw the cut-out photos afterward, and carried them around with her—it was incredible to think that she believed her family was still alive.

When he (or they) had finished with the note, it suddenly occurred to Starkweather that Mrs. Ward was still upstairs. As he later recalled the event, "she was up there about forty-five minutes." It struck him as peculiar, but he was not worried as he climbed the stairs to look for her, since Mrs. Ward had told him there were no guns in the house. As Charlie later spun the tale for Elmer Scheele, however, someone had been less than candid. When he went upstairs that afternoon, Mrs. Ward allegedly produced a rifle and "took a shot at me."

"Where were you when she took a shot at you?" Scheele asked.

"To the hallway and about five feet south of her," Charlie replied. "And she just stepped out of the boy's room and she took a shot at me with the .22. . . . [S]he was standing either in the room or right in the doorway in that room right above the library."

"Did that shot strike you?"

"No," said Charlie, stating the obvious. "I didn't see a thing about it. . . . [S]he ran on by me. . . . [S]he started going for the top of the steps. . . . I had the knife. . . . I threw the knife at her. . . . It struck her in the back. . . . [S]he was moaning and groaning."

"Did she fall?" Scheele asked.

"Halfway," said Starkweather. "I caught her . . . underneath the arms. . . . [S]he wasn't all the way to the floor. . . . I dragged her into her bedroom. . . . [S]he was still talking to me, she wasn't dead. . . . I laid her on her bed and just left her there."

"What did you do with the knife?"

"I—I pulled it out. I pulled it out. . . . I run on down the stairs and Caril was awake then, and I gave her a gun. . . . I told her to go in and watch the maid."

"What did you do then?" the prosecutor asked.

"I ran back upstairs," Charlie told him. "I was going to put a Band-Aid or something on there to keep her from bleeding. . . . I walked in there and she was trying to get to the phone, so I moved the phone . . . in the outside of the room there."

"Then what did you do?"

"After that," said Starkweather, "I hit the dog. . . . She had a dog there. . . . A black one. . . . I couldn't get near. . . . It was trying to bite my hand off. . . . Well, I picked up the .22 and he stood up and started barking, and I hit him with it. . . . Why, I hit him just like it was a baseball bat . . . with the butt end. . . . [H]e didn't move at all."

"Then what did you do?" Scheele repeated himself, numbed by the recital of violence.

"Well, I put the rope around her, or I took a sheet and cut the sheet and put a piece of sheet around her mouth and hands. . . . [A]fter that, I bound her feet and hands and covered her up."

"What did you cover her with?"

"A blanket," Charlie said.

In Starkweather's recital of events, Clara Ward spent the rest of the day in that bed, and suffered no more harm from Charlie or Caril Ann before they left the house—a version flatly contradicted by forensic evidence of multiple stab wounds. When he had finished tying up his wounded prisoner, Starkweather said, he went downstairs and told Caril what had happened. It was her idea, he claimed, to keep the incident a secret from the housekeeper, for fear that Lillian would "go apeshit."

By that time, Charlie told authorities, he was increasingly concerned about the risk of someone spotting Bob Jensen's Ford. With Caril Ann standing guard inside the house, he backed Clara's Packard out of the garage and parked Jensen's car in its place, nosing the big Packard up behind the Ford, to help conceal the stolen car. Back inside the house, he started ransacking cupboards and closets, rifling through drawers, in search of any other guns or valuables. It was a meager haul, all things considered: gloves and binoculars, a white shirt for Charlie and a "westy-looking" jacket for Caril, and some other women's clothing she would never have a chance to wear.

It was approaching 6:00 P.M. when Lauer Ward came home, fresh from an afternoon meeting with Governor Anderson. They had discussed the recent spate of homicides attributed to Charlie Starkweather, and Anderson recalled that Ward was visibly upset as he excused himself. He made a quick stop at a liquor store and chatted with the owner briefly, then drove home. Ward must have overlooked the hot Ford parked in his garage, but there was no way to miss Charlie, waiting in the kitchen with a rifle pointed at Ward's head.

Starkweather told police that he assured Ward everything was fine, that he and Caril Ann simply meant to tie him up and take his car. In that account, Ward verbally agreed, then made a grab for Charlie's gun. They grappled for it, lurching toward the basement stairs, and Ward went tumbling down. When Charlie flicked the lights on, he could see Ward lying at the bottom of the steps and staring up at him. Ward's .22, which Charlie said had fallen with him and discharged on impact with the basement floor, was lying by Ward's side.

Starkweather claimed that he then ran downstairs, in time to wrest the gun away from Ward. Defiantly, Ward snatched up an electric iron and raised it overhead, prepared to strike. "I just cocked the gun and pointed it at him," Charlie told Elmer Scheele, "and he put his hand back down. . . . I told him that nothing was wrong [!] and nothing was going to happen. . . . [H]e put the iron down on the floor."

Ward wasn't finished making trouble yet, however. As they reached the stairs, Starkweather said, he made a break for it, and Charlie fired a shot into his back. Still moving, Ward dashed through the kitchen to the living room. Starkweather said he had the front door open, when a second bullet brought him down. It was a head shot, Charlie's specialty, delivered from about five feet away. "I asked him if he was all right," said Charlie, "and he didn't answer."

Beyond that point, Starkweather's several statements to authorities were bogged down in hopeless contradictions. First, he tried to tell police that Caril was innocent of any wrongdoing at the Ward residence, but his subsequent statements clearly implicated her in two premeditated homicides—the slayings of Clara Ward and Lillian Fencl.

When Charlie's several stories are condensed, the gist of them is this: He claimed that Lillian ran downstairs after Lauer Ward was killed, and Charlie feared to follow her, because Caril thought the maid might have a gun. Eventually, Fencl came up on her own, unarmed, and Charlie took her to an upstairs bedroom, where he tied her up— unharmed—and left Caril Ann to watch her. Back downstairs, he bagged some canned goods for their flight and smeared shoe polish in his hair, to change the color. Finally, he called Caril down to dab the parts he couldn't see.

When that was done, he told authorities, "We left. . . . I locked the front door and I turned off all the lights, and I gave [Caril] the guns and told her to go on out and put them in the car." They spurned Ward's Chevrolet in favor of the stylish Packard, Charlie leaving the house after he stole ten dollars from Lillian Fencl and "about seven dollars" from Clara Ward's nightstand.

"Now," Scheele asked, "did you at any time use your knife on Mrs. Ward after you threw it at her the first time?"

"No," Charlie said, "she was alive when I left."

"Did you at any time use your knife on the maid?"

"Why?" Charlie asked, apparently surprised. "Ain't the maid alive?"

Scheele ignored the question. "Did you ever touch Mrs. Ward with your knife?"

"Well, was she stabbed?" asked Charlie. "No, I never touched her with the knife."

Charlie would stand by those denials to the bitter end, but

all three victims in that house *were* stabbed. As in the case of Carol King, forensic evidence described the weapon as a double-edged knife with a narrow blade, unlike Starkweather's hunting knife. Forensic pathologist Erwin D. Zeman also ruled out knives found on the premises, and no weapon matching the wounds was ever found. (At one point, Charlie told police he might have left a double-edged knife at the Bartlett house, but it was missing, too. If it existed, and was left behind on January 27, clearly it could not have been employed in killings *after* Charlie fled the house on Belmont Avenue.)

It comes as no surprise that Caril Ann told a very different story of events of January 28. When Charlie came downstairs from tracking Mrs. Ward, Caril said, he told her he had stabbed the older woman in the throat with Velda Bartlett's kitchen knife. Caril grudgingly admitted washing off the knife, then pouring perfume on the rugs and one of the chairs outside Mrs. Ward's bedroom, to disguise the stench of violent death. She never went *inside* the bedroom, Caril insisted, but instead went back downstairs and drank some pop while watching out for Clara's husband. After warning Charlie that Lauer Ward was home, Caril said she ducked into a bathroom, and remained there until Ward was dead. That done, she had emerged to wait with Charlie for a while, and see if any neighbors actively responded to the gunfire. No one came to check it out, she said, and finally they took the housekeeper upstairs.

"What did he do when you went upstairs, Caril?" Dale Fahrnbruch asked.

"He said for her to sit down in the chair," she said, "and I was looking out the window."

"What room were you in at that time?"

"One of the bedrooms."

"Was the light on?" Fahrnbruch asked.

"No."

"Did you have anything in your hands other than the gun?"

"The light," she said. "The flashlight."

"And the maid was sitting in a chair in that bedroom?"

"Yes."

"Then what happened, Caril? You were looking out the window?"

"Well," she said, "he took a sheet and started tearing it, and then he started tying her wrists, and I told him why didn't he let her lay down on the bed, because she would get tired from sitting up all night. I didn't know he was going to kill her then. And then he made her lay down on the bed and started tying her wrists."

"How did he tie her wrists?" asked Fahrnbruch.

"With both hands together," Caril replied.

"So that the little fingers touched each other?"

"Yes, I think so. And then he tied them to the bedpost."

"Were her hands over her head or not?"

"Yes."

"Then what else did he do?"

"He tied her feet," Caril explained. "To the end of the bed. She kept saying to turn on the light, she was scared of the dark."

"Did somebody turn on the light?" Fahrnbruch asked.

"No."

"Did you hold the flashlight for him while he was tying her up?"

"I don't remember," Caril said, sounding flustered. "I was looking out the window, and he started stabbing her, and she started screaming and hollering."

"Do you know what he stabbed her with?"

"My mother's knife," Caril said.

"Did he say anything while he was stabbing her?"

"No, he put a pillow over her face."

"Did he stab her more than once . . . twice?"

"Yes," Caril said. "I heard it. Every time he stabbed her, she moaned."

"About how many times did he stab her?"

"More than five."

"Was she laying facedown on the bed, or faceup?"

"Faceup," Caril said.

"Now," Fahrnbruch prodded, "was she laying that way when he tied her up? Did her hands continue to be tied to the top of the bed?"

"No, she broke them loose," Caril said, betraying that she had done more than simply *listen* to the crime. "While he was stabbing her."

"And what had he tied her to the top of the bed with?"

"A sheet."

"What about her feet? Were they still tied to the bottom of the bed?"

"Yes," Caril replied.

"And then what happened, after he had got done stabbing her?"

"He said he didn't think she was ever going to die," Caril reported. "And then he said to shine the flashlight over there. And he cut the strips holding her legs and covered her over."

"What did he cover her up with?"

"A blanket that laid on the bed," Caril replied. "I seen the blood on the bed, but I didn't see the stabs."

"You held the flashlight while he was cutting the legs from the bed [*sic*]?"

"Yes."

"Did you hold the light while he covered her up?"

"Yes," Caril said. "I held it on the floor."

"Where were you standing when he was doing that?"

"By the bed," she replied.

"Were you looking out the window, Caril?"

"Yes," she insisted. "To see if anyone was coming. . . . He told me to shine the flashlight on his arm. There was bloodstains all over his shirt, over the cuff of his shirt. . . . He told me to find a clean shirt for him."

"What did you do?"

"I went and found a white shirt."

Charlie and Caril later agreed that a kitchen knife was thrown out of the Packard, during their final flight from Lincoln, but no such knife was ever found, despite a search by Sheriff Karnopp's deputies. Pathologist Zeman could not rule out such a weapon being used on the Lincoln victims, but he frankly doubted it. "Kitchen knives are generally flimsy," he reported. "These wounds were made with a rigid blade, and probably one with a double cutting edge." A more likely weapon, Zeman said, was something on the order of a bayonet or a stiletto.

The confusion in stories told by Charlie and Caril Ann inevitably hurt Caril's plea of innocence. At first, authorities believed that Charlie was trying to shield her from prosecution, but he muffed it by admitting that he didn't know the women in Ward's house were dead. Later, he seemed to change his tune, implying that Caril may have killed the maid. "I don't know," he told police. "Either she said the maid was trying to get away, and she didn't know whether to stab her or not. Maybe she did, I don't know." Still later, he reversed a part of Caril Ann's story, telling prosecutors it was *Caril* who said "the maid wouldn't die." Caril Ann's supporters blame those later statements on the vengeful spirit of a murderer condemned to die, intent on taking "his girl" with him to the chair.

And yet . . .

James Reinhardt notes that a jailhouse polygraph test confirmed Charlie's statement that he left Clara Ward alive and tied to her bed, covered with a blanket. When found by police, her body was on the floor, half-covered by two beds drawn together, and her clothing had been partially removed.

Before they left the house, Caril said, the phone rang, and she answered it. An unknown caller asked to speak with "Mrs. Ward," and Caril replied, "They're all asleep." Before the disembodied voice could ask more questions, she hung up the phone.

The 1956 Packard was no hot-rod, but it would do all right for a getaway car, Charlie reckoned. Leaving the Wards' house, the redhead was momentarily at a loss for what to do next. He drove around Lincoln, aimlessly, for fifteen or twenty minutes, before some compulsion drew him back to Caril Ann's house on Belmont Avenue. There,

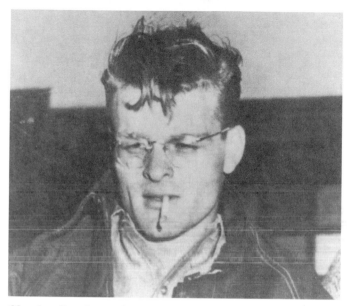

Charles Starkweather, teenage rebel, self-made in the
mold of movie idol James Dean
Courtesy of The Nebraska State Historical Society

Caril Fugate
with two-year-
old half-sister
Betty Bartlett
*Courtesy of The
Nebraska State
Historical
Society*

Charlie and Caril in happy days, before the murder spree
Bettmann Newsphotos

The Bartlett home, an unlikely setting for mass murder in January 1958
Courtesy of The Nebraska State Historical Society

Trapdoor leading to "the cave" where Robert Jensen and Carol King were murdered
Courtesy of The Nebraska State Historical Society

Starkweather's parents followed the manhunt
through sensational press reports.
Courtesy of The Nebraska State Historical Society

Caril Fugate in custody, following the Wyoming arrest
Courtesy of The Nebraska State Historical Society

Starkweather caged, defiant to the bitter end
Bettmann Newsphotos

Caril appears in court for one of her pretrial hearings.
Courtesy of The Nebraska State Historical Society

Popular in death as he never was in life, Charlie draws tourists to his cemetery plot.

Courtesy of The Nebraska State Historical Society

they saw the porch light burning, with a car parked in the driveway.

Charlie drove on past and out to Highway 34, westbound, toward Washington and Charlie's vision of the perfect sanctuary. The police had missed him so far; how would they pursue him to another state? They were in Seward County, Caril would later say, when she climbed into the back seat of the stolen car and changed her shirt. Somewhere along that same stretch, she recalled, she tossed her old shirt and her mother's kitchen knife out of the car.

It was approaching 10:00 P.M. when they stopped for gas, on the outskirts of Grand Island. Station proprietor Walter Cummings was off on an errand, and his wife apologized to Charlie for not knowing how to operate the gas pumps. When she glanced outside, five minutes later, the Packard was still sitting there, and Mrs. Cummings went back out to see if anything was wrong. No, Charlie told her, but "he might be back later."

Leaving Grand Island, he chose Highway 2, the main drag through central Nebraska. With any luck, it would take them as far as Alliance, in Box Butte County, and they could pick a new route from there, for the run to Wyoming. It felt good to be in motion, leaving the cops and the carnage behind.

Before the sun came up the next morning, Charlie told himself, they would be free and clear.

13

Shoot to Kill

Fred Ward was getting worried as the time crept up on half past eight on Wednesday morning, January 29. His cousin Lauer was always punctual for work. If something happened to detain him, he would call the office and explain, tell everyone approximately when they should expect him. Lauer was perfectly dependable.

Except today.

Another time, Fred might have shrugged it off, but everyone in Lincoln was on edge that morning, with the recent spate of murders. There were six bodies found in just two days. It was a massacre unrivaled in Ward's lifetime, and the press was doting on the gruesome details.

BENNETT FAMILY SLAIN

TOT AND PARENTS FOUND DEAD IN APPARENT MURDER

3 MORE BODIES FOUND

BENNETT VICTIMS BRING TOLL TO 6

Any time now, Ward imagined that the story would go national. The *Omaha World Herald,* lying on his desk, had done its best to set the proper mood.

FEAR ROUSES COUNTRYSIDE WITH MULTIPLE KILLER AT LARGE

Bennett, Neb.—Terror stalked the countryside Tuesday night. Farm houses became armed camps and grim-lipped men and women here, 16 miles southeast of Lincoln, burned lights far past the usual bedtime.

There was only one conversation topic, a gun-crazy teenage murder suspect and his 14-year-old girlfriend. . . .

Horror mounted in Lincoln and throughout eastern Nebraska as dusk fell and the word got around that three more killings had been added to the triple murder discovered in Lincoln Monday. . . .

Volunteer posses were formed.

As the night wore on the lights in the small town and farm houses continued to glow.

No women and children walked the streets.

Terror stalked the countryside.

It was all great melodrama from a distance, in the papers or on television, but the story lost its ghoulish fascination if you happened to be living in the middle of the killing zone. It seemed ridiculous to think that anything would happen to Ward's cousin, living in the wealthy neighborhood he occupied, and yet . . .

How simple it would be to put his mind at ease.

Fred pushed the newspaper aside and reached out for the telephone.

The night had been a long and sleepless one for prosecutor Elmer Scheele. He had been standing by at St. Elizabeth's Hospital when Dr. Zeman did the autopsies on Robert Jensen and Carol King. By morning, Starkweather and Fugate had been "positively" sighted in Missouri, Iowa, and Kansas, not to mention the increasing number of near misses in Nebraska. Lincoln's mayor had offered a five-hundred-dollar reward for the fugitives, while John Carter, head of the local garbageman's union, contributed another hundred dollars to safeguard his profession's good name. Now FBI agents were joining the search, assuming that their quarry must have fled the state. Once Starkweather and Fugate crossed the border in a stolen car, they would be federal fugitives.

Just like John Dillinger.

Except that Dillinger was only wanted for a single murder when the G-men gunned him down.

Scheele didn't know what he should do about the girl. The papers had it right, where Caril Ann was concerned: Nobody knew if she was still alive or not—and if she was, whether she stayed with Charlie out of fear, or for the hell of it. A trigger-happy punk was one thing, but a homicidal teenage girl defied all logic. Still, the prosecutor had to cover all his bets. If Caril was found alive, unharmed, there was a decent chance they would be looking at two murder trials instead of one.

By Wednesday, Elmer Scheele knew they would be extremely fortunate if no one else was killed. Starkweather was a mad-dog killer, plain and simple, but he wasn't Scheele's only concern at the moment. Local hardware stores and sporting goods emporiums were selling out of guns and ammunition. There had been at least one shooting incident near Bennett overnight, and Scheele would not have been surprised if there was worse in store, come sundown. Already that morning, a group of a hundred-odd vigilantes had turned up outside Scheele's office, in the county courthouse, demanding to know why Starkweather had not been caught.

If they or others like them ran into the fugitives, thought Scheele, the net result could be a bloodbath.

He would have to keep his fingers crossed and hope that the police found Charlie first. They were already fanning out to search the city, block by block, prepared to shoot on sight if there was any hint of danger to themselves or unarmed citizens, but Scheele had no good reason to believe Starkweather would be found inside the city limits. Maybe the young punk was crazy, but he couldn't be *that* stupid.

Charlie and Caril Ann were miles away by now.

They had to be.

It was approaching noon when Fred Ward made the short drive to his cousin's house on South Twenty-fourth Street. No one answered his knock, so Fred used his key and walked into the middle of a waking nightmare.

Lauer Ward lay just inside the entrance to the living room, as if he had been cut down when he entered, without having time to shed his coat. Starkweather claimed his victim had been fleeing toward the street, but the forensic evidence disputed him. Ward had been shot twice, in the throat and temple, but there was no bullet in his back to coincide with Charlie's story of a struggle climaxed by a shooting on the basement stairs. Ward had been *stabbed* between the shoulder blades, however, after he was down, already dead or dying on the floor.

Upstairs, in one of the bedrooms, Clara Ward lay on the floor between two beds that had been drawn together, in a seeming effort to conceal her body. Dressed in a nightgown, with nothing underneath, she had one knife wound in her back, but Clara had been facing her killer when the blade fell repeatedly, ripping into her throat and chest. Nearby, her poodle, Suzy, lay cowering under one of the beds, still clinging to life despite a broken neck.

Lillian Fencl was the last victim found, tied to the bed in another room, stabbed repeatedly in the chest and stomach, with superfluous gashes marking her legs, arms, and hands. Her eyes and mouth were open, as if she had spent her final moments crying out to heaven for a mercy that had been denied.

The sole unscathed survivor of the massacre was Queenie, the retriever, barking from her prison in the downstairs bathroom, as Fred staggered to the nearest telephone and called police.

Investigators did not have to rack their brains to come up with two likely suspects in the latest triple murder. They had victims shot with .22s and stabbed repeatedly, with special violence demonstrated toward the women. They had newspapers riddled with holes, where photographs of Charlie and Caril Ann had been cut out. And, by 12:25 P.M., they had Bob Jensen's missing car, recovered from the Wards' garage.

Case closed—if only they could find their suspects.

Word went out that Charlie and Caril Ann had fled the latest crime scene in a black 1956 Packard. It was another stroke of luck, as far as lawmen were concerned.

A big, expensive car like that would not be hard to find.

News of the latest homicides hit Lincoln like a giant meteor, impacting at a thousand miles per hour from the silent void of space. The shock waves spread at once, by word of mouth and through the press, but there was something *alien* about the whole experience, defying common values of the time. Modern Nebraskans had no frame of reference to help them cope with savage predators in human form. Perhaps their great-grandparents would have understood that kind of blood lust, if the killers had been Indians, but in the last months of the 1950s, there was nothing to prevent hysteria from spreading like a prairie fire.

Before the massacre on South Twenty-fourth Street, residents of Lincoln and the environs had consoled themselves with the belief, approaching certainty, that Charlie and Caril Ann had escaped, made tracks, gone *somewhere else* to stage the final act of their peculiar, suicidal passion play. Now they were back, if they had ever left, and no one in the capital was safe.

It had been one thing, for most Lincolnites, while Charlie was "killing his own." His first known victims had been "white trash," from the wrong side of the tracks, and number four—no one was making any links to Colvert yet—had been an aging recluse Charlie knew for years. Bob Jensen and Carol King were good kids, granted, but they had been *teenagers,* and therefore prone to trouble, even if it crept up on them from behind.

But now, the rules went out the window. Charlie and Caril Ann were killing "quality," invading mansions of the rich and famous, preying on the town's elite—all, as it seemed, with absolute impunity. They struck and disappeared by night, left only bodies in their wake, no witnesses. Police had known what they were driving since the Bartlett massacre, had issued bulletins complete with photographs, but nothing did the trick.

It felt like chasing rabid mongrels through a maze, with all the lights off, so you couldn't really tell if you were chasing *them,* or they were after *you.*

Too late, lawmen began erecting roadblocks on the highways leading in and out of Lincoln. They had no idea where Starkweather had gone, or if Caril Ann was even still alive, but anyone could spot a Packard tooling down the highway. Spotter planes were sent aloft, to give the search a new dimension. If police were ever going to catch a break in the case, it had to come soon.

Governor Anderson, as one of the last persons to see Lauer Ward alive, was doubly traumatized by the death of his friends. The ink was barely dry on headlines reading 3 MORE BODIES FOUND, when Anderson mobilized two hundred members of the Nebraska National Guard. They hit the streets in combat gear, cruising in Jeeps equipped with .30-caliber machine guns, loaded M-1 rifles in their hands. The soldiers turned up no new evidence and played no part in Charlie's capture, when it came, but it was reassuring just to see them on the street, prepared for battle.

Even so, Lancaster County residents still put more faith in personal protection than they did in uniforms. Don

Stokes, a local hardware dealer, sold forty guns in the space of two hours on Wednesday, requiring four trips to the warehouse for supplies. Some of the citizens who tried to join a sheriff's posse, forming at the courthouse, had been sipping courage from a bottle and were turned away, along with others who appeared hysterical.

Indeed, hysteria was the prevailing mood in Lincoln on that Wednesday afternoon. The city's telephone exchange was paralyzed by calls—the greatest jam since V-J Day in 1945—from would-be witnesses who swore that they had seen the youthful killers cruising in Ward's Packard, strolling down the street, or browsing at some local store. Some spotted Charlie on their very doorsteps, but in every case, the fugitives turned out to be deliverymen. Schools closed in Lincoln, armed parents driving their children home to hide behind locked doors. A college student who resembled Charlie Starkweather went into hiding for the duration, frightened of showing his face on the streets.

One caller, who neglected to identify himself, tipped lawmen that the fugitives were on their way to rob Lincoln's National Bank of Commerce. National Guardsmen rushed over to surround the bank, but Charlie stood them up. It took a while for the tense soldiers to decide they had been victims of a hoax.

Elsewhere, as members of the Guard and sheriff's posse started searching house to house, they found themselves welcomed with open arms. Housewives served coffee and hot chocolate, cookies—nothing was too good for the men who had turned out in frigid weather to help exorcise the demon in their midst.

As dusk came on, Lincoln assumed the aspect of a postapocalyptic ghost town. There was little traffic on the streets, except for squad cars, Jeeps, a few commercial vehicles whose business could not wait. The city's restaurants and theaters went begging, while their patrons stayed at home and watched TV . . . or listened for an unaccustomed noise from outside.

Rev. Peter Raible, of the Lincoln Unitarian Church, would

later use the terror as a sermon topic, seeking to explain the feelings Charlie and Caril Ann evoked in Lincolnites. "At the height of the Starkweather manhunt," he said, "all of us believed that a ruthless killer roamed our city. We had no idea where he was; we knew that our personal chances of meeting him were slight; but we also knew that he struck suddenly, apparently at random and without warning. Many housewives were home alone; families were divided among home, school and work. This isolation led to a growing panic. We were afraid, and we were alone."

The city's frightened residents could not have known that Death had passed them by, this time. Charlie was gone, already miles away and running for his life.

To the end of the line.

14

Trapdoor

Seward, Nebraska, lies twenty-five miles west of Lincoln, on U.S. Highway 34. The state's most wanted fugitives were almost there, on Tuesday night, when Caril Ann climbed into the back seat of the Packard to change clothes. The plaid shirt she was wearing had been featured in a photo on the front page of the *Lincoln Star,* and she was worried that she might be recognized. Two shirts went out the window after she had changed—hers, and an old blue one of Charlie's. Homicide detectives later speculated that it may have been near Seward where she ditched one of her mother's kitchen knives, but it was never found.

Charlie was near exhaustion, fighting symptoms of a nasty winter cold, but he was wired by the excitement of the murders, too. Somewhere beyond Aurora, rolling toward Grand Island, he asked Caril for sex. If we believe his later statement to authorities, he was refused in no uncertain terms.

"You've had yours for the day," Caril said.

Dale Fahrnbruch later tried to clarify the point. "Had you had it that day before with Caril?" he asked.

"No," Charlie replied, "I didn't have it that day with her."

"What did she mean," Fahrnbruch pressed, "that you already had it that day?"

"Well, she probably thought I screwed old lady Ward," Charlie said.

"Well, did you?"

Charlie sneered at the idea. "Hell, no."

In fact, autopsy findings would confirm that neither female victim in the latest massacre was raped. Caril did not have the benefits of science at her fingertips, however. She was working on pure instinct, and her mood was unforgiving. Charlie Starkweather was out of luck.

A little after 1:00 A.M., the couple reached Grand Island, stopping at a combination all-night gas station and drive-in restaurant. They filled the Packard's tank and had the night attendant take a look under the hood. No problem with the oil or water. Charlie bought four cheeseburgers to go, with fries and coffee. Now that his hair was black and plastered down with shoe polish, nobody looked at Charlie twice.

It was the same thing when they stopped at Broken Bow, on State Road 2, at 2:00 A.M. Ed Bolen had the night shift at the Bow Oil service station, and was killing time when Charlie pulled in off the highway. Bolen topped the Packard off, and Charlie followed him back to the office, asking about highway maps. He was particularly interested in Washington and Utah. Bolen couldn't help him, but he did give Charlie road maps of Nebraska and Wyoming.

This was a strange one, Bolen thought, with his bowlegs and funny-looking hair, as if someone had tried to dye it, but they couldn't get it right. There was a lost-child quality about him, too, which made the night attendant stop him halfway out the door.

"Where are you heading?" Bolen asked the teenage stranger. "Maybe I can help you with directions."

Charlie thought about it for a moment, pocketing the maps. At last, he shook his head. "I guess it really don't matter," he said.

"Suit yourself."

Bolen leaned on the counter and watched the sleek luxury car pull away.

Charlie kept driving, north and west on Highway 2, but he was running out of steam. Fatigue and the affliction labeled "turnpike trance" in public safety bulletins were lulling him to sleep. Near 4:00 A.M., he almost lost it, jolted back from dreamland as the Packard veered off-road and nearly capsized in a ditch. He saved it, barely, but the near miss was enough to tell Charlie that he had pushed himself too far.

Caril Ann was dozing when the car swerved off the pavement, and she woke up frightened, furious at Starkweather for nearly killing them. They squabbled, Charlie telling her he needed sleep, Caril Ann incredulous when he suggested stopping where they were, beside the open road. She wanted to keep going; Charlie said he couldn't drive another hundred yards without some rest.

When they had bickered for a while, Starkweather came up with a compromise. If Caril Ann would have sex with him, he thought that he could stay awake another hour, maybe more.

"You want to do it right here on the highway?" she demanded.

"Sure, why not? There's nobody around."

Caril knew an ultimatum when she heard one. It was either put out on the spot, or run the risk of having a patrolman happen by while Charlie caught his forty winks. Reluctantly, she gave him what he wanted, but it didn't help. A few miles farther down the road, he started yawning, finally pulled off into a rest stop—picnic tables, toilets, and a drinking fountain screened by trees against the prairie wind. In moments, they were both asleep.

They did not see the trooper who pulled in to use the men's room, sometime after 4:00 A.M. He scrutinized the car and saw a boy asleep behind the wheel, but there were no outstanding wants or warrants on a Packard, nothing on a black-haired youth. The trooper shrugged it off and got back in his car, eastbound, toward Broken Bow.

Truck driver Maynard Behrends was headed in the opposite direction—toward Alliance, out in Box Butte County—when he came up on the rest stop at 4:45. He saw the Packard, thinking to himself that it was not the kind of vehicle you normally saw parked along the roadside, miles from anywhere.

Behrends slowed down, to see if there was anybody in the car, but Charlie and Caril Ann were slumped down in their seats. The vehicle looked empty, making Behrends wonder if it may have broken down and forced the driver to proceed on foot, in search of help. He jotted down the number from its license tag—Nebraska 2-17415—and kept an eye out for the stranded owner, all the way to Seneca, but there was no one to be seen along the road.

It was approaching 6:00 A.M. when Charlie woke up, stiff and cold. He switched the Packard's engine on and got the heater running, left Caril mumbling in her sleep as he pulled out onto the empty road.

Weeks later, he would tell James Reinhardt that his feelings for Caril Ann had already begun to change. Charlie still *wanted* her, but not so much for sex—much less for love. Above all else, he needed Caril Ann as a witness to his final days. By dawn on Wednesday, January 29, Starkweather was oppressed by a sensation that "the end of the trail was not far off." He lived in dread of being gunned down by the law, alone, without a girl to watch him die and scream his name as he lay twitching in a pool of blood.

He drove through tiny Ellsworth, still a hundred miles from the Wyoming border, then decided that the Packard needed gas and doubled back. Roy Graham was on duty at the filling station Charlie chose, and while the black-haired youth before him bore no great resemblance to the state's most wanted fugitive, he acted "jumpy." Once the Packard left his station, Graham telephoned the state patrol, but there was little he could tell them. A report was broadcast, but it brought police no closer to their quarry.

Maynard Behrends was returning from Alliance to his

base, at Broken Bow, when he was startled to behold the Packard from the rest stop, headed west. This time, he saw the occupants, surprised that two young people would be driving such a flashy car. It felt like something worth reporting, but he waited on the call until he made it back to Broken Bow.

Too late.

The couple drove on through Alliance, north on Highway 2, and stopped before they reached Berea for another thirty-minute nap. In Crawford, forty miles from the Wyoming line, they bought more gas. Charlie had covered up his dye job with a straw hat that belonged to August Meyer, and several witnesses remembered him because the hat looked out of place in winter. Still, it was no crime to wear a goofy hat, and no one thought to call the state patrol.

It would be after noon before they knew that Charlie Starkweather had made his getaway from Lincoln in a Packard, and by that time he was gone.

At noon, while Fred Ward was en route to check his cousin's house, the killers stopped again, at an isolated filling station and café near the Wyoming border, west of Harrison. They topped the Packard off again, bought candy bars and nine bottles of Pepsi-Cola, then continued west on U.S. Highway 20. Fifteen minutes later, they were in Wyoming.

It was still not good enough, but they were getting there.

Wyoming calls itself the Equality State, and all things being equal, Charlie knew he still had trouble coming if the law caught up to him. But he was trying to relax, and decided to dawdle along the highway at one third the speed limit, acting like a tourist who has nowhere to go and all day to get there. After ninety minutes in Wyoming, Charlie and Caril Ann had covered barely half the sixty-six-mile distance from the state line to the town of Douglas, seat of Converse County.

It was half past one when Charlie heard the news that Lincoln lawmen had discovered Lauer Ward, his wife, and maid. Bob Jensen's Ford had been retrieved from Ward's garage; the word was out for every cop in the Midwest to keep an eye peeled for the missing Packard. The announcer spoke of panic in the streets of Lincoln, soldiers mobilized, and searches house to house.

It was a kick to think of all the squares in Lincoln "going ape" that way, a sign that Starkweather had really shown them something, gotten to them in a major way. It was a kind of righteous payback for the SOBs who had been laughing at him since that first day, back in kindergarten. He was teaching them a lesson they would not forget.

But he was frightened, too. Escaping from Nebraska gave him hope, but it was marginal at best. No matter how he wished it, Charlie knew the odds against evading capture must be astronomical.

"Everything was closing in on us fast," he told Reinhardt, "like a trap door that starts falling when the animal moves toward it. There was only one way of escape, and that was toward the trap-door. The faster we moved, the faster it seemed to fall."

In Douglas, Charlie was convinced he had been recognized, despite the hat and dye job. In his mind, it seemed that everyone was staring at the Packard with Nebraska plates, two kids inside who should have had a beat-up junker, rather than a rich man's car. He made his way through town and picked up U.S. Highway 87, westbound.

They would have to ditch the car, he realized. And they would have to do it soon.

Merle Collison was thirty-seven, a father of five from Great Falls, Montana, who earned his living as a traveling shoe salesman. He had been driving since the crack of dawn on January 29, and serious fatigue was setting in by early afternoon. Afraid of nodding off behind the wheel, he pulled his brand-new Buick over to the side of Highway 87, east of Casper in Natrona County, drew his overcoat around him, and lay down across the broad front seat to catch a nap. He would be fine, once he had rested, and his customers could wait for a while. It wasn't like the shoe stores on his route were going anywhere.

Unknown to Collison, grim Death was rolling up behind him, looking for a ride.

Ten miles from Douglas, headed west, Starkweather thought his luck had changed. A car was parked beside the highway, seemingly abandoned. Charlie parked behind it, checked both ways for any traffic as he went to check it out. Unfortunately, though, the doors were locked, and peering through the window, one hand cupped against the glass, he saw no keys in the ignition switch.

Strike one.

Charlie drove on another mile and change before he saw the Buick on the south side of the highway, near the turnoff for Ayers Natural Bridge Park. He stopped and walked across the two-lane blacktop, looked inside, and saw a man asleep on the front seat. He tried the door and found it locked.

No problem.

Charlie tapped the driver's window with his knuckles, kept it up until the stranger woke, and looked at him with bleary eyes. "Unlock your door," he said.

"What for?" Merle Collison inquired.

"We're trading cars," said Charlie.

Was he serious? The salesman shook his head. "Forget it."

Charlie didn't argue, simply walked back to the Packard for a moment, then returned. When he came back, he had a rifle in his hands.

The details of what happened next depend on who was telling it, and when. This much we know from autopsy reports: Merle Collison was shot nine times—once in the nose, once in the cheek, once in the neck, twice in the chest, once in the left arm, once in the right wrist, and twice in the left leg. However, only two shots pierced the Buick's window, indicating that the driver's door was open when the final seven rounds were fired.

The salesman's murder clearly troubled Starkweather. Nine bullets pumped into a prostrate man eliminated even the most flimsy claim of self-defense and painted Charlie as a craven coward. It was even worse than stabbing Clara Ward, who, after all, had "brought it on herself" by trying to escape.

In fact, Charlie would later tell authorities, it was Caril Ann who killed Merle Collison. "I shot him," he explained in a letter to Elmer Scheele, "but Caril finished him off." According to Charlie, his rifle had jammed after the second shot, and he called out for Caril to bring another gun. Before she reached the Buick, Collison had opened up his door, agreeing to let Charlie have the car, but then he made a grab for Charlie, trying to fight back.

"Caril was standing beside the car," Charlie wrote. "[H]e had a lot of fight left in him. . . . Caril began shooting at him. . . . [W]hile she was shooting he said something about a wife and kids. . . . Caril said that was too bad and was calling him a lot of names."

It's possible, of course, but Caril denied it to the bitter end, and we have only Charlie's word that she participated in the final slaying of their bloody spree.

Whoever finished off Collison, his body sprawled across the Buick's seat and sagging toward the floor presented Charlie with another obstacle. Caril Ann would later tell Dale Fahrnbruch that she climbed into the Buick's back seat to avoid the blood, but her display of squeamishness turned out to be the least of Charlie's problems. Sitting in the driver's seat, he got the motor started, but for some reason could not release the parking brake. No matter how he strained and cursed, the lever would not budge.

At one point in the struggle, Caril said Charlie leaned across the seat toward Collison and asked him, "Man? Man? Are you dead?"

There was no answer from the corpse, no offer of assistance with the stubborn brake. Starkweather launched into another fit of cursing, while Caril sat behind him, staring out the window at the frozen fields beyond.

Joe Sprinkle was a twenty-nine-year-old geologist from Casper, bound for Douglas on that Wednesday afternoon.

Some ten miles from his destination, Sprinkle crested a rise and saw two cars ahead, one parked on either side of the road. The vehicle on his side of the highway was a Buick with Wyoming tags; the other, facing westward, was a stylish Packard with Nebraska plates. He could see no one in the Packard, but a young girl occupied the back seat of the Buick, staring at him as he passed.

It was a strange scene, but he might have let it go, except for Charlie. Glancing in his rearview mirror, Sprinkle saw a young man climb out of the Packard on the driver's side and make his way across the blacktop toward the Buick. Sprinkle thought the two cars might have been involved in a collision, and he slowed, then made a U-turn, doubling back to see if he could help.

Pulling up behind the Buick, Sprinkle was in time to see the young man get in on the driver's side. Joe parked and walked up to the Buick, still not fearing any danger to himself. As he drew closer, he could see the young man grappling with the Buick's hand brake.

"Can I help you?" Sprinkle asked.

When Charlie straightened up and turned to face the good Samaritan, he had a rifle in his hands. "Help me release the brake," he ordered, "or I'll kill you."

Almost before the threat had time to register, Joe Sprinkle saw the corpse sprawled on the Buick's seat and knew he was a witness to cold-blooded murder. There was no time to connect the grisly scene to news reports of Charlie Starkweather. It was enough to know the young man with the rifle was a killer who would almost certainly not hesitate to silence a potential prosecution witness.

"All I saw was the gun barrel," Sprinkle later told reporters, "and every time I looked it got bigger. I thought I'd be killed anyway, so I tried to get the gun."

Stalling for time, he leaned past Charlie, reaching for the Buick's brake lever, then grabbed the rifle's barrel with both hands. A fierce tug of war began, Starkweather punching Joe with one hand, while his other gripped the .22. Despite his years of schoolyard brawling, though, Charlie was outmatched by his adversary's six-foot stature and 180 pounds. No matter how he cursed, kicked, punched, and grappled, Sprinkle held on to the weapon for dear life, dragging his teenage would-be killer from the Buick, out into the middle of the road.

Natrona County sheriff's deputy Bill Romer had company that afternoon, en route from Casper to a routine job in Douglas, fifty miles away. A friend named Sidney Baldry had accompanied him, to kill some time, and they discussed the Starkweather manhunt as they were rolling east on Highway 87. Both agreed that Charlie and Caril Ann were doubtless far away by now, if they had any smarts at all.

The best part of their journey was behind them, when they spied a milk truck up ahead, stopped in the middle of the eastbound lane. Romer was swinging out to pass the truck, when he discovered that a car had blocked the westbound lane, as well. A couple stood beside it, watching two men wrestle in the middle of the highway.

Romer took a closer look, and saw the men were fighting for a rifle. Stepping out of his patrol car, he was moving toward the two combatants when a young girl leaped out of a Buick, parked along the shoulder of the road, and ran to intercept him.

"Take me to the police!" she cried, as if his uniform meant nothing to her.

"Well," Romer said, "I'm a deputy sheriff."

At that, the girl burst into tears and said, "He's killed a man!"

Romer glanced back at the combatants. "Where?" he asked.

She pointed toward the Buick. "There."

"Who is he?"

Awkward seconds passed while Caril Ann struggled to pronounce the name. "Charles Starkweather!"

At that point, Charlie seemed to glance up from his struggle with the larger man, to recognize the sheriff's car and uniform. Abruptly, he released the .22, Joe Sprinkle lurching backward in the absence of resistance, tumbling down into a roadside gravel pit. Starkweather sprinted to the Packard, whipped it through a squealing turn, and took off back toward Douglas, rubber smoking in his wake.

Bill Romer grabbed Caril Ann and dragged her to his cruiser, shoved her in the driver's side so that she had no exit, wedged between himself and Baldry. Reaching for his two-way radio, he raised Bill Morton, dispatcher for the Wyoming Highway Patrol in Casper, calling for a roadblock on Highway 87, west of Douglas. Morton said that he would place a call to Douglas, try to get the men and guns in place as soon as possible.

That done, Romer took off in hot pursuit of Charlie's stolen Packard, trailing it eastbound for several miles. He did not plan to brace the fugitive himself, but wanted to be sure Starkweather did not double back and thus defeat the roadblock, which—he hoped—would soon be forming up ahead of him. When Romer satisfied himself that Charlie did not plan to turn around and make a run for Casper, he broke off pursuit and drove back to the roadside murder scene.

It seemed a long ride back, but Caril Ann filled the time by talking. "I seen him kill ten people," she told Romer. "He killed my mother, stepfather, stepsister, a boy and a girl, a farmhand, and three other people. I was there and seen it all."

"What happened?" Romer asked.

"My mom and Charlie were having an argument and she slapped him," Caril replied, thus sealing her fate at her subsequent trial. "Charlie hit her back and my stepfather saw him. Charlie killed him, my mom, and stepsister. The baby was crying, so Charlie took the barrel of his gun and pushed it in her throat."

Romer and Baldry would remember Caril Ann's words that day, and the admission would come back to haunt her at her murder trial.

Police Chief Robert Ainslie took the call in Douglas. Charlie Starkweather was headed his way in a killing hurry, driving hell for leather in a big ol' Packard, ten dead bodies on his rap sheet. Ten they *knew* about.

At least he hadn't killed a lawman yet, but there was nothing stopping Charlie if he felt like it.

Ainslie sped over to the Converse County sheriff's office, warning them that he was on his way. Sheriff Earl Heflin was emerging from the courthouse as the chief arrived, toting a .30–30 lever-action carbine that emphasized his resemblance to a Wild West cowboy. With the boots and the ten-gallon hat, a .38 revolver riding on his hip, Sheriff Heflin could have been auditioning for *Gunsmoke*. Tall and rugged-looking, Heflin was the polar opposite of Ainslie—a short, bespectacled man who looked more like a certified accountant than the town's chief law enforcement officer. Appearances can be deceiving, though, and Sheriff Heflin liked to joke with friends that when he practiced with his guns, he "couldn't hit the broad side of a barn."

That afternoon, the odd couple of law enforcement was the only thing that stood between Charles Starkweather and freedom. If he blew through Douglas, he could take off to the north or south, slip into Colorado or Montana, maybe double back and use the side roads heading eastward, toward Montana.

If they lost him here, the whole damned circus would begin again.

As alert as the two lawmen were, they almost missed their prey. Five miles due west of Douglas, they met Charlie coming back toward town, but did not recognize his vehicle. Much later, when the smoke cleared, one report would claim that Deputy Romer had broadcast an incorrect description of the car. In any case, Ainslie and Heflin glimpsed Nebraska plates before the Packard passed them, burning up the highway at 100 mph. They also got a quick look at the driver: black hair, leather jacket, maybe glasses. It was nothing much like what they had been told of Charlie Starkweather, but there was no one else around.

Chief Ainslie goosed his cruiser through a tight U-turn and shot off in pursuit. Starkweather had a decent lead until they entered downtown Douglas, and the spotty traffic slowed him down a bit. The squad car rolled up close behind him, siren wailing, red lights flashing. Sheriff Heflin drew his .38 and started shooting at the Packard's tires, the sounds of gunfire scattering pedestrians on Main Street. Dodging bullets, Charlie zigzagged through the slower traffic, the police car close behind him. We can only guess whether he was frightened or exhilarated by the chase, and he would take that secret to his grave.

At Center Street, a red light had the flow of traffic stalled. Chief Ainslie saw his chance and took it, ramming Charlie from behind. Their bumpers locked, and for a moment Ainslie thought he had the fugitive, but then Starkweather stood on the accelerator, and the Packard's bumper fell away.

A few more minutes, and the open highway lay before them, eastbound. Charlie unleashed everything the Packard had, while Ainslie and the sheriff clung tenaciously behind him, the squad car's speedometer needle trembling at 120 mph. Sheriff Heflin tried his carbine, leaning out the window, cold wind whipping in his face. His third or fourth shot drilled the Packard's broad rear window, transforming the safety glass into a milky glaze.

Charlie kept going for a few more seconds, pouring on the speed, but when he popped up from a low dip in the highway, Ainslie and the sheriff saw his brake lights flash. A moment later, they were shocked to see that he was stopped dead in the middle of the two-lane highway.

Their man was armed, a ten-time killer who had managed to evade the largest manhunt in Nebraska history. Ainslie and Heflin took no chances, parking well back from the Packard, crouched behind their open doors and waiting until Charlie suddenly appeared. They yelled at him to raise his hands, but he ignored them. Ainslie aimed a bullet at the ground near Charlie's feet, and ordered him to lie down on the pavement. Rather than obeying the instruction, Charlie reached around behind his back, and Ainslie fired *another* warning shot. A moment later, Heflin and the chief could see that Starkweather was simply tucking in his shirt. It took a third shot from the cruiser to convince him they were serious about his lying down.

Too cool.

As they approached him cautiously and snapped a pair of handcuffs on his wrists, the lawmen saw that Starkweather was bleeding freely from one ear, apparently where flying glass had nicked him. Charlie knew it, too, and started whining as they dragged him to his feet.

"I'm shot!" he said. "You shot me!"

"Come on, it's just a scratch," said Sheriff Heflin, who would later tell the press: "He thought he was bleeding to death. That's the kind of yellow son of a bitch he is."

At the cruiser, Charlie complained that his cuffs were too tight. If Heflin did not loosen them, he groused, he would refuse to talk about his crimes. When he was comfy in the back seat of the police car, Heflin asked Charlie why he had stopped so abruptly in the middle of the highway.

Charlie shrugged, as if the answer should be obvious. "I would have hit head-on with somebody, anyway," he replied.

As they turned back toward Douglas, Charlie had one parting thought. "Don't be rough on the girl," he told his captors. "She didn't have anything to do with it."

15

Buried Alive

Caril Ann was singing a similar tune on the ride into Douglas, with Deputy Romer and Sid Baldry. "She told me she had always been a hostage," Romer subsequently told the press, "but did not say one way or another that she tried to get away from Starkweather. She said that her home in Lincoln had been the headquarters for a group of two or three teenagers with Starkweather who planned to rob a Lincoln bank. She had been held captive in the Bartlett home and they had left only when the other teenagers chickened out on the bank robbery plan."

That was a lie, of course. There was no gang, no holdup plan. Caril Ann had tried a variation of the same line on her sister, four days earlier, but it would not hold water. Worse, from Caril Ann's point of view, before the ride was over, she had doomed her own defense. As Romer told the hungry media, "She told me she had seen all nine murders in Nebraska."

That simple statement blew Caril's alibi—to wit, that she had only stayed with Charlie out of fear for her family's

204

safety. If Caril knew they were dead all along, had in fact witnessed their murders, then her story was a lie.

She may have recognized her error, albeit too late, for Romer noted that she "finally wound down and became unintelligible. I couldn't tell for sure what she was saying sometimes. Her memory seemed to get progressively worse as we got her near the jail."

The Converse County lockup was a kind of Mayberry affair, in those days, with living quarters for Sheriff Heflin and his wife on the premises. Hazel Heflin took charge of Caril, and saw her safely situated in a women's cell, upstairs. In Mrs. Heflin's words, Caril "smelled" and "needed a bath pretty bad," but the teenager refused to bathe or even change her dirty clothes. A doctor came to visit, but he left without examining the prisoner, since Caril would not allow him close enough to touch her. She was finally sedated, and spent most of her remaining time in Douglas in a groggy daze.

Charlie was no bouquet of roses, himself, slouching into the jail with his shirt torn and bloody, his clothes filthy from two days on the road, shoe polish clotted in his hair. He did not mind a bath, but balked at talking to authorities at first. His only comment was to tell Heflin and Ainslie, "You wouldn't have caught me if I hadn't stopped. If I'da had a gun, I would've shot you." Fortunately for the officers, Starkweather's only weapons on that last wild ride had been his hunting knife and the useless .32 revolver that he had been carrying since Monday afternoon in hope of finding cartridges.

Charlie was playing dumb, but the police already had his first of several statements, taken from his jacket pocket at the time of his arrest. That curious letter, penned at Lauer Ward's home and addressed "for the law only," was written in Charlie's shaky handwriting but seemed to be Caril's story, though she had refused to sign it when it was completed. It ignored the Colvert, Meyer, King, and Jensen murders, and described the massacre on Belmont Avenue as a joint endeavor, Charlie shooting Marion Bartlett in self-defense, while Caril Ann "stopped" her mother and bludgeoned Betty Jean with the rifle. It would do for starters, but it would not be the last word on the case, by any means.

The news of Charlie's capture in Wyoming brought a palpable relief to Lincoln. After two tense days, the local vigilantes could stand down, Guardsmen return to the monotony of normal jobs, housewives resume their workaday routines. Sheriff Merle Karnopp was delighted to receive the bulletin. "I hate to think what might have happened after dark Wednesday if they hadn't been captured," he said. "People would have been shooting at anything that moved. There were a lot of armed men who had been drinking who were roaming around town."

The work of Lincoln's law enforcement officers was only getting started, though. Police Lieutenant Eugene Henninger was at the Converse County jail by 9:30 P.M., having flown in with a couple of reporters from the *Kansas City Star*. He found the lockup already besieged by journalists, with Sheriff Heflin caught up in the middle of it all. As Henninger described the scene to William Allen, years after the fact, "[Heflin] said I couldn't see Charlie—he was his prisoner and nobody else was getting in to see him. He gave me a hell of a time. I finally told him, 'Look, we don't know how many more people he shot in Nebraska who might still be alive. We need to find out so we can get to them.'"

Grudgingly, Heflin led Henninger to his prize captive's cell, told him, "There's the yellow son of a bitch," and left them alone. Charlie was pleased to see someone from home, even a stranger with a badge, and Henninger soon had him talking. Before long, he was writing out his first formal statement in the case, and his story kept changing as he went along.

In the Wyoming statement, Charlie admitted killing all three members of Caril Ann's family while Caril was at school. He described the trip to August Meyer's farm, but skipped over the old man's slaying. Charlie seemed to admit the murders of Jensen and King, while stating that he "didn't want to shoot him or her." Upon returning to the car, he said, he found Caril Ann listening to a radio report of her family's murder—yet another blow to her shaky alibi—before they drove back to Lincoln. As for the Wards, Charlie was adamant that when he left their mansion there was "only one dead person in the house." Merle Collison's cold-blooded murder was another act of self-defense, in Charlie's view. The shoe salesman had promised "he would not do any wrong," but then he broke his word and grabbed for Charlie's rifle, whereupon Starkweather had been forced to shoot him "about three or five times." Again, there was no mention of the Colvert homicide.

Starkweather's state of mind after the murder spree remains as much a subject of debate as the specific details of his crimes. Some thirty hours after his arrest, he told Merle Karnopp that he "slept like a log" in Sheriff Heflin's jail, but Charlie had a different tale for James Reinhardt, months later. "Exhausted as I was, I couldn't sleep," he wrote from death row. "I simply laid there, staring at a couple of names that had been scratched into the steel wall, and was lost in my own thoughts. I said to myself Why? Why, why, had everything had to happen to me?—it wasn't fair, and it wasn't right, then everything was blankly, so bungling [sic]. I tried to condense it together, but all I could think of was—it wasn't just."

From there, Charlie launched into another long-winded recital of privations suffered in his childhood, concluding that "a kid who's been hated will go on hatin' 'til he's crazy or dead. I'm not dead, and I'm not crazy."

Back in Lincoln, Elmer Scheele and company agreed with Charlie's latter statement, but they meant to see him dead with all deliberate speed.

On Thursday morning, January 30, Sheriff Heflin formally charged Charlie Starkweather with first-degree murder in the slaying of victim Merle Collison. It was a capital offense, and normal circumstances would have called for Charlie to stand trial for his life in Wyoming, but Governor

Milward Simpson was a staunch opponent of capital punishment, already on record as saying that he would commute any death sentence won in the case to a term of life imprisonment. The good news, from Nebraska's point of view, was that Simpson had no objection to sending Charlie home. If asked, Simpson said, he would sign extradition papers "in a jiffy."

Back in Lincoln, that was all Governor Victor Anderson needed to hear.

While Charlie waited for the governors of two states to decide his fate, he took another fling at writing, this time to his parents. The letter read:

> Dear Mon and dad,
>   In a way i hate to write this or maybe you will not read it but if you will I would like to have you read it, it will help a lot.
>   I'm sorry for what i did in a lot of ways cause I knew I hurt everybody and you and mon did all you could to rise me up right and you all ways help me when I got in bad with something. But this time i would like you not to do anything to help me out. i hope you will understand, i know my sister and brothers even nom that this will take a long time befor people stop looking at them in a funny way. So it would make me happy if everybody will go on just like anything didn't happen. the cops up here have been more than nice to me but these dam reporters—the next one that comes in here he is going to get a glass of water, but dad im not real sorry for what i did cause for the first time me and Caril had more fun, she help me a lot, but if she comes back don't hate her she had not a thing to do with the killing. All we wanted to do is get out of town. tell every body to take care. Chuck. P.S. tell Bob VonBruck [sic] to think of some body besids him "he help to cause this."

Charlie never elaborated on his grudge against Caril's brother-in-law, but he would nurse it though his final months of life and take it to his grave.

Late Thursday afternoon, Elmer Scheele and Sheriff Karnopp led a six-man extradition party aboard an Air National Guard C-47 transport for the flight to Douglas. Charlie seemed elated by Karnopp's arrival, asking to see his "buddy" without delay, greeting the sheriff from his cell with a cheery "How's Dennis?" He spoke freely to the Nebraska lawmen, explaining that he had always wanted to be an outlaw, driven from childhood by the need to "be somebody." None of it was really *his* fault, after all.

Scheele introduced himself to Charlie with the comment that he would do everything within his power to put Charlie on death row. Starkweather grinned at that and signed the extradition waiver, as did Caril—although she later claimed that she had no idea what she was signing. Scheele dismissed the claim as one more lie, maintaining that the paperwork was carefully explained to both suspects and that "they knew what they were doing." Charlie, unaware of Milward Simpson's promise for a commutation or the fact that Wyoming had executed no one in two decades, joked that he had signed the extradition waiver since "Wyoming uses the gas chamber, and I don't like the smell of gas."

With all the paperwork in order, Elmer Scheele saw no point in delaying their departure. Charlie and Caril Ann had balked at flying, but the prosecutor didn't mind a long drive back to Lincoln, as it gave him time to question Starkweather. A four-car caravan was hastily arranged, Caril Ann accompanied by Hazel Heflin, without handcuffs, while her boyfriend made the trip in clanking chains. They drove as far as Gering, in Nebraska's Scotts Bluff County, before stopping for the night at a local jailhouse. En route, Charlie confessed to Robert Colvert's murder, thereby adding one more victim to the final body count.

The story got around that Charlie was afraid to fly, reporters having fun at his expense, but Sheriff Karnopp gave a different version of events to William Allen. "Charlie wasn't afraid of anything of that nature," Karnopp insisted. "He was a daredevil. He wanted to put off being put in prison as long as possible so that he might have more time and opportunity to escape. He was always looking for a chance to get away."

It sounds like Charlie, but his running days were over. All that waited for him now were courtrooms, prison walls, and the electric chair.

Next morning, standing on the toilet in his cell, Charlie used a borrowed pencil to inscribe his third written confession on the jailhouse wall. It read:

Caril is the one who said to go to Washington state.

by the time any body will read this i will be dead for all the killings *then they cannot give caril the chair to.*

from Lincoln Nebraska they got us Jan 29, 1958.

1958 Kill 11 persons
Charles kill 9) all men
Caril kill   2) all girls
        11

They have so many cops and people watching us leave i can't add all of them of.

Charlie decorated his note with a drawing of an arrow-pierced heart. Inside the heart, he wrote, "Charles Starkweather and Caril Fugate."

At a glance, his math was way off base; the final body count included six male victims and five females. Later on, defense attorneys would maintain that Charlie's problem with arithmetic was evidence of his insanity, but Sheriff Karnopp had a more prosaic explanation, drawing on the final line of Charlie's note. Starkweather simply didn't have the time to make a proper head count, said the sheriff, rushing as he was to finish off the note before he had to leave for Lincoln.

Karnopp brought the cuffs and shackles with him when he came to Charlie's cell that morning, trusting no one else to do the honors. The handcuffs were in place when Charlie said, "I gotta use the bathroom."

"Sure," the sheriff told him, "go ahead."

"Well, take off the handcuffs," Charlie said. "I can't go with them on."

Karnopp shook his head. "You know I can't do that, Charlie."

"How come? I'll pee my pants."

"I can't help that," said Karnopp fearing the escape attempt he had been watching for since they left Douglas, Thursday night.

"All right then," Charlie said at last. "I just won't go."

Gertrude Karnopp joined the caravan in Gering, freeing Hazel Heflin to go home. Before she left Nebraska, Mrs. Heflin spoke to members of the press and said of Caril Ann, "I don't think she knows her mother is dead."

It was the first major shift in Caril's story, veering sharply away from her Wednesday statement to Bill Romer, and she kept up the façade with Gertrude Karnopp, asking, "Are my folks dead?" When the sheriff's wife made no reply, Caril asked, "Who killed them?"

"Don't you know, Caril?" Mrs. Karnopp asked.

Caril said she had received the shocking news from Sheriff Warick's wife, in Gering, just that morning. From there, she went on to describe August Meyer's death and the murders that followed, remarking of Lillian Fencl that it seemed the maid would never die. Caril Ann complained that Clara Ward's clothes were too big for her, despite the fact that she was wearing a blouse and suede jacket stolen from the dead woman's closet. Rubbing absentmindedly at a bloodstain on the sleeve, she asked Mrs. Karnopp, "Isn't this the prettiest jacket, though?"

It was in speaking of her family that Caril ran into problems, time and time again. That morning, she described a telegram she had received from her sister Barbara, at the Douglas lockup, pledging moral support. "But you just wait," Caril said. "She won't have a thing to do with me when we get back."

Forgetting her ruse of the moment, Caril went on to tell Mrs. Karnopp that the newspapers were wrong in stating that "the bodies" had been shot where they were found. In fact, she said, they had been killed inside the house, then dragged outside.

"Which bodies do you mean, Caril?" Mrs. Karnopp asked.

Caril seemed to realize what she had said, and hesitated prior to answering. "Mr. Meyer was shot in the house," she replied, "and then drug outside."

Too late to save herself, Caril lapsed back into sullen silence and amused herself for the remainder of the trip by twisting Kleenex tissues into paper dolls.

There is a myth, still popular in certain circles, that Caril Ann was pregnant when arrested, that she bore a child in prison, and the baby was adopted by her sister. In fact, Gertrude Karnopp reports that Caril was menstruating on the trip back to Lincoln, ruling out any possibility of a secret birth.

There was no Son of Starkweather.

Crowds lined the route as Charlie and Caril Ann returned to Lincoln, gawkers straining for a glimpse of the teenagers who had terrorized a state. Charlie ignored his public, but Caril Ann was pleased to see them, smiling, waving, trying once to roll the window down, before she was restrained by Mrs. Karnopp. She had nothing in the way of smiles for Charlie, though, and seemed to grow more angry at him by the mile as they approached their final destination. When the convoy made a pit stop in North Platte, Caril held one of her paper dolls up to the window, where Charlie could see it, and wrung the doll's neck.

Security was paramount in Elmer Scheele's consideration as the caravan rolled into Lincoln, and it cut both ways. He could no more afford to have his famous prisoners picked off by angry vigilantes than he could allow them to escape. With that in mind, Karnopp and Scheele bypassed the city lockup and the county jail, proceeding directly to the state penitentiary, where Charlie was sequestered in the hospital. From there, the lawmen drove Caril Ann to the state hospital nearby, and got her settled in a private room.

Next morning, Charlie had a date with Elmer Scheele, to give his version of the rampage. Scheele began his grilling with some questions about Charlie's family, his education, and his employment history, before he got around to Robert Colvert's slaying in December. Charlie described the crime in detail, clinging to the self-defense scenario, before they moved on to the Bartlett massacre.

Caril was at school, Starkweather said, when he had visited the shabby house on Belmont Avenue. The Bartletts gave him "dirty looks," and Velda "told me not to come around anymore." Curiously, Velda's butcher knife vanished in Charlie's description of the ensuing fight, but he still managed to describe her slaying as an act of self-defense.

"Mrs. Bartlett came running" after her husband was shot, Charlie said. "She was screaming, and I shot her."

"And what was she doing when you shot her?" Scheele asked.

"Well, she picked up the hammer that he had."

"And what did she do after she picked up the hammer?"

"Well, she—she just got to standing up," Charlie said, "and I shot her."

"And then what happened?"

"Well, she wasn't dead," Charlie replied, "and I hit her with the butt of the gun."

"More than once?"

"Yes."

"Do you know how many times?"

"I don't know."

While he was killing Velda, Charlie said, young Betty Jean was "hollering pretty loud," and he had thrown his hunting knife at her, the pommel striking her "in the neck or the head, or the chest." After that, he "hit her a couple of times with the gun," and she finally lay silent.

Charlie told the prosecutor that he had the bodies hidden and the house cleaned up before Caril Ann got home from school. He had been killing time by throwing his knife at the walls when she arrived, and Charlie ducked behind the door to surprise her.

"And what did you do when she came in?" Scheele asked.

"Nothing," Charlie said. "Just talked to her."

"What did you tell her?"

"Her parents were someplace else."

"Where did you tell her they were?"

Charlie shrugged. "At this old couple's house."

He repeated the preposterous tale of anonymous strangers taking the Bartletts hostage as part of a bank-robbing plot.

"Did she question you about that story?" Scheele inquired.

"No," Charlie answered, "not too much."

Nor, seemingly, had Caril been curious about the long delay, six days with no word on the robbery, no contact from the kidnap gang or from her missing parents. It was ludicrous, but Scheele let Charlie talk, describing how they left the Belmont house and drove toward Bennett.

"Did Caril know at that time what had happened to her family?" the prosecutor asked.

"No," Charlie said, "I don't believe she did."

August Meyer's slaying was another unavoidable incident, in Charlie's version, the old man firing at him without warning, Charlie forced to return fire or die. He did not remember Howard Genuchi helping them out of the ditch, in the wake of that murder, but cut to the abduction of Bob Jensen and Carol King.

Scheele was intent on pinning down Caril's role, if any, in that double homicide. "Did Caril have any weapon?" he inquired.

"Yes," Charlie said, "she was watching him with the four-ten."

"Did Caril have the four-ten in her hands at all times that you were in the car with this young boy and young girl?"

"Yes."

Caril Ann had waited in the car, said Charlie, while he marched his captives to the old school basement, but his description of the killings left critical questions unanswered.

"What did you do when you got there?" Scheele asked.

"Why, I told [Jensen] to go on down in there."

"What did he do?"

"Well, he started down in," Charlie said.

"And what happened then?"

"Well, I don't know, but he——"

"Where was the girl with him?" Scheele interrupted.

"She was just about ready to go down."

"She was just starting down into the cave cellar, too?"

"Yes. He came a-flying up. He said something. I don't know what he said."

"And what happened then?"

"Well," Charlie said, "he pushed her out of the way and started to come toward me, and I shot him."

"And did you shoot him more than once?"

"I think so."

"Could it have been a number of times?"

"Two or three," Charlie said.

"Or more?"

"Or more, it could be."

"What happened when you shot him?"

"He fell, turned around a couple of times, and fell back down in there," Charlie said. "Then she started screaming, and I shot her. . . . I pushed her on down; she was about—well, she wasn't even at the bottom of the steps when I left her. I just pushed her right down the—well, out of sight of the top steps and put the door over and left."

No stripping of the body after Carol was shot, no stabbing

of her genitals. Caril Ann was waiting in the car when he got back, said Charlie, and they drove away, discussing plans to make a run for Washington. Scheele did not press the point.

In discussing the Ward case, Charlie described tying Clara Ward and Lillian Fencl to beds in separate rooms, but claimed that both were still alive, with Caril Ann guarding them, when he went down to dye his hair with shoe polish.

"I did the front," he said, "and then I called Caril and told her to come on down. She did the back and the sides."

"Did you ever go back upstairs?" Scheele asked.

"I never, no."

"Did Caril?"

"Went back up and got my knife," Charlie said.

"How long was Caril up there, that time?"

"Not very long."

"And what did you do then?" Scheele asked.

"We left."

The rest of Starkweather's recital was a simple travelogue. Scheele did not ask about the slaying of Merle Collison; that was Wyoming's problem. He had one last question, though, before he left.

Had Caril Ann ever tried to get away from Starkweather while they were on the road?

"No," Charlie said, "she never did. And she had all the chance, she wanted to."

It was 8:15 P.M. on Sunday, February 2, when deputy prosecutor Dale Fahrnbruch arrived to question Caril at the state hospital. He was accompanied by Gertrude Karnopp, Dr. Edwin A. Coats, and court reporter Audrey Wheeler. After establishing her age and former residence, Fahrnbruch addressed the slaying of her relatives. Caril tried to tell the same story as Charlie, but she couldn't seem to pull it off.

"Caril," Fahrnbruch said, "what happened when you came home from school on that Tuesday?"

"I came in," she said, "and I opened the door and walked in, and he was standing behind the door. I don't remember whether he grabbed me or not. He told me—he said for me to sit down on the couch, or chair, and then I asked him where my folks were, because they were out there and they were gone, and then he told me that story."

"What story was that?" Fahrnbruch pressed.

"He told me my folks were over at that old lady's house where he had the hot-rod, I guess that's what you call it, and he said if I done what he told me, then they wouldn't be hurt. I asked him how they got over there, and he said he had come in and my mother had told him to get out, and he asked them if they were going along peacefully, and he said my mother kept telling him to get out, and they grabbed my little sister, and then they asked him if he was going peacefully, and he said he would."

"What did you think about that?" Fahrnbruch asked.

"Well, I didn't believe him at first. I kept saying, 'I don't believe you.' Then I went out into the kitchen and I either plugged in the coffee, or he did."

"And then what happened, after you plugged in the coffee?"

"I don't remember what went on in the house."

"What went on in the house?" Fahrnbruch asked.

"No."

"What do you mean, Caril?"

"I don't remember it all."

"You don't remember it all?"

"I don't remember it all."

"What do you mean you don't remember it all?"

"I don't remember what went on."

The performance was vintage Caril, with ambiguity—"either he did or I did"—followed by sudden attacks of amnesia when she felt herself veering onto thin ice. There was no mention of a holdup being planned—indeed, no motive whatsoever for the aging neighbors to abduct her family. Caril *did* remember changing clothes and watching television, though, along with certain conversations.

"Did you and he talk back and forth?" Fahrnbruch asked.

"Talked about my folks," Caril Ann replied.

"What did you say, and what did he say about your folks?"

"I asked him if I could talk to them and see them, if they were all right, and he assured me they were all right."

"Did you stay in the house?"

"Yes."

"And how many times would you say, Caril, that you stayed in the house while he went away?"

"Almost every night."

If Fahrnbruch caught the glitch, he gave no sign. "Now Caril," he continued, "Chuck has told me he tied you up the second night and that is the only time. Is that right?"

She dodged the question, replying, "He tied me up when he left the house, and he didn't tie me up tight so it hurt."

"Could you get loose?" asked Fahrnbruch.

"Well, what do you mean?"

"Well, what did he tie you up with?"

"My mother's dishtowel."

"Now Caril, I have talked to the people that have interviewed Chuck, and they tell me that he told them that there was only one night he tied you up. Is he wrong when he says that?"

"Yes."

Caril's statement on the death of August Meyer was equally ambiguous. They had walked over to the barn with Meyer, she said, but Meyer was "on the porch" when Charlie shot him in the head. The weapon was her stepfather's .410 shotgun, which Caril Ann described as "a 45." She "didn't look at [Meyer]" but "seen the body," watching while Starkweather dragged it to the shed.

"Did Chuck say why he shot him?" Fahrnbruch asked.

"I don't remember."

"Did you help put Mr. Meyer in that little house?"

"No," she insisted. "I picked up his hat."

"You picked up his hat?"

"And threw it inside."

Caril Ann agreed with Charlie that she had been carrying

her stepdad's shotgun on the night ride back and forth from August Meyer's farm, with Bob Jensen and Carol King.

"What happened when the car was stopped?" asked Fahrnbruch.

"Well, he told him to get out."

"Who told *who* to get out?"

"Chuck told the boy to get out," she replied, "and I pointed the gun at the girl. I put it on the back seat and told her to get out."

Tightening the noose. "You mean you pointed the gun at the girl and told her to get out?"

"Yes," she said.

"Why did you do that, Caril?"

"Because he told him to get out."

"He told the driver to get out?"

"He told them *both* to get out."

Caril's story of the killings in the cellar was predictably confused. According to her statement, she sat waiting in the car while Charlie spent "a half hour or an hour" with the captives, underground. She heard at least two shots, as they were starting down the stairs, but finally admitted that "it could have been more." In passing, she admitted taking four dollars from Bob Jensen's wallet, thereby sealing her fate on a robbery charge.

In regard to the Ward-Fencl murders, Caril described Charlie going upstairs to look for Clara Ward, returning sometime later with the news that "she was dead upstairs in the bedroom."

"Okay, Caril," Fahrnbruch said. "What happened after Charles told you that Mrs. Ward was dead upstairs?"

"Well, I asked him how he killed her."

"What did he say?"

"He said he stabbed her in the throat."

"And what did you say?"

"I just said I didn't—well, I didn't say nothing."

"What did he do then," Fahrnbruch asked, "after he told you that?"

"He had a knife," Caril answered, "and he told me to go in the bathroom and wash it off."

"Where did you wash it off?"

"In the downstairs bathroom."

"Now Caril," Fahrnbruch continued, "did you ever have a gun in your hands while you were in the Ward house?"

"Yes."

"And what gun did you have in your hands?"

"A .22," she said.

"And was that loaded at the time?"

"Yes."

"And what did you do with that gun, Caril?"

"I pointed it at the maid."

"And why did you do that?"

"Because he told me to."

Caril told the prosecutor she was hiding in the downstairs bathroom when Lauer Ward was killed, and while she heard one shot, she only had Starkweather's version of events, described after the fact. Ward was alive and moaning on the floor when she emerged from hiding, and they took the maid upstairs, where Charlie tied her to a bed. Once more, Caril managed to avert her eyes from murder, staring out the window while Charlie stabbed Lillian Fencl. Caril Ann knew he had stabbed her "more than five" times, however, because "[e]very time he stabbed her, she moaned."

Caril Ann may have believed that her peculiar description of events would get her off the hook, but she was wrong. On February 3, both she and Starkweather were charged with two counts of first-degree murder in the death of Robert Jensen: specifically, premeditated murder and murder during the commission of a robbery. Despite their youth, they would be tried as adults. If convicted, they could ride the lightning in the state's electric chair.

The choice to prosecute on one case only was a judgment call. Nine other slayings in Nebraska would be swept aside, along with several dozen lesser charges ranging from petty theft and reckless driving to armed robbery, "inciting a riot," and various federal counts involving interstate crimes. Elmer Scheele would be criticized in some quarters for not "throwing the book" at Charlie and Caril, but in fact, he chose his mark judiciously: malicious robbery and murder of an all-American teenager, with confessions on record from both defendants. If Scheele couldn't nail them for Jensen, his cause was hopeless, and the other counts were window dressing.

They could only execute the killers once.

While Elmer Scheele was laying out his strategy, Nebraska law enforcement was enduring a storm of criticism for its failure to corral the "mad-dog" teenagers before they ran up such a body count. The heat was so intense, with accusations of malfeasance, negligence, and a potential cover-up of sloppy work, that an outsider was employed to study the investigation and report his findings.

Harold Robinson was an ex-FBI agent, employed with the California Department of Justice at the time of the Nebraska rampage. His investigation focused chiefly on the Colvert murder and the Bartlett massacre, since a timely solution in either case would have saved seven lives. Particular criticism focused on the massacre on Belmont, where police had twice visited the murder scene, once with Charlie still inside the house, but had detected nothing that would put them on alert.

Beginning with the Colvert case, Robinson noted that police had followed their normal procedure for investigating a robbery-homicide. It was no fault of detectives, he concluded, that employees at the service station never got around to learning Charlie's name. Old Mrs. Kamp had been no help at the secondhand clothing shop, when she described her suspicious customer as a "male, unkempt individual, approximately twenty-five to thirty years of age." Indeed, the most promising lead—Rodney Starkweather's statement to police that Charlie had borrowed his 12-gauge in November and returned it shortly after the Colvert slaying, was only recorded after the three Bartlett corpses were found. In conclusion, Robinson reported that police investigation of the Colvert case "wasn't inadequate in any material aspect."

The Bartlett case was harder to explain away, but Robinson managed. Lincoln police investigated thousands of domestic complaints each year, he noted, and the first visit to Belmont Avenue, on January 25, was unremarkable. Caril Ann was calm and rational; she had done nothing to make Officers Soukup and Kahler suspicious, said nothing that would put them on alert. On January 27, when detectives searched the house with Pansy Street, there were no bullet holes, no bloodstains, nothing to suggest foul play. It was "regrettable" that no one searched the outbuildings that morning, Robinson concluded, "but it must be borne in mind that the primary reason for them going to the premises was not to conduct a search but to satisfy Mrs. Pansy Street concerning the subject matter of her complaint."

Of six "criticisms" contained in Robinson's final report, two called for higher police salaries, one noted a high rate of personnel turnover at Lincoln P.D., and a fourth called for centralization of criminal records held by city, state, and county forces (totally irrelevant to Charlie's case, since he had never been arrested). The only direct criticism of active behavior in the case was aimed at civilians, specifically withholding of pertinent information by Crest station employees and the trio who found Colvert's body. On the flip side, Robinson signed off with a seven-point commendation of Nebraska lawmen, noting their "complete cooperation and assistance" with his own investigation, adequate coordination of the statewide manhunt, and "commendable actions by officers at the Bartlett home before the Bartlett bodies were discovered."

Under the circumstances, it was probably a fair report, but some in Lincoln—notably survivors of the Bartlett clan—dismissed it as a whitewash. To the grieving friends and relatives of murdered victims, it was simply one more case where the police investigated their own behavior and absolved themselves of any fault. Some of that bitterness, inevitably dulled by passing time, would linger to the present day, but there was nothing to be done.

The suspects were in custody, and one of them, at least, was on his way to the electric chair.

On Friday, February 21, Charlie took time away from smoking in his prison cell and wrote to Pansy Street. The letter read:

> Dear Mrs. Street:
>
> i hope mrs. street that you will read this and not destroying it befor you do read it. i'n writing this to tell you, that i'n sorry for the sorrou we have gave you and there are a lot of others we hurt also. but i'n sorry for you cause you lost your daughter and i know hou you must love her, flo i'n not asking you to give in any way, but i had to tell you that "i'n sorry" and i would not blame you for hating. Someday i'n going to write you another letter, telling you what started and cause this to happen the way it did. i hope you will read it too, "if you do nay hate some other people to and naybe you'll know that i'n not the only one to blanc for what happen. i wish there was a way to re-pay you for what has happen. "but there's not." Tell your daughter and some that i'n sorry.
>
> Chuck Starkweather

The promised second letter never came. If Pansy Street was disappointed, she concealed it well.

On February 27, Dale Fahrnbruch and Lt. Henninger went back to get another statement from Charlie. They skipped Bob Colvert's murder and went straight to Belmont Avenue, discovering that Charlie's tale had changed dramatically with passing time. Caril wasn't *really* still at school, he told them now, when the three murders were committed in her home. In fact, she had been present when

223

the fight broke out, he said, though she was in the bathroom when he shot her stepfather. The gunshot brought her out, and she had grabbed his gun to threaten Velda Bartlett when the woman pulled a kitchen knife on Charlie. It was Starkweather who killed the woman and Caril's little sister, though, and dragged their bodies to the shed out back.

It was in this statement that Charlie blew away the hostage alibi, describing how the two of them had worked it out together, after Caril Ann's friend from school had dropped by on the morning after.

"What's the next thing that you did," Fahrnbruch asked him, "after the girl was there?"

"Well," Charlie said, "we started talking about what the hell we'd do if we ever got caught. . . . [W]e was trying to make up a story, and it didn't work too well. . . . I thought if we got caught we'd make up like she was a hostage, you know, and we'd start messing around and make it look like it."

In fact, Charlie described their sojourn in the house as something of an orgy, making love "every night and morning," with a marathon performance of "five or six times on Sunday." His description of the August Meyer slaying and the Jensen-King abduction was unchanged . . . until he got back to The Cave. At that point, Charlie finally admitted pulling down Carol's jeans and panties, but he denied any sexual contact and offered no explanation for the postmortem stab wounds. Moving on to the last triple murder, Charlie repeated his earlier claim that only Lauer Ward had been killed, to the best of his knowledge, before they bailed out of the house.

"Now, Charlie," Fahrnbruch said, "you've previously told us about Caril's activities, and now you've changed your story as to exactly what she's done during all this time. What is the reason that you changed your story?"

Charlie shrugged. "Well, I don't know."

"Are you now telling the truth relative to Caril's activities?"

"Yes."

"Have you told us about everything that you know about what she did?"

"Well," Charlie said, "there might be a lot of things, but I can't remember them all at one time."

"And those other things about her in these previous statements are untrue, some of them?"

"They ain't nothing in them other statements that are untrue," Charlie said. "I just didn't tell you anything about her."

"What was the reason for not wanting to tell?"

"Because I thought she could get away with it easier."

A month later, on March 28, Charlie got the urge to write another letter. This one was addressed to Elmer Scheele, and it revised his story once again, further incriminating Caril.

Dear Mr. Scheele:
    i'n writing this at ny own free will and well sign it when done. It would take to much paper to tell why i change ny mind of what happen in Caril f part of Killing Carol King? i Know my folks can tell you why i'n writing this. When i kill the boy out at the cave by the school house, he drop on the steps and landed on the floor in the cave. the King girl never ran or said anything i told her to stay right where she was i gone on down into the cave and he was moving a little, show i got up out of the cave and Carol King was standing right where i left here. "i think she was Shock" i went to the car to get a flash light Caril fugate was sitting in the front and with the 4.10, i gone down into the cave and was down there about 15 to 25 min. then i got scared and ran out of the cave and told King to go down into the cave, and not even stay intull she got down she was on about the 2'd step and ran to the car, i was so dan scared i back of into a dichd, we got out of car to see what happen, i and caril went on back up to the cave and told carol

King to come on up. i gave the 22 cal. to caril fugate and told her to watch her, gone on back down to the car and was on the side jacking the car body up, then i heard a shot and ran back to the cave, caril said that King started to run and had to shot her. caril went on to car and got it. i put the King girl in the cave, on about the 2 or 3 step from the top. the rest is in the statemind i gave you. when we got the car out i caril walk up to the cave and pass the door and some boards on the opening of the cave, if there is any details you would like to Know about the King case come out or asked ny folks to asked me, and i'll tell you, and the nan that got Kill in wyoing, caril and i both shot hin! My writing is a little of a mess, but i hope you can read it.

In addition to changing his story of King's death, Charlie also misplaced her body (found on top of Jensen's, at the bottom of the stairs), failed to explain the stab wounds, and apparently withdrew his own confession to pulling down her pants. It was confusing, at the very least, and Caril's supporters—now, as then—insist the letter was a cruel, transparent bid to take her with him on his last trip, to death row.

On April 9, Starkweather wrote to Scheele again, reiterating his charges against Caril and stating his reasons. "I'll be convicted for what I did and that's okay," he wrote. "But I'll be damned if I'll be sentenced for what I didn't do." He closed the letter by describing Caril Ann as the most trigger-happy person he had ever seen.

With Charlie under lock and key, his parents took their share of flack for nurturing a monster. Guy Starkweather was angry at the criticism, describing himself in media interviews as one of Charlie's potential victims. "I don't think Charlie would have hesitated to shoot me," Guy said. "They say a man will not go against his own flesh and blood, but that's not the case now." As for public recriminations,

Charlie's father said, "I'm tired of taking the blame for this. What could I have done? He was old enough to make his own decisions."

Helen Starkweather tried a different tack, with a letter addressed to "the interested parties of Lincoln," published in the *Lincoln Journal* on May 17.

> I have heard there are comments on my statement of my "six problems and one catastrophe." I will admit what happened to Charles in that week was a catastrophe, few can deny that. I did not mean that I had raised six problems in the definition that the dictionary gives to the word problem. What I mean was I had problems to be met. Every mother and father has. Each child at some time or other has a different problem and has come to me and his father for a solution. Sometimes the answer we gave was the same as far as the other children, sometimes different, according to how we felt we could best get the answer across to the child's understanding.
>
> As the pace of this old world is set today one cannot deny there are numerous problems that children and youth find hard to cope with. What with the atomic bomb, the speed of our planes being faster than sound, Sputnik and our own Vanguard, I think we parents wonder what our world is coming to so we should see what our young folks are up against.
>
> Do you parents believe that you can always give an answer to your children and know that they have fully grasped the meaning? I don't think so.
>
> Every mother and father knows that each child is a separate individual, each with different ideas and thoughts. We love each and every one of our children, one no more than the other. There are problems for a parent to meet in the years of raising a family, sometimes small, other times large.
>
> We have taught our children that when they come

up against something they do not understand not to dodge it but to face it to the best of their ability.

I think all of us at some time in our life, probably mostly in younger years, met with something that was really an obstacle, but with the help and understanding of our parents we surmounted that obstacle and were better persons because of it.

When one of my children came to me with a problem and were seeking the best explanation I could give, I hope they understood. My problem was, did they? Anything that needs thinking and working out is a problem, mathematics or diagraming a sentence for an English lesson. That is what I meant by six problems and a catastrophe.

We all have a big problem on our hands sometimes in trying to understand our children. I truly hope everyone understands what I am trying to get across.

I thank you all very much.

As for Charlie, by that time, he was already looking forward to his trial and counting on a death sentence. In fact, he was looking forward to it.

"Better to be left to rot on some high hill behind a rock, and be remembered," he later wrote, "than to be buried alive in some stinking place."

16

"Nobody Remembers a Crazy Man"

The press went after Charlie with a vengeance, speculating on the motive for his crimes and milking the disaster dry. He wasn't O. J. Simpson, but for 1958, Starkweather was a fair facsimile. And as the future football star, while publicly acquitted on a double murder charge, would come to represent (for some) the problem of domestic violence in America, so Charlie was the poster boy for rampant "juvenile delinquency."

The *Omaha World Herald*'s approach was typical, lamenting that Starkweather could not be dismissed as "a case apart, a biological accident, a monstrous freak of nature." Rather, the editors declared, he was a *symptom* of a greater illness, the "uniform" of sideburns, tight blue jeans, and leather jacket coupled with a "snarling contempt for discipline, the blazing hate for restraint." James Dean and Elvis were on everybody's mind when the editorial concluded that certain unnamed "influences are pulling some youngsters away from the orbit of the home, the school, and the church, and into the asphalt jungle. That is the problem."

For Charlie and Caril Ann, however, the problem was staying alive. The odds were poor, especially in Charlie's case, but there was still an outside chance that he could beat the chair. The first step was to get a full-time lawyer on the case—which took some time in those days, with the legal revolution of the 1960s still some years ahead. The young defendants had been in custody for over two weeks when Judge Harry Spencer got around to appointing Caril's defense counsel on Saturday, February 15. Lincolnite John McArthur, a forty-seven-year-old lawyer and Seventh-Day Adventist, was surprised by his selection—and by the flood of angry, hateful calls that followed. How could he defend a heartless little bitch like that? the callers wondered. Was there something wrong with *him?*

Caril missed her own preliminary hearing on March 7, her attorney showing up alone to file a writ of prohibition with the court. In simple terms, McArthur sought a transfer of her case to juvenile court because of her age. Judge Herbert Ronin took the motion under advisement and postponed the hearing until March 29.

Charlie, meanwhile, was getting by with the services of attorney Hal Bauer, from Lincoln's Legal Aid Bureau. It was Monday, March 10, before Bauer thought to ask Judge Spencer for help. The judge belatedly decided that Starkweather's case was too complex for one attorney, so he fingered two more: fifty-two-year-old William Matschullat and fifty-four-year-old T. Clement Gaughan. "The whole world is going to be watching this trial," Judge Spencer cautioned his selected pigeons, "and I want to appoint someone who will see that justice is served."

Not that securing justice meant getting anybody off the hook, of course. Convictions were anticipated by all hands—as good as guaranteed in Charlie's case—and lawyer Gaughan took the job with visible reluctance, planning on no more than a protection of his client's basic rights. "I'll do what I can," he told the press, "but I can't pull rabbits out of a hat." As they prepared for trial, Starkweather's lawyers divided their assignments, Matschullat accepting the responsibility for briefs and research, while Gaughan would be on the firing line in court.

Two days later, on March 12, Elmer Scheele filed a brief in response to McArthur's petition for a writ of prohibition on Caril Ann. The media was already bogged down in legalese, but Scheele was happy to explain the move. If Caril Ann was tried as a juvenile, the maximum sentence for her crimes—including potential conviction of first-degree murder—would be detention until she turned twenty-one, less than seven years down the road. The same conviction as an adult would limit the sentencing options to death or life imprisonment. Scheele did not mean to see Caril wriggle through the net by playing on her tender years.

On Saturday, March 22, reporters braved freezing rain to attend a press conference called by the prosecutor. Scheele unveiled an eight-page FBI report including positive ballistics tests, review of handwriting, bloodstains, and other microscopic evidence. The gist of it was obvious: Scheele had the utmost confidence that he would bury Charlie and Caril Ann, beginning with Starkweather's trial, already scheduled for May 5.

The major stumbling block, for lawyers Matschullat and Gaughan, was their client. Charlie didn't care if he survived; in fact, he made it clear that he *preferred* death over life imprisonment. His plea that everyone he killed—four women and a child included—had been beaten, shot, and stabbed in "self-defense" was so preposterous, so arrogant, that jurors would be virtually guaranteed to put him in the chair.

There was no hope of getting Charlie off, but Matschullat and Gaughan still believed that they could save his life by pleading him insane. The sheer brutality of Charlie's actions, coupled with a seeming lack of motive, argued for insanity, but the attorneys hit a brick wall when they broached the subject with their client. Charlie stubbornly resisted the suggestion that he "cop a plea," and members of his family likewise opposed the strategy, perhaps afraid that any claim of madness would somehow transfer itself to them. For Charlie's part, he openly admired the prosecutor's stated plan of putting him to death. "Scheele knowed I wasn't crazy," Charlie said. "He didn't try to kid nobody."

Heedless of resistance, Matschullat and Gaughan took their losing battle seriously, working overtime to prove that Starkweather had lost touch with reality before his murder spree. The prestigious Menninger Clinic, in Topeka, Kansas, agreed to study Starkweather, but only if he could be left in their exclusive care "as long as necessary," possibly for months. The state was not about to loose its grip on Charlie for an hour, much less weeks on end, so the attorneys had to shop around.

At first, they found the doors of Lincoln's mental health professionals closed tightly in their faces, local experts bitterly reluctant to involve themselves with Charlie's case. Two psychiatrists from Kansas City, Dr. Nathan Greenbaum and Dr. John O'Hearne, volunteered to examine Charlie before a Lincoln practitioner, Dr. John Steinman, finally agreed to participate in the tests. Greenbaum and Steinman thought that Starkweather was legally insane—that is to say, "incapable of having any premeditation" before Bob Jensen's death, or of planning *any* homicide "with the knowledge that he would be hurting people because of the murder." In short, as one of Charlie's new supporters put it, "Pumping bullets into a human is no different to Starkweather than pumping bullets into a rabbit."

Elmer Scheele may well have shared that view of Charlie's grand indifference to the toll of human suffering, but he was not concerned with attitude. To prove his case, the prosecutor merely had to demonstrate that Starkweather was "sane" when he fired six shots into Robert Jensen's skull. In legal terms, under the nineteenth-century "McNaghten Rule," that simply meant that (a) the killer understood the nature of his act—i.e., that shooting someone in the head may cause that person's death—and (b) that he knew killing people was a crime.

Charlie resisted every effort of the lawyers and psychiatrists to save his life, refusing to sit still for polygraph examinations or an electroencephalograph that might have demonstrated brain damage. (A perforated eardrum led the doctors to suspect that Charlie may have suffered from a serious infection during childhood, possibly with damage to his gray matter.) At last, Charlie's attorneys were compelled to act on his behalf, despite resistance from their client. "The plea will be changed to not guilty by reason of insanity," Clement Gaughan told reporters, "whether Charlie likes it or not."

It was the final insult in a life distinguished by humiliation from age five, and Charlie was determined not to let it pass. In jail, before his trial, he told James Reinhardt he "would rather burn" than be regarded as insane. Starkweather had his image to consider, after all. As he explained to Reinhardt, "Nobody remembers a crazy man."

Dr. O'Hearne, meanwhile, was busy disagreeing with his Kansas City colleague, flatly contradicting the idea that Charlie was incapable of planning crimes or understanding their result. Instead, he painted Charlie as a character consumed by fear and anger, stemming from a blighted childhood.

"I think the family environment didn't teach him to be an ordinary person," O'Hearne said. "I think the person he fears most, reasonably or unreasonably, is his father, and this is something that to other people might seem unnatural—that his father who has been incapacitated from work for years from arthritis is the man who to him was the biggest threat. I think he has certain mixed feelings toward his parents. I think he has loyalty for them. I think also there is a deep down anger and hostility. I think that his subsequent actions point out what some of those feelings might have been. I think he took out on other people some of his feelings he may have had toward his family."

I think . . .

Elmer Scheele was more interested in demonstrable fact, if any such thing can be derived from psychological examinations. He commissioned Charles Munson, a clinical psychologist at the Nebraska State Hospital, to visit Charlie in prison on April 2 and April 10, administering a marathon battery of tests that included Rorschach, Bender-Gestalt and Stress-Bender-Gestalt, the Wechsler Intelligence Scale for Adults, the Thematic Apperception Test, a wide-range achievement test, the Draw-a-Person test, and the Minnesota Multiphasic Personality Inventory. Not only was Starkweather sane, Munson concluded, but he also possessed above-average intelligence, with an IQ rating of 110—one point above "average." Defense psychiatrists rated him at 97, still well within the "normal" range, but Munson ascribed their lower test results to Charlie's well-known hostile attitude toward the insanity defense.

It would remain for Charlie's parents, rather than the trained psychologists, to note how he had changed once Caril Ann walked into his life. She was the one, in Charlie's words, who "brought everything out," approving and encouraging the antisocial urges he had struggled to suppress before they met. Caril Ann had been his audience and cheerleader, the rooting section he had craved since kindergarten, proud of his ability to drive fast cars and make a tricky head shot when the chips were down. In Charlie's mind, at least, the murder spree had been as much for *her* as for himself, a demonstration of his "manhood" to the one he loved.

But things had changed since the arrest, and he was having second thoughts about their love affair.

And so was Caril Ann.

After additional postponements, John McArthur's writ of prohibition was rejected by the district court, but the

Nebraska attorney general's office granted him permission to proceed with an appeal to the state supreme court. McArthur thought he had a solid case, according to state law, which read:

> When in any county where a juvenile court is held, a child under the age of sixteen years is arrested with or without a warrant, such child may . . . be taken directly before such court, or if the child is taken before a justice of the peace or police magistrate, it shall be the duty of such justice of the peace or police magistrate to transfer the case to such court. . . .

The rules seemed clear enough, but most states also have provisions whereby minors over certain ages may be tried as adults, if their crimes are serious enough. If Caril Ann went that route, she could be looking at the chair.

By April, it was clear to all concerned that Caril would not face trial before that fall, or maybe later. A deputy attorney general asked the state supreme court to dispose of McArthur's appeal before summer adjournment, but McArthur objected to the "rush," and his objection was sustained. Consideration of his motion was postponed until the court's fall term.

Meanwhile, the clock was ticking in Lincoln, and time was money. Harold Robinson was billing the state $1,790 for his review of police procedures, and Lancaster County's commissioner reported that the Starkweather case had already cost taxpayers $3,784. It is a measure of our changing times that the amount was considered extreme.

But justice always has a price.

Criminologist James Reinhardt was unique among the experts drawn to interview Charles Starkweather, in that he had no axe to grind, no paying customer to satisfy with his conclusions. For over thirty hours, both before and after Charlie's trial, he delved into the killer's psyche, viewed

Starkweather's "art" and listened to his rambling, often melodramatic descriptions of a life consumed by hatred. On the side, Reinhardt interviewed Charlie's relatives, former classmates, old teachers and counselors, co-workers at various menial jobs, even employees at the secondhand shops where Starkweather bought his clothes. When Charlie went to trial, Reinhardt was watching from the gallery reserved for newsmen, hanging on his every word.

From their first interview in prison, Charlie never deviated from his fear that "[t]hey might try to prove me insane." If "they" succeeded, Charlie feared, his name and bloody deeds would be forgotten, passed off as the actions of a lunatic, deserving no respect. He was initially suspicious, thinking Reinhardt may have been employed by the defense, but over time he saw the visitor as one more forum for his tale of childhood deprivation and abuse, the story of a young man "forced" to kill in "self-defense." At length, when he began to ramble on about his dreams and waking visions of the Reaper, Charlie had apparently decided that Reinhardt did not intend to paint him as a madman.

Above all else, Reinhardt made out an "awful sense of *failure*" in the stories Charlie told. He was embarrassed by the act of hauling garbage, which he viewed as proper work for "nincompoops." More to the point, he said, "a girl deserves better'n a garbage hauler." In Charlie's view, "a kid ain't no good without money," even if he has to kill for it. At times, when Charlie clammed up or declared that "[t]here is nothing left worth talking about," Reinhardt drew him out with flattery, reminding him that great *haters* are often remembered far longer than lovers. That notion intrigued Charlie, prompting him to ask if Reinhardt thought his life would "ever be made into a movie," or if it "would get on television."

In fact, it would do both, but Charlie would not be around to see it.

At one point, Charlie claimed to have "found Jesus" in his cell, but the experience made little outward difference in his attitude. Reinhardt notes that Charlie "never really showed much enthusiasm" for his newfound religion, employing it more as a lament or lame excuse than as a guide for what life still remained to him. "Jesus," he complained, "wouldn't a let me be treated the way I was treated." On the other hand, religion gave Charlie another "out" when he was asked why he had killed. "I guess," he replied, "the devil was in me."

His conversion was suspect at best, and it brought no remorse for his victims. Rather, he continued to regard the homicides he had committed as a string of "necessary" acts. "These people," he told Reinhardt, "were in my way. They got in my way, and I killed them."

Marion Bartlett, for instance, had brought death on himself, in Charlie's view, because he "wanted to break me and Caril up." Velda Bartlett, in her turn, was "coming at me with a knife." And little Betty Jean? "She was yellin'," Charlie grumbled. "You could hear her for a mile."

In retrospect, however, he denied the toddler's murder. "I hit the kid," he told Reinhardt, "but I didn't kill her."

"Well," Reinhardt replied, "you beat the child on the head with the butt of your gun."

"Sure I did," Charlie said. "There wasn't nothin' else to do . . . and her yellin!" Changing his story again, almost before the words were out of his mouth. "You think I killed Caril's little sister, but I didn't. Yes, I hit her with a gun, but I didn't kill her. Why would I want to kill a baby?"

Why, indeed? "Well," Reinhardt said, "I don't know. She was crying . . . "

"The old man and her mom was dead," Charlie answered. "What could she do? We couldn't have her around."

"Charles," Reinhardt asked, "have you ever felt any remorse or shame for bashing in the head of that little girl?"

"I told you why we had to kill her," Charlie said. "It's all done. What good is crying about it now?"

It was the same, with variations, for his other victims. Bob Jensen (shot in the back of the head) was "comin' toward me." August Meyer? "I knowed the old man had a gun." Lauer Ward "wouldn't stop when I told him to." Merle Collison had to die "because I wanted his car." Small loss, in Charlie's view. "Them people," he remarked, "ain't no deader with a bullet hole through them than before."

It was more difficult, at first, for Charlie to analyze his motives, but he was learning as he went along. "Misery, fear, hate," he told Reinhardt in one of their sessions. "I guess I was frustrated. *That's what everybody's been saying.* Anyhow, I got fed up bein' everybody's nobody, bein' unresponsible. That's what they was sayin'. Well, I got responsible, didn't I?" [Emphasis added]

The longer he sat in jail, the more philosophical Charlie became. In one of their later sessions, he told Reinhardt, "I used to think that I'd like to live in a kind of world where a kid didn't have to have the right kind of friends to be somebody, where people didn't pay no attention to the kinda clothes you wore or what you looked like. Somehow, I got an idea that the next world is more like the one I wanted."

Killing others was a means to that end, in Charlie's view, since he had never truly thought he could escape. "Maybe the end will come fast," he told Reinhardt. "Anyhow, it'll come to a man, not a mouse."

And he would take Caril with him, if he could.

In interviews before the trial, Reinhardt noted that Charlie still spoke of his love for Caril Ann. She was a girl who "always wanted to do what I wanted to do," someone he could "count on when the going was tough."

"Caril would give me anything," he said. "She would rather give it to me than to let someone else have it. We planned to go away where we could be alone together. Our folks were down on us. We wanted to get married. Her folks objected, and my old man had ordered me out of the house for letting Caril drive my car. Sure, he asked me to come back, but I knowed it would all happen again. Everybody was determined to separate me and Caril. She was all I had; I was all she had. Without each other, there was no reason to live."

By the time they went to court in separate trials, however, Charlie's attitude had changed. He testified against her voluntarily and helped send her to prison. By his own admission, he no longer cared if Caril Ann lived or died, although he sometimes wondered if he would be privileged to "see her from the other side."

Reinhardt finally concluded that Charlie "suffered severe inner conflicts," including a need to exaggerate the very physical characteristics that made him the butt of cruel jokes in school. Nothing was really *his* fault if he had been marked at birth, by Mother Nature, and humiliated by his peers through childhood, adolescence, on into the workaday routine of "throwin' trash." In Reinhardt's estimation, Charlie "wanted people to believe that he suffered" endless indignities, but at the same time, he "depended upon the generosity of the people he distrusted to justify his hate." Without his persecutors, Charlie was reduced to being simply "everybody's nobody," a loser who had no one but himself to blame. "Like a malignant disease in the bloodstream," Reinhardt wrote, "his sickening discontent spread to every facet of the personality. By the time he was nineteen no potential interest remained unaffected."

Charlie killed, in short, because he fantasized that murdering would make him "somebody," the way it did in movies and on television, but his dream went sour on him. "I was in it," he said, "and it wasn't the way I had wanted it. It was faster, time was shorter. There was no escape. The end was sure."

Was Charlie Starkweather insane? The experts disagreed in court, and jurors finally decided he was not, but the McNaghten Rule is often criticized as backward, out of touch with modern understanding of the human mind and mental illness. It has been replaced, in many jurisdictions, with guidelines that identify a range of mental defects and diseases.

Still, the man or woman who can kill without remorse, sometimes repeatedly, breaks all the rules. We used to call them "psychopaths," but that tag was too easily confused with the *psychotic* who has broken contact with reality. More recently, such predators were labeled "sociopaths," but even that designation was deemed too pejorative by advocates of "political correctness." Today, professionals inform us that most repeat offenders, including serial killers, are victims of APD—"antisocial personality disorder."

Simply put, in layman's terms, they have no conscience.

An appeals court, weighing Charlie's death sentence, had this to say about his state of mind:

> It's true Charles Starkweather was unable to fit himself normally into human society from the time he started school and he possessed only subnormal mental facilities. His inability to comprehend the reactions of normal people forced him to live apart, even from his own family, and ultimately made it possible for him to look back upon the death of eleven people at his own hands without the slightest trace of remorse or conscience.
>
> His own delusions and imagination convinced him that it was necessary to kill almost everyone in what he considered to be "self-defense."

That aside, however, he was obviously "sane" within the context of prevailing law. Slow wits or not, he knew enough to borrow guns or steal them, rob his victims, put together minimal disguises, plot his getaway from half a dozen crime scenes. He had purchased ammunition, gasoline, and road maps, all without appearing to hallucinate that he was living on the planet Mars.

And Charlie knew that once his gun was loaded, once he aimed it at another human being and pulled the trigger, death would be the probable result.

It was enough to put him in the chair.

17

Self-Defense

The case labeled *State of Nebraska v. Charles Raymond Starkweather* officially opened on Monday, May 5, 1958, with Judge Harry Spencer presiding. The morning's warmth bore no resemblance to the frigid winter days when Charlie and Caril Ann were on the run. Lancaster County's aging courthouse was not air-conditioned, and it would become a sweatbox as the trial proceeded, with the windows shut for reasons of security.

There had been apprehension on the part of certain Lincolnites that "Charlie's gang" might try to spring him when he went to court, but the only teenagers who showed up on that first day were a dozen boys from Bennett who had sworn to kill the redhead in revenge for Robert Jensen's murder. Dressed in boots and blue jeans, T-shirts with the sleeves rolled up to bare their shoulders, they resembled "juvenile delinquents" in their own right, but they brought no weapons and dispersed without a protest when a pair of Sheriff Karnopp's deputies advised them to move on.

Starkweather, when he finally arrived from prison, was a study in contrast. Surrounded by uniformed officers, with plainclothes detectives salted through the crowd and snipers peering down from nearby rooftops, Charlie showed up in a tan suit, tie, black shoes. He had received a haircut, under protest, and had put on fifteen pounds in jail. The changes were cosmetic, though: His sneering grin was still the same, and as he climbed the courthouse steps, he swung the chain connecting him to Sheriff Karnopp like a jump rope.

Charlie had the moves down pat and never gave up playing to the cameras, perpetually self-conscious in the way he cocked his head and held his cigarette, the way he swaggered in and out of court. He knew just how James Dean would do it, if he were alive and standing trial for murder with the outcome guaranteed.

He played it cool.

It took four days to seat the jury, and while Charlie made no secret of his boredom through the tedious voir dire procedure, spectators were lined up hours in advance to fill the court's 150 seats. They gaped at Charlie, hung on every word the judge and lawyers said, while journalists relayed the action nationwide.

It was the hottest show in town.

The final jury was composed of seven women and five men. Four of the women—Miriam McCully, Adeline Muehlbeier, Evelyn Russell, and Mrs. George McDonald, Jr.—listed their occupation as housewives; Mildred Fagerberg worked at a department store in Lincoln, while Beatrice Volkmer was employed at a rubber plant, and Ellen Heuer worked in a bookstore. Among the men, Anders Hallbert was a carpenter, John Svoboda worked for the railroad, Oliver Rosenberg was a hospital employee, Alvin Christiansen was an electronics specialist, and Raymond Swanson was a salesman. None of them were Charlie's peers, in any sense, but they would have to do.

Jury selection was completed at 2:45 P.M. on Thursday, May 8, and Judge Spencer called a recess until half past three. When court reopened, Elmer Scheele was ready with the opening remarks for what would surely be the biggest case of his career.

"The state intends to pursue a conviction of first-degree murder in this case," he told the jury. "In order to do that, we will prove that a murder was committed, that Charles Starkweather did it, that he killed with premeditation—which, let me remind you, can be a matter of only a few minutes—and that the murder was done while committing a felony, in this case, robbery."

He sketched a bare-bones outline of the crime, from Charlie and Caril leaving Lincoln on the morning of January 27, to their stop at August Meyer's place, through the abduction, robbery, and murder of Bob Jensen and Carol King. Scheele promised autopsy results and crime-scene photographs, together with a statement from the killer, in which Charlie owned up to his crime.

"In closing, members of the jury," Scheele went on, "let me remind you that Charles Starkweather is presumed sane, but if evidence of insanity is made by the defense, it will be the duty of the state to prove that Starkweather is indeed sane, and liable for these despicable acts of extreme violence. I can assure you that we will do exactly that, if needed."

As Scheele sat down, Clem Gaughan rose to speak for the defense.

"We do not deny that Starkweather killed Jensen," he said, "but the defense is insanity, and we will try to show why he killed. Starkweather is an odd young man whose IQ has always been subnormal. At one time a test showed him to be only a grade or two above an idiot. He didn't have the things other boys had and was forced to scrounge for whatever he could. Charlie was held back in the sixth grade and did worse the second year than the first. Finally, he was promoted only because he was getting too big for the other boys in the class."

As Gaughan spoke, running him down, Starkweather

clutched the table, glaring, showing concentration for the first time in the trial, so far. If looks could kill, Clem Gaughan would have bumped the body count to twelve.

"Charlie was never able to adjust for his deficiencies," the lawyer said, piling it on. "Instead, things got worse. He suffered several severe blows on the head over the years that affected him tremendously. He has severe headaches which have made a significant impact on his behavior.

"Charlie has not cooperated with us, and even in life and death circumstances, he did not have reasonable responses. He has experienced delusions and will testify that he killed everyone in 'self-defense.'

"But that is Charles Starkweather's story. The defense is insanity."

With that, court was adjourned, and Charlie was returned to prison, scowling for the cameras as he left the courthouse. Clearly, standing trial for murder wasn't going to be quite as much fun as he had imagined.

Scheele spent the last day of the trial's first week on testimony describing the crime, giving jurors a feel for murder's impact on the victim's family. Robert Jensen, Sr., was first on the stand, dabbing tears from his eyes as he described his son's recovery from polio in 1951, working up to the night when he had last seen Bob alive.

"Now what happened later that night," Scheele asked, "as far as Robert is concerned? Did he come home?"

"No, he did not."

Scheele led him through the night of waiting, Warren King's appearance on the Jensen doorstep, their eventual report to the police.

"Now," Scheele continued, "when was Robert's funeral held, Mr. Jensen?"

"The following Friday afternoon."

"There in Bennett?"

"Yes, sir."

"At the family church?"

"Yes, sir."

"And you viewed the body?"

"Yes, sir."

Less than half an hour on the witness stand, and Jensen was identifying relics from a shattered life: a photo of his son, Bob's watch and high school jacket, a snapshot of Bob's car, a seat cushion and blanket taken from the Ford.

Next up was Warren King, describing sister Carol's involvement with the church and high school band, her role as an assistant cheerleader. By the time he started to repeat the story of his fruitless search with Robert Jensen, members of the jury had begun to see what Scheele was getting at.

Charlie had not simply gunned down a pair of teenage hooligans like himself. He had murdered a piece of America's future.

Scheele's third witness was I. W. Weaver, a county engineer who came prepared with diagrams to plot the murder site. State Trooper Winston Flower was next, describing how he photographed the cellar and its lifeless occupants. While he was on the stand, the jury viewed his handiwork, long-distance shots to start with, drawing closer frame by frame, until they showed the bloodstained walls and steps. Exhibit 16 was a photo of Carol King, her breasts and buttocks bared, her body smeared with blood. The last shot was a close-up view of Jensen, lying crumpled in a pool of blood, once Carol's body had been hoisted off of him.

And the parade of witnesses continued. Ernest Hunt and Dennis Nelson described Bob Jensen's visit to their service station on the night he died. Merle Boldt recalled his search for the missing teenagers and the sighting of Charlie's old Ford on the muddy lane leading to August Meyer's house. Homer Tate and Marvin Krueger described Charlie's two visits to Tate's filling station, fixing a flat tire and stocking up on ammunition. Howard Genuchi told of pulling Charlie's car out of the mud, while Leo Schwenke recounted his discovery of Bob Jensen's schoolbooks alongside Highway 2. Patrolman John O'Neal picked up the story with his identification of Charlie's car, while Everett Broening added grim drama with his discovery of the two corpses.

Friday's last witness was pathologist Dr. Erwin Zeman, a veteran of more than 2,000 autopsies who had performed the postmortem examination on young Robert Jensen. In clinical tones, he described Jensen's death from multiple close-range gunshot wounds to the head, each bullet striking with explosive force. Assorted minor bruises on the body, Dr. Zeman said, were probably sustained as Jensen tumbled down the stairs, already dead before he hit the concrete floor.

The jurors took that image home with them on Friday afternoon, to ponder through a weekend that was suddenly less bright and cheerful than it should have been.

On Monday the twelfth, Scheele began linking Charlie to the double slaying with a string of witnesses from law enforcement. FBI ballistics expert Robert Zimmer led the way, with testimony that a .22-caliber rifle recovered in Wyoming, at the scene of Merle Collison's murder, had fired the bullets extracted from Bob Jensen's skull. Harold Smith, lately retired from the highway patrol, described his recovery of spent .22 casings near the storm cellar where King and Jensen died. Louis Meyer, August's brother, brought the game full circle by identifying the Wyoming weapon as his brother's gun. As another link, Deputy Sheriff William Johnson testified that he had found a license plate from Charlie's car close by The Cave.

Establishing the fact of robbery was no great challenge, either. Robert Jensen had already testified that Bob was carrying five dollars when he left home on the night he died. Now Deputy Robert Anderson described his search of Jensen's wallet, at the autopsy. It seemed empty at first, but he found one dollar folded into a "secret compartment," making five when it was added to the four Caril stole. Freelance stenographer Elmer Shamburg had recorded

Charlie's statements at the penitentiary, including full confessions to the double slaying, and he testified that Starkweather had spoken voluntarily, without threats or promises from the prosecution.

Sheriff Karnopp was next on the witness stand, explaining that he found Bob Jensen's wristwatch lying broken in the cellar east of Bennett. It had stopped on impact with the floor, said Karnopp, not because it had run down.

Starkweather's final chase and capture was described in duplicate. Deputy Romer told his story of arriving on the scene brief moments after victim Collison was killed, recovering the Jensen murder weapon, and pursuing Charlie in the Packard while he radioed ahead to Douglas. Sheriff Heflin took the story up from there, describing his wild ride with Chief Bob Ainslie and the fusillade of shots that finally brought Charlie to a halt. Attorney Gaughan asked if Charlie had, at any time, appeared to grasp the sheer enormity of what he'd done. Heflin responded in the negative, but then reversed himself on redirect from Elmer Scheele. What he had *meant* to say, the sheriff testified, was that while Charlie seemed aware of his offenses, he showed no remorse.

The first clinker surfaced before lunch, while Lincoln's assistant police chief, Eugene Masters, was on the witness stand. Clem Gaughan seized the opportunity to introduce two of Charlie's written statements—his letter addressed "for the law only" and the victim tabulation from his cell in Gering—which described Caril as an active partner in the murder spree. That afternoon, Charlie's defenders introduced the letter to his parents, written from Wyoming, in which he declared that while Caril "had not a thing to do with the killing," she had "helped a lot" on the road.

The point, apparently, was not to spread the guilt around, but to depict Starkweather as delusional, unable to recall the details of the most dramatic incidents in his short life. The letters clearly troubled Caril's attorney, though. "I won't believe it until she tells me," said McArthur, in response to questions from the press. "She's never even suggested such a thing."

On Tuesday, Elmer Scheele wrapped up the prosecution's case by reading excerpts from the statements Charlie had made to himself and Dale Fahrnbruch, back in February. The prosecutor took his time—all day, in fact—and concentrated on the parts of Charlie's rambling narrative that dealt specifically with Robert Jensen's death.

> SCHEELE: Now, who was that man that asked you if he could help you?
>
> STARKWEATHER: It was that kid, I don't know his name.
>
> SCHEELE: Can you describe him to me?
>
> STARKWEATHER: He was tall and big and wore glasses.
>
> SCHEELE: Did you go back to the old schoolhouse grounds?
>
> STARKWEATHER: Yes.
>
> SCHEELE: And what happened there?
>
> STARKWEATHER: Why, I told him . . . to walk to the . . . to that hole there. I was going to put that lid on and then cover it up with that timber of that schoolhouse, you know, that . . . and we got to the schoolhouse and I told him to go down in there.
>
> SCHEELE: And what weapon did you have in your possession at that time?
>
> STARKWEATHER: The twenty-two caliber.
>
> SCHEELE: Did Caril have any weapon?
>
> STARKWEATHER: Yes; she was watching him with a four-ten.
>
> SCHEELE: Did Caril have the four-ten in her hands at all times that you were in the car with this young boy and young girl?
>
> STARKWEATHER: Yes.

SCHEELE: So, then you got out of the car and Caril got out of the car?

STARKWEATHER: No; Caril stayed in the car.

SCHEELE: And where did you go when you got out of the car?

STARKWEATHER: We walked up to the hole.

SCHEELE: What did you do when you got there?

STARKWEATHER: Why, I told him to go down in there.

SCHEELE: What did he do?

STARKWEATHER: Well, he started down in.

SCHEELE: And what happened then?

STARKWEATHER: Well, I don't know, but he—

SCHEELE: Where was the girl with him?

STARKWEATHER: She was just about ready to go down.

SCHEELE: She was starting down into the cave cellar too?

STARKWEATHER: Yes; he came a-flying up, he said something, I don't know what he said.

SCHEELE: And what happened then?

STARKWEATHER: Well, he pushed her out of the way and started to come toward me, and I shot him.

SCHEELE: What happened when you shot him?

STARKWEATHER: He fell, turned around a couple of times, and fell back down in there. . . . Then she started screaming, and I shot her . . . I pushed her on down. . . .

It was nearly 3:00 P.M. before Scheele finished reading, closed the binder, and removed his glasses.

"The state rests," he said.

The defense began presenting witnesses on Wednesday, striving for an image of their client as a young man who had drawn a losing hand at birth and gone downhill from there. Optometrists Leonard Fitch and J. E. Burress led the parade, confirming that they had tested Charlie's eyes and fitted him for his first pair of glasses three years earlier. Without the spectacles, his eyesight was atrocious and presumably had had some adverse impact on his younger life—although it never seemed to hinder him when he was shooting squirrels or rabbits on the run.

John Hedge was next, recalling Charlie's days at the Western Newspaper Union, eliciting a red-faced scowl from the defendant when he described Charlie as the "dumbest man who ever worked for me." Three of Charlie's co-workers were also called to talk about the day the handle of a paper baler slipped and struck him on the head. He had been dazed, at first, but showed up bright and early the next morning, without any visible aftereffects from the incident. The three also recalled joking with Charlie about what he did with "all that money" from the Crest station robbery, in December 1957, but they had no reason to suspect that he had actually been involved.

The first of Charlie's relatives to testify was half-aunt Elsie Neal. She told the court that Charlie had been visibly upset when he dropped by her house on Friday, January 24. When she had asked him what was wrong, he talked about an argument with Velda Bartlett, over Caril Ann. Reluctantly, the witness also testified that Guy Starkweather had asked her to keep Charlie's frequent headaches a secret from the defense team.

Next up, Clem Gaughan introduced the statement Starkweather had made in his Wyoming jail cell. It marked the jury's first exposure to the Ward and Bartlett murders, and while Charlie confessed to three more slayings in the statement, Gaughan was not concerned about making his client seem more guilty. Rather, he was counting on the jurors to pick out discrepancies between that statement and the others read by Elmer Scheele—specifically, Starkweather's claim that Caril had clubbed her half-sister to death.

Gaughan's last move before lunch was a reading of

Charlie's seven-page handwritten statement, including the claim that when he left Lauer Ward's mansion "there was only one dead person in the house." Again, since none of the Bartlett-Ward killings pertained to the trial, Gaughan's aim was not putting the heat on Caril Ann, but rather convincing the jury that Charlie was hopelessly mad, so far gone that he couldn't recall whom he killed from one day to the next. It was a risky ploy, but given Charlie's numerous confessions, it appeared to be the only strategy with any hope of saving him from the electric chair.

The first afternoon witness was Hal Bauer, from Legal Aid, who had filed the March 10 petition seeking a lawyer for Charlie. He pointed out that Charlie had no counsel when he signed his last two statements at the penitentiary, and that he had not signed papers requesting a lawyer until March 6. It looked bad for the cops, until Elmer Scheele rose on cross-examination and led Bauer through a crash course in Nebraska's criminal law. Still years away from the revolution in prisoner's rights, Nebraska county courts had no power to appoint attorneys for indigent suspects. First, a hearing was required, at which the defendant was bound over for trial in district court. Only then could a full-time lawyer be appointed by the district judge. Hal Bauer had been sent from Legal Aid to represent Starkweather at his preliminary hearing, which was waived on Bauer's advice. Thereafter, Charlie had been eligible for a lawyer and, in fact, had been supplied with two. The letter of the law had been observed.

The afternoon began to drag as Gaughan called on several more of Charlie's relatives to talk about his sterling character. He was a nice boy, each of them agreed, as if by rote. None had expected him to run amok, nor did they linger on his love of guns and shooting anything that moved.

The day's last witness was Dr. Julius Humann, director of guidance for the Lincoln public schools. He talked about Starkweather's less than brilliant academic record, reeling off the IQ stats that placed Charlie in the "dull-normal" range. It was another slap in the face, this total stranger running Charlie down and making him look stupid with the whole world watching, but Dr. Humann's testimony was mercifully brief. Charlie regained his sneer and swagger as court was adjourned for the day, going back to his public, back to the cameras.

Back to his cell.

Thursday's testimony began with Bob Von Busch describing five years of friendship with Charlie, filling in details of life in the Starkweather home. Bob recalled Charlie paying rent to his father, and quoted Guy's complaints, once Charlie started dating Caril Ann, that he was spending too much money on the girl. One of their arguments had led to Charlie punching out a window, but the final break had come when Guy objected to Caril driving Charlie's car. Gaughan was touching all the bases: troubled home life, brooding rage, a fragile mind about to snap.

Starkweather's parents had been scheduled to testify on Thursday, but Guy pulled a no-show, balking until he was served with a subpoena to appear. The incident highlighted Guy's peculiar leaning toward the prosecution and refusal to cooperate with Charlie's lawyers. (Once, in court, when Scheele had scored a telling point against his son, it was reported that Guy called out, "Way to go, Elmer!") Overall, Guy seemed less troubled by the thought of Charlie's death than by the fear that someone would attach the "crazy" label to his family.

Helen Starkweather was another story altogether: nervous, weary, beaten down by the incessant scrutiny of newsmen and her neighbors. When she took the stand on Thursday morning, she admitted that she did not like the way his lawyers were presenting Charlie's case. Her son was not a madman, she insisted; rather, he had been seduced and led astray by Caril Ann Fugate.

"You don't feel there is anything mentally wrong with Charlie, is that right?" Gaughan asked.

"Not at the present time," she said.

"Mrs. Starkweather," he pressed, "in order to be fair with you and in order to be fair with everybody else, is there anything, while you are sitting on that witness stand, that you can think of that you want to tell the jury?"

"Yes, sir," she replied. "It was right after Charles started going with Miss Fugate. Before that, he was the best of friends with his brother. They were together constantly, no arguing or anything. But soon after he started going with Caril, it seemed like his family was pushed behind and his whole life centered around her. That's the way it seemed to me. He wanted to be with her. She seemed to have a hold on him."

"You think he was a different boy after that?" Gaughan asked.

"Yes, sir."

"Of course, that was also about the time he got hit on the head with this baler handle, wasn't it, Mrs. Starkweather?"

"I think he started going with her just before that, yes."

Charlie followed his mother to the stand, responding tersely to Gaughan's questions, clearly ill at ease with the attorney.

"What was your first school?" Gaughan asked.

"Saratoga."

"Did you have any fights with the other kids?"

"The second day I was there," Charlie said.

"Did you have any other trouble while you were there?"

"Couldn't see the blackboard half the time."

"You don't trust people, do you Charlie?"

"Myself."

Gaughan driving home the point. "You trust me a little bit, don't you?"

"No."

"You're naturally suspicious, aren't you?"

"Yeah." Starkweather seeming proud of that.

"You don't like people, do you Charlie?"

"A little bit."

Gaughan was patient, counting on the jurors to see Charlie's animosity toward his own lawyer as another sign of irrationality. He worked his way around to Charlie getting beaned while he was working at the paper company.

"Did your head hurt the next morning?" Gaughan asked.

"I got drunk that night," Charlie said, "and it hurt worse."

"What did you do that night?"

"I got pretty well pickled. I don't remember what happened."

"Do you still have headaches?"

"Yeah."

"How often do you have them?"

Charlie seemed to smell a trap. "Once in a while."

"How often?" Gaughan prodded. "Once a day, once a week, once a month?"

"Every other day, sometimes."

"Are they bad headaches?"

"Some of them," Charlie acknowledged.

"Did you tell your mother and father about them?"

"No."

"Why not?"

A shrug. "I didn't tell 'em."

"Did you yell at people on the street while you were driving in the garbage truck?"

"I'd yell at some old guy and tell him how to drive," said Charlie.

Gaughan cut to the chase. "Why did you kill, Charlie?"

"In self-defense, the ones I killed."

"Do you feel any remorse for the people you killed?"

Charlie stiffened. "I won't answer that."

"Why were you mad at Caril Fugate, at The Cave?"

"For what she did," Starkweather said.

"What did she do?"

"Shot Carol King."

Again: "Do you feel any remorse for the people you killed?"

"I won't answer that."

Charlie was visibly relieved as Gaughan took his seat and

Elmer Scheele stood up. He had a quick smile for the prosecutor, treating Scheele as if he were a long-lost friend. For his part, Scheele was already looking down the road to the next trial.

"Now, the reason you told me to begin with that you shot Carol King was because you were trying to protect Caril Fugate, is that right?"

"Yes, sir," Starkweather said.

"That's all."

Before the daily lunch break, Gaughan read into the record Charlie's letter dated April 19, to Elmer Scheele, in which he called Caril Ann "the trigger-happy person i ever seen." It had been she who shot Carol King and later finished off Merle Collison, while "calling hin about every nane below gods sun while shoting him." Charlie told Scheele that his original description of the double murder at The Cave was false, but pledged that "this will tell the truth and the part in what Caril fugate did."

That afternoon, when court resumed, Gaughan introduced the full text of Charlie's jailhouse confessions to Scheele and Dale Fahrnbruch. The prosecution objected, noting that much of the dialogue was irrelevant to Bob Jensen's murder, but the objection was overruled. Jurors and spectators alike seemed distracted as Gaughan began to read the first confession, but he forged ahead. At one point, William Matschullat was forced to wake his client up. It came as a relief to all concerned when Judge Spencer interrupted Gaughan's recital and adjourned court for the day.

The tedious reading resumed on Friday morning, May 16, but Gaughan cut it short after an hour, calling Guy Starkweather to the stand. Guy had provided various reporters with a string of pithy quotes since Charlie's capture, and the media was looking forward to his testimony.

Gaughan came directly to the point. "Do you think your son is crazy, Mr. Starkweather?"

"He never done nothing to act crazy to me," Guy replied.

"You think Charles knows the difference between right and wrong, do you, Mr. Starkweather?"

"He knew the difference between right and wrong when he was living with me, yes sir."

"Do you think he has the ability or the—do you think he has the ability to exercise the knowledge of the difference between right and wrong?"

"I know Charles is rather good mechanically, yes."

"You didn't get the question," Gaughan said. "I think the question I asked you was if you thought Charlie exercised the knowledge that he had of differences between right and wrong in these incidents that he is alleged to have committed."

"No," Guy admitted. "No, I don't."

"You don't think he used that knowledge?"

"I don't think he used good judgment, no."

It was something less than a rousing defense of his son, but it was the best Guy could do. When he had been excused, Judge Spencer asked if the defense had any other witnesses on hand. Gaughan replied that he would question the psychiatrists on Monday, and court was adjourned for the weekend.

Outside, as Charlie was escorted to the sheriff's car, a press photographer from Iowa got in his face, and Charlie punched him for his trouble. When Charlie made the trek again, the same photographer stepped forward with a sheepish smile and told him, "No hard feelings, Charlie."

Starkweather glared back at him and said, "Next time, I'll kick you in the teeth."

To Sheriff Karnopp, it was simply one more sign that Charlie needed watching every moment that he spent outside of prison. "I never knew what he was going to try next," Karnopp told author William Allen. "I half-expected he would make a break for it."

On Monday, May 19, Gaughan began to call his psychiatric experts, hoping to convince the jury that his client fit the legal definition of insanity. Dr. Nathan Greenbaum was the first to take the stand.

"Now," Gaughan asked the witness, "have you determined any findings, or did you come to any conclusions as a result of your determination as it has to do with the person of Charles Starkweather?"

"My conclusions," Greenbaum replied, "based on my observations and examinations, leads [sic] me to the opinion that Charles Starkweather is suffering from a severe warping of the emotional faculties. That is, he is unable to experience feelings that other people do. People don't mean anything to him. They are no more than a stick or a piece of wood to this boy. And this is one of the symptoms of a very serious disease of the mind. He has grown apart and isolated from other people, as if he has never become a member of society, as if he has never become domesticated by society."

Greenbaum had delivered the classic definition of a psychopath, although he shied away from using labels.

"Would you say, Doctor, that this is something that has been with him for a long time?"

"Yes, sir."

"Doctor," Gaughan continued, "have you found or come to any other conclusions concerning the causes, or things you might have found in your diagnosis, which Charles Starkweather is suffering from at this time or which he has at this time?"

"Yes," the Kansas City specialist replied. "Another important factor which we have found is that he lacks the capacity for control which is part of normal people. In the case of the defendant, there is a short-circuiting of the process that makes us stop before we commit certain acts; the moment the impulse comes upon him he acts immediately. He is unable to stop."

"Do you feel, Doctor, that if you had examined this boy six months ago, before he committed any crime, that you could have predicted the very thing that would happen, did happen?"

"Without any question," Greenbaum said. "I could not have predicted specific details. I would have said something like this: 'This boy is dangerously sick and is capable of committing dangerous and violent acts.'"

"Doctor," Gaughan asked, "do you have an opinion based upon your findings that the defendant killed Robert Jensen on January 28, 1958 [*sic*], near Bennett, Nebraska—do you have an opinion as to whether this defendant was mentally capable of deliberating and premeditating the act he committed?"

"I have an opinion," Greenbaum said. "And I believe he was not. Charles Starkweather was completely detached from people, and he does not have the ability most people have to control anger—that the moment he had an impulse, he acted on it. He is dangerously sick and needs to be put under maximum security because he is dangerous. He tends to perceive things in a somewhat distorted way. He will pick out things which are not important because of his particular way of looking at things. The act of killing meant no more to him than stepping on a bug."

In fact, Greenbaum said, it would be fitting to compare Charlie with "a creature out of a jungle," apparently tamed, but liable to break loose at any time. "It is further true," he said, "that when such a creature tastes blood, it breaks through and a wild rampage occurs in which a primitive impulse comes back."

Scheele wasn't buying it, determined to pin Greenbaum down on cross-examination.

"Doctor," he began, "did Charles Starkweather, on January 27, 1958, possess mental capacity to ask the driver of an automobile in which he was riding, while he was armed with a .22-caliber pump rifle and sitting in the back seat of the automobile, 'I asked him if he had a billfold, if he had any money?'"

"And the question?" Greenbaum queried.

"Did he have sufficient mental capacity to do that?"

"I believe so."

"And understand the nature and purpose of that act?"

"Theoretically."

"Did he possess enough mental capacity on that date to purchase .22-caliber rifle bullets for a .22 rifle?"

"Could have," Greenbaum allowed.

"Did he, in your opinion?"

"It was possible that he did, yes."

"And to buy gasoline for his vehicle?"

"Yes."

"And to know the use for which road maps are intended and distributed?"

"Yes."

"And to know that if you pull the trigger of a loaded firearm a bullet will come out?"

"Yes."

"And to know that if the bullet strikes a human being in a vital spot, the effect the bullet will have on the person?"

"Yes."

With those admissions on the record, Scheele tried to extract the formal name of Charlie's illness, but Greenbaum stubbornly refused to label it as paranoia, schizophrenia, or any other well-known malady. The prosecutor finally gave up, and Clement Gaughan rose on redirect, to clarify the point.

"Now, Doctor, you told Mr. Scheele that you would not categorize, that you would not diagnose this case in single terms. Now, Mr. Scheele has made considerable out of that, and I would like to have you explain to the jury why you would not do that."

"We could call it ABC disease or XYZ disease," Greenbaum replied. "There is no single word at this time that describes every manifestation of this disease. Giving a name to it would not make it disappear. I would like to use an illustration. Say I have a bookcase that is full of books, and you want to organize them or categorize them. Now, you can do it in different ways. You can say you're going to put all the tall books together, or all the short books together, and all the medium-size books together. That would be one way, but it still wouldn't tell you much about what the books are like. Or you could put the blue books together, the black books, the red books, the thin books, the thick books, and history here, language there, and so on. If you're interested in any one book, you still have to look in that one. While it helped you in one way to sort it out, it still doesn't tell you anything about the individual."

On that vague note, the court adjourned for lunch. When everyone was back in place, Gaughan called Dr. John O'Hearne to amplify his Kansas City colleague's testimony.

"I wonder," the attorney asked, "if you could tell the jury generally what the result of your findings and conclusions are?"

"The result of the physical and neurological examination," O'Hearne replied, "a special examination of his nervous system, disclosed a short, stocky young fellow with breasts somewhat large but muscularly developed, with tenderness in the spot where we usually expect it to be if a peptic ulcer is present, with a hole in his left eardrum, which apparently has been there for a long time, with decreased deep tendon reflexes—the one where the doctor hits you in the knee and the foot flies up. Charles hardly moved on examinations such as these."

If he was physically unresponsive, though, O'Hearne found Charlie volatile in temperament and quick to anger. It appeared that his performance suffered under stress.

"If things would come at him one at a time," O'Hearne said, "slowly as in a routine job, he would be able to handle these things, but if things began to flood in on him, such as work not going right, the sprinkler in the ceiling coming on, or somebody yelling and a whistle going all at once, I don't think he could function. He would be like a frightened animal."

"Now, Doctor, from your testimony that you have given," Gaughan continued, "do you have an opinion as to whether the defendant, at the time he killed Robert Jensen, had a sufficient degree of reason to know that he was doing an act he ought not to do? Is there any doubt that Charlie was in this type of state when he committed all the murders?"

"Well," O'Hearne replied, "if we could have stopped him right in the middle of it and asked him, like a school kid, 'Is it wrong to kill or steal?' the answer out of his mouth would have been yes. Perhaps I can give you an example of this. Words come easily, and I think they came correctly, to Charlie. But perhaps I can illustrate with an example. On the continuing examination here this morning, when I asked him how he liked what was going on, he said he didn't like it. I said, 'What would you do about it?' He said, 'If I had a grenade I would show you.' I said, 'What?' He said, 'A bomb.' I said, 'What would you do with a bomb?' He said, 'I would kill Greenbaum with it.' I said, 'What would you do to the other people in the courtroom?' He said, 'To hell with them.' Anybody that says something he disagrees with, like his ex-boss there, he wants to shoot him. He wants to bomb them. He wants to bomb Greenbaum."

It is doubtful that O'Hearne's description helped Starkweather's cause. On cross-examination, Elmer Scheele again set out to demonstrate that Charlie fit the legal definition of a sane defendant.

"Is it your opinion," Scheele asked, "that the defendant, Charles Starkweather, was unable to form premeditation prior to the death of Robert Jensen based in part, at least, on the premise that the death of Robert Jensen and the robbery of Robert Jensen took place at the same time?"

"Let me see if I understand," O'Hearne replied. "You are asking me if I believe that he was able to premeditate under those conditions the death and robbery of Robert Jensen. The answer is no."

"Now," Scheele pressed on, "immediately following the death of Robert Jensen, Starkweather was able to cover up evidence of that crime, wasn't he?"

"From what he told me, that wasn't the next thing that happened."

"But he did, very shortly thereafter, cover up the entrance to The Cave where the body of Robert Jensen lay, did he not?"

"I am not real clear in my memory," O'Hearne replied, "whether he said he tried to cover it or not."

"And he had presence of mind when he did get the car unstuck, and mental ability sufficient to enable him to get out of that area completely, didn't he?"

"No," O'Hearne said. "By virtue of the fact that, after riding around on the highway for a while, he came back, parked the stolen car on the streets of Lincoln, Nebraska, and slept in the car."

"But he was able to form and carry out these plans," Scheele insisted, "to cover up evidence of the crime, to avoid apprehension and detection, and to plan and to carry out an escape, was he not?"

"Well, he worked on his escape," O'Hearne admitted, grudgingly.

"He did all these things, didn't he?"

"And crossed the state line, too," the doctor said.

"And knew and understood what he was doing at the time he did it?"

"I assume," O'Hearne granted, "that he even knew that crossing the state line would get him in with the federal authorities."

"When you add up the sum total of the acts he performed after the death of Robert Jensen, the following day and up to the date of his capture, then it has significance. The composite sum total of these acts?"

"That is the point I am trying to make," O'Hearne said. "No one single thing makes sense."

"But added together they do make sense?"

"Yes."

"That's all," the prosecutor said.

And on that sour note for the defense, court was adjourned.

Clement Gaughan called his final witness on the morning of Tuesday, May 20. Dr. John Steinman was the only

Lincoln psychiatrist who had been willing to speak out on Charlie's behalf, and it was hoped that his testimony would sway the jury toward a finding that Starkweather was insane.

When the preliminaries were disposed of, Gaughan asked Steinman, "And from your examinations and observations, based upon your experience and examinations, did you come to any conclusions?"

"I did," Steinman replied. "At the time of my examination, that Charles Starkweather was not of a normally healthy mind. I would say he had a diseased or sick mind."

"Now, Doctor, based on your examination and findings, is the diseased mind of the defendant, as you have described, such that he is unable to adapt himself to the realities of society with which he is in contact?"

"Yes," Steinman said, "I believe that is true. Perhaps I can best illustrate that with a statement he made to me when I first interviewed him. In talking about his eyesight, his marksmanship, he said, 'I'm not as good a shot as they say I am. One thing, though, I am quick on the draw.' He said, 'That is no good. I get that from watching television.' He said, 'That is no good even for a lawman because there is no use you can do with it, being quick on the draw, except for a lawman.'"

"Is it or is it not true," Gaughan asked, "that the defendant is unable to feel normal emotions like his fellow human beings with his diseased mind?"

"I would say that his range of emotions is limited," Steinman said, "that he feels perhaps two that we are familiar with: anger and fear, or anxiety. The other shadings of emotion—pity, sympathy, the feeling of attachment to another individual—is [sic] something that I think he is striving for but actually only has a dim recognition of. When I asked him what happened and how he felt through this when he committed these acts, he has always come back with the same thing: 'Self-defense.' I said, 'Self-defense, how is that?' He said, 'Haven't you ever felt what it is like to have a cop chase you?' He will admit fear, but if I were to say he was yellow or a coward he would get angry."

"We have testimony," Gaughan said, "given by family and friends about Chuck's behavior during and after the murders—that he was happy, cheerful, gay, no different than before. What would that indicate?"

"I would say that it would indicate a diseased mind," Steinman replied. "A person who had committed the act of killing three people, including a young child, and then returned to friends and family and appeared to be normal and cheerful was not able to feel things the way other people would."

In Steinman's opinion, Charlie demonstrated clear-cut signs of paranoia that was bound to make him dangerous. "An individual should not turn his back on a person suffering from paranoia," Steinman said. "A paranoid is distrustful of a person in retreat and feels the individual may return to harm him."

Dr. Steinman noted that Charlie displayed considerable ability in some areas, such as auto mechanics, and recalled his IQ score of 97, but the numerous misspellings and grammatical mistakes apparent in his letters were described as signs of how his mind malfunctioned under stress.

On cross-examination, Elmer Scheele ran true to form, focused on proving Charlie had been capable of planning crimes and carrying them out.

"Doctor Steinman," the prosecutor asked, "did he say or do anything prior to Robert Jensen's death that would outwardly disclose his intention to rob Robert Jensen of his automobile?"

"Yes," Steinman said. "According to the statement, he said he was going to take his car."

"Did he at or about that time outwardly display any intention to rob Robert Jensen of his money?"

"I don't believe he outwardly displayed any until some moment—I am not quite sure. From the statement, I got the impression, somehow, that Caril Fugate suggested to him that he ask where they had any money, I take it."

"Could it be, Doctor," Scheele pressed on, "that according to the statement he was the one that asked Jensen if he had any money?"

"He asked Jensen, but that was prompted by Caril's reminder. 'Better ask them if they have some money,' or something of that sort."

"Doctor, did Charles Starkweather rob Robert Jensen of his money?"

"I am pretty sure," Steinman admitted.

"And did he carry out his intention, later on, to rob Robert Jensen of his automobile?"

"Yes. I don't believe that was his original intention."

"And he knew and appreciated and understood that if he shot Robert Jensen in the head with that .22-caliber six times it would be fatal, didn't he?"

"I think he knew," Steinman said, "but perhaps his reaction could be characterized best by what he says his response was after the Bartlett killings. He said, 'We were in a hell of a mess.'"

"At any rate," Scheele said, "he carried out his intention to use the gun if it became necessary, didn't he?"

"Yes."

"And it did have fatal results, as far as Robert Jensen was concerned?"

"Yes."

"So his action on the intention was effectively carried out?"

"Yes."

"That's all," Scheele said.

There were no questions for the witness on redirect, and Judge Spencer adjourned court for the day.

It was the prosecution's task, on Wednesday, to rebut the testimony of defense psychiatrists and prove that Starkweather was sane, responsible for his behavior, and a fitting candidate for the electric chair. Charles Munson, from the Nebraska State Hospital, was Scheele's first witness of the day.

"Do you have an opinion," the prosecutor asked, "as a result of your examination and tests of Charles R. Starkweather, as to whether or not he was legally sane, as defined in McNaghten's Rule, on the dates you saw him?"

"If he was . . ." Munson faltered. "Do I have an opinion as to whether he was legally insane at that time?"

"Yes."

"Yes."

"What is your opinion in that regard?" Scheele asked.

"My opinion is that Charles R. Starkweather is or was legally sane at the time I saw him."

"Do you have an opinion as to whether or not he was legally sane on January 27, 1958?"

"I do," Munson replied.

"What is your opinion in that regard?"

"My opinion is that Charles R. Starkweather was legally sane as of January 27, 1958."

On cross-examination, Gaughan spent most of his time attacking Munson's credentials, pointing out that Munson was not a physician, did not hold a Ph.D., nor even a master's degree in psychology. As a state employee and a prosecution witness, Gaughan intimated, he was bound to testify that Starkweather was sane.

Dr. Edwin Coats, employed at the Nebraska State Hospital since 1938, was next on the stand. Unlike Munson, he was a specialist in neuropsychiatry, and Elmer Scheele was anxious to elicit his opinion on the claim that Charlie was delusional.

"Now, Doctor," Scheele began, "during the course of your examination, did you find any evidence or indications that Charles R. Starkweather was suffering from delusions?"

"No, sir," Coats replied.

"Or hallucinations?"

"No, sir."

"What were your findings with reference to Charles R. Starkweather?"

"I found he was a cooperative, pleasant young man,"

Coats said. "He readily admitted to the things, the crimes, with which he was charged. He was at all times cooperative. He seemed oriented; he knew where he was and who we were and our relationship to him."

"Doctor, did you find Charles R. Starkweather to be psychotic?"

"No, sir."

"Did you find him to be suffering from a form of medically recognized form of insanity or mental illness to a degree that he would be a fit subject for commitment to a mental institution?"

"No," Coats replied. "I found him suffering from a personality disorder, but not to the extent that he would be committable."

Scheele's final witness in rebuttal was Dr. Robert Stein, head of neurology and psychiatry at Lincoln General Hospital since 1946 and a frequent expert witness for the state. His task was to complete the portrait of Starkweather as a volatile but sane young man who killed because he wanted to, without compulsion from an "inner voice" or any other psychiatric cause.

"And did you make a diagnosis of the defendant upon the completion of your examination?" Scheele asked.

"I made the diagnosis," Stein replied, "that Charles had a personality disorder characterized by emotional instability, considerable emotional insecurity, and impulsiveness; that this would fit into a category under the antisocial type of personality disorder; that he was legally sane."

"Now, at the time you saw him, did he appear to you, Doctor, in your opinion, to know the difference between right and wrong?"

"He did," Stein said.

"In your opinion," Scheele continued, "did he possess that same mental ability on December 1, 1957, during the month of January 1958, and specifically on January 27, 1958?"

"He did."

"Is murder itself a normal act?" Scheele asked.

"No, it is not."

"But is the act of murder in and by itself a criterion of insanity?"

"It is not."

"Or mental illness?"

"It is not."

"And did Charles R. Starkweather relate to you during the course of your being in his presence his acts in attempting to cover up evidence of the various acts he committed, his attempts to avoid detection and apprehension, and to escape?"

"Yes," Stein said, "he did."

Stein told the court that Charlie understood the situation he had blundered into with his spate of killing, knew the penalty that he would face if captured. More to the point, his mind was capable of planning crimes—specifically, the robbery and homicide of Robert Jensen on the night of January 27, 1958.

It was 11:40 A.M. when the defense rested its case. Judge Spencer sent the jurors home, but warned them that the next time they came into court, they would be staying until they had reached a verdict in the case.

A little after nine o'clock on Thursday, Dale Fahrnbruch opened final arguments for the state, recapping the events before and after Robert Jensen's murder, reminding the jury of Charlie's apparent premeditation and his efforts, however clumsy, to avoid detection of the crime. There was no argument about the fact that Starkweather had robbed and killed Bob Jensen, but premeditation was required to put him on death row.

"Didn't he shoot, purposely, six shots into the side of Jensen's head?" Fahrnbruch asked the jury. "He made six decisions when he shot Robert Jensen, a decision every time he pulled the trigger. Every possible fact relative to the Jensen case that is capable of corroboration from physical facts backs up Starkweather's statements. Yet the defense does not want you to believe them. You, the jury, must decide what protection you are going to give to the community. Do you want evidence of malice? Remember the picture of Jensen's head. Do you want intent? What about the shotgun sawed off because it would spread more? Self-defense? It would be more accurate to term it self-preservation to avoid detection and apprehension."

William Matschullat, silent through most of the trial, was the first to speak up in Charlie's defense, making a forthright bid for pity.

"He who sets that boy in the electric chair will have a terrific responsibility," Matschullat said. "There will be days and months in the future when you will wonder about it. This could happen to your son or daughter. We are not here so much to save Charlie but to see that other boys and girls will have a chance for a fair trial, representation. Think of the men we rehabilitate after a war. If you can do it for millions, you can do it for one other—a brethren of your own community. The state's case has made Charlie out as eligible to be an officer in the U.S. Army. That's ridiculous! Saying he was a 'friendly lad,' 'cheerful,' 'cooperative,' with an IQ of 110, a little better than average—yours or mine!"

He waited, letting that sink in, before he delivered the punch line. "Are we going to push this boy down in the electric chair if he has a deranged mind? Why should we kill the boy? Let's kill the devil in him!"

Clem Gaughan took the floor as Matschullat sat down, striking a similar tone, spreading the blame around.

"This boy is a product of our society," he said. "Our society that spawned this individual is looking for a scapegoat. Caril Fugate should get the same punishment as this lad, and I can tell you right now that she is never going to get the death penalty. In many ways, I think I know this lad as well as anyone alive does. His life, my life, are almost parallels until our nineteenth birthday. I stand here and weep unashamedly. Society treated me exactly as it treated Charles Starkweather. But the Good Lord gave me, possibly, a little better parents."

Gaughan understood the fear that lurks in every juror's

mind with an insanity defense: the possibility that a sadistic killer may be someday judged as sane, and freed to kill again. He did his best to sweep those fears aside, while making sure the jurors felt their share of guilt for Charlie's plight.

"I assure you," the attorney said, "that even an act of congress will not take him out of the state hospital. The society that spawned this young lad has set up rules for the insane. The Bible commandment which says 'Thou shalt not kill' applies as much to you as to Starkweather. If you return a death verdict I will take you to the death house so you can see him with his trousers cut to the knees, with his arms bare, his head shaved, the electrodes attached. And when the switch is pulled, you will see the electricity snap and the smoke come from his head, his hair stand on end as the electricity goes through his body. You will see him jerk in the straps and see him fall forward. That is your responsibility, not mine. Ladies and gentlemen, I ask you for the life of Charles Starkweather."

Elmer Scheele was on his feet as Gaughan walked back to the defense table. The prosecutor was grim-faced as he took center stage and began to address the jury.

"That was one of the most emotional appeals I have ever heard," Scheele said. "Such appeals are common when you have a weak case, or no case at all. Then you must distract the jury's attention from the facts. I've got to rely entirely on you twelve ladies and gentlemen to judge this case on facts of evidence. It is unfair and ridiculous to attempt to place blame on society and ask you to do nothing as far as Charles Starkweather, because the blame is on society. Let us get back to earth, get our feet on the ground, if justice is to be accomplished and society is to be given the protection it deserves.

"I can be emotional too," Scheele went on. "I could describe how it felt to go to Robert Colvert's home in December and talk to his widow, the pregnant wife of a dead man. I could describe the sight I saw in the small abandoned toilet and chicken house behind the Bartlett home . . . the August Meyer farm and what I found there . . . the storm cellar and what I saw there. I could take you to the Ward home to tell you what I saw there, and how the relatives felt when they identified the bodies. But I don't want to put you through that. It took me weeks to get those things out of my mind. Now, let's get our feet back on the ground. It's time to face up to our responsibilities."

Scheele reminded the jurors that psychiatrists for both sides in the case had agreed that Charlie knew right from wrong, the only legal test of sanity that could apply in court. The facts spoke for themselves, as to Starkweather's planning, his ability to carry out a plan, the will to cover up his tracks. In Scheele's view, the defense allusions to a "short circuit" in Charlie's brain were ruse, concocted to deceive the jury into "grasping the straw of insanity," and he urged them not to fall for it. As for the various confessions introduced, he pointed out that they were parallel and accurate in all respects, except where Charlie had tried to protect Caril Ann, in the early days after his arrest.

"I have never asked for the death penalty while serving the last four years as county attorney," Scheele said, "but it is one of the duties I have had to face up to since I took my oath of office. This jury has to go all the way to protect this community—our families, yours and mine—from the defendant. I am asking for the death penalty. Can we take a chance and gamble with the safety of persons in this community? It is the only solution, the one answer, for the fate of a confessed slayer."

Judge Spencer briefed the jurors on their several options. If they happened to believe there was a reasonable doubt that Charlie Starkweather had robbed and murdered Robert Jensen, they were charged to find him not guilty. As an alternative, if they believed he did the crimes but was deranged, within the narrow bounds of the McNaghten Rule, they could return a verdict of not guilty by reason of insanity. If Starkweather was sane *and* guilty, they had four remaining options: guilty of first-degree murder with a recommendation of death; guilty of first-degree murder with a sentence of life imprisonment; guilty of second-degree murder (that is, without premeditation); or guilty of manslaughter (an inadvertent homicide resulting from criminally negligent or malicious behavior).

It was 5:25 P.M. when the jurors retired to deliberate, but they broke for supper at six o'clock and were driven to the nearby Lincoln Hotel, returning to continue their deliberations some two hours later. There would be no verdict that night, and jurors were returned to the hotel, no going home this time, until their work was done. On Friday morning, they resumed, a break for lunch, and it was 2:14 P.M. before the bell rang to announce a verdict had been reached.

Three quarters of an hour later, with Judge Spencer on the bench, the various attorneys in their places, Charlie slouching in his seat, and the gallery packed, the court clerk read the jury's verdict. The defendant was guilty and sentenced to die.

Charlie had been expecting it, and there was no emotional display. He turned to William Matschullat and yawned, then smiled at Sheriff Karnopp as the officers surrounded him, to take him out.

Guy Starkweather was philosophical in speaking to the press. "The Lord giveth," he said, "and the Lord taketh away. Let's all go out and get a steak."

18

"I Don't Care If She Lives or Dies"

Caril Ann had staked her hopes on John McArthur's writ of prohibition, which would take her case to juvenile court. She was still waiting in her prison cell when word came down on Charlie's sentence, reminding her that she could go that way, as well, if things went wrong. It was June 7 when Judge Spencer set the date of Charlie's execution for December 17, but even in the 1950s that was being optimistic, with appeals still going on.

On Thursday, July 3, the Nebraska Supreme Court disposed of McArthur's writ with a decision that "[j]uvenile courts do not have the sole or exclusive jurisdiction of children under eighteen years of age who have violated our laws." Caril Ann was ordered to stand trial for Robert Jensen's murder as an adult, in Lancaster County Superior District Court, where Charlie had received his death sentence. She would be the youngest female in American history to stand trial for first-degree murder. Caril didn't know, as yet, that Elmer Scheele would not be asking for the death sentence in her case, as he had with Starkweather.

That choice was almost certainly decided on the basis of her gender, in an age when most Americans found it difficult to swallow that a female, much less one who turned fifteen in prison, could be capable of vicious, "manly" crimes. More than a decade would elapse before Joe Average read about the Manson tribe, longer yet before he heard of Patty Hearst and the so-called Symbionese Liberation Army. By the 1980s, with names like Velma Barfield, Aileen Wuornos, and Blanche Moore broadcast from coast to coast on CNN, the shock value of female killers would be lost, and jurors would be more inclined to vote for death across the board, although the sentences were rarely carried out.

Caril's trial was set to open on October 27, 1958. One week before that date, McArthur and a new addition to the legal team, Merril Reller, held a press conference at the state hospital, where their client was confined. According to the ground rules, TV reporter Ninette Beaver, already convinced of Caril's innocence, would be the only one allowed to speak; other reporters in the audience would have to write their questions down, hand them to Beaver, and suffer in silence if she chose to ignore them. The order didn't go down well, but McArthur was adamant. "That's the way it's going to be," he said. "Otherwise, we'll call the whole thing off."

Describing that press conference years later, in a book that pleaded for Caril Ann's release, even Beaver was struck by Caril's demeanor. Smiling at compliments on her new sweater and skirt one moment, she "changed into a hard-faced, angry young woman" as the questioning began, glaring at the crowd with stony eyes and speaking in "a clipped, brittle voice." She had nothing but scorn for Charlie now, telling her audience why they almost always went to movies on their dates. "He couldn't dance," she explained, "because he was so bowlegged."

"Had you gone with him for quite a while?" Beaver asked.

"Yes," Caril said, "I went with him a year before, and

then I told him I didn't want to see him again, but he came back. . . . And that Sunday [i.e., two days before the Bartlett massacre] I told him to leave, and I told him I didn't ever want to see him again."

Why had she decided to break up with Charlie?

"I think he's crazy," Caril replied.

"Do you still think that?" Beaver asked.

"Yes, I do."

"Did you ever break down and cry and beg Charlie to let you go," Beaver prompted, "or anything like that?"

"Yes," Caril answered, taking the cue. "I cried all the way."

The interview went on in that vein for forty-five minutes, Caril Ann insisting that she had been blameless in the killings, didn't know her family was dead until she heard it in the Gering jail, that Charlie was deranged and she had been his helpless slave. She had considered life in prison and the possibility of death, but said that she was not concerned. "I don't think I have anything to worry about," she told her audience. "The Lord knows I'm innocent, and I know it, and the people who are involved know it, too."

Beaver's colleagues were inclined to view Caril's press conference as a strategic blunder. She had come off sounding tough and overconfident, all claims of innocence aside, glaring defiantly into the cameras when tears and some expression of remorse would almost certainly have served her better. If prospective jurors viewed the broadcast, they would have a hard time thinking of Caril Fugate as a frightened little girl.

Caril's trial began on schedule, bright and early on the twenty-seventh, with another crowded courtroom. Still, there was a different *feel* about this crowd of gawking spectators; they seemed more curious than terrified, less awestruck than amused. The premier monster had been dealt with, after all. It was his consort's turn.

Preliminary motions went more swiftly in Caril Ann's

case than they had for Charlie, in the absence of a do-or-die insanity defense. Caril claimed that she was innocent, another hapless victim of the man already sitting on death row, and she was counting on a jury to believe her. By the time court was adjourned that afternoon, Elmer Scheele had accepted thirty-three potential jurors.

John McArthur started grilling them on Tuesday, asking each when he or she was born, then adding fourteen years and asking what the would-be juror had been doing at that age, attempting to build sympathy for Caril. "Have you ever been threatened with a deadly weapon?" he asked each in turn. "Have you ever had to make a decision while under great stress? Are you aware that there is a vast difference between merely being physically present when a crime is committed and actually aiding or abetting to commit the crime?"

By three o'clock on Wednesday afternoon, the twenty-ninth, Scheele and McArthur had agreed on seven men and five women. Instead of breaking for the day, Judge Spencer went ahead with opening arguments, Scheele leading off as spokesman for the state. Once more, he sketched the now familiar details of the Jensen murder, walking through the bloody night of January 27. There was no substantial doubt about the facts. Scheele's case, like that of the defense, would hinge on whether Caril Ann Fugate was a hostage or an active, willing member of the murder team.

To fit that role, she did not have to wield a knife or pull a trigger. Charlie's later story of the Carol King murder notwithstanding, it would be enough to hang Caril Ann if she participated in the kidnapping and robbery that led to murder in The Cave. "All the time they were in Jensen's car with Robert Jensen driving and Carol King sitting beside him," Scheele said, "Charles Starkweather was sitting directly behind Jensen with a loaded gun, while Caril Fugate sat beside him holding in her hands at all times the loaded four-ten shotgun." She had taken money from the victim's wallet, thereby aiding and abetting in the robbery, while holding Carol King at gunpoint made her a kidnapper. Caril

Ann had known her family was dead, Scheele told the jury, and there had been ample opportunity for her to flee the house. "But she, instead of doing that, voluntarily accompanied him up to, through, and after the date of January 27."

John McArthur had a different take on things. "There is a basic problem which has been overlooked here," he told the court. "This girl was introduced into this horrible sequence of events by opening a door and having a gun stuck in her face." He challenged Scheele's assertion that Caril Ann had known about her family's massacre. Instead, she had been terrorized by Charlie's threats and had accompanied him out of fear, not only for her relatives, but for herself. Despite that fear, though, she had tried to warn her sister, her grandmother, even the police. It wasn't Caril's fault that the warnings were misunderstood or carelessly ignored. The public had been misinformed by media reports about the crime spree, into thinking that Caril Ann was Charlie's lover and accomplice. If the jurors *really* understood her, they would see that she was nothing but a frightened, helpless child.

On that note, court was finally adjourned.

Caril's trial began in earnest on Thursday morning, October 30, with a replay of the witnesses from Charlie's trial: Robert Jensen repeated his story of January 27 and identified Bob's wallet; Warren King described the impact of Carol's murder on his family; I. W. Weaver brought his diagrams of the abandoned school site; and Dr. Zeman took his second jury through the list of injuries sustained by Jensen on the night he died. The testimony wrapped at noon, and court was adjourned for the day so that a juror could attend the funeral of his sister-in-law.

Friday morning, it was more of the same, with photographs presented of the area around the cave. When Scheele prepared to introduce the victim photographs, however, John McArthur rose to object, claiming gaps in the vital foundational evidence. Judge Spencer sustained the objection, never raised at Charlie's trial, and the gruesome photos were sidelined, unseen by the jury.

So far, the evidence had been routine, establishing the fact of murder, but without connecting Caril Ann to the crime. Deputy Bill Romer meant to change all that when he was summoned after lunch, repeating his account of how he met Caril at the Collison murder scene, taking her with him as he chased the stolen Packard east, toward Douglas. He described Caril blurting out, "He's going to kill me!" and his ultimate determination that the "he" in question was Charles Starkweather.

"And did you have any further conversation with Caril Fugate?" Scheele inquired.

"Yes, sir, I did," the deputy replied. "She told me that she had seen Mr. Starkweather kill ten people."

"Did she say who she had seen him kill?"

"Yes, sir, she did." No hesitation as he laid it out before the jury. "She said she had seen him kill her mother, her stepfather, her stepsister, and a boy and a girl, and a farmhand and three other people."

Ninette Beaver, watching the exchange, reports that Caril "looked flushed" and gnawed her lower lip as Romer testified. His word alone would be enough to blow her tale of ignorance about the slaughter of her family, and he was not done yet. Romer went on to say that Caril's demeanor changed dramatically, once she was notified of Charlie's capture.

"Up until that time," he testified, "she had been crying and was fairly hysterical, and at that, as soon as we heard that Starkweather was in custody, she stopped her crying."

"Had she been talking rather freely prior to that time?" Scheele asked.

"Yes, sir, she had," Romer said. "She didn't talk anymore after that."

The implication was obvious: Caril Ann had been acting, with her tears and "hysteria," perhaps banking on the notion that Charlie would escape or be gunned down. After all, he had promised the cops wouldn't take him alive. Now, with the man himself in custody and fit to talk, there was a chance her own role in the crimes would be revealed.

McArthur rose to cross-examine, knowing he would have to find a crack in Romer's story if he meant to save his client from a life in prison or a date with the electric chair. The deputy admitted that Caril Ann had given "an impression" that she feared Starkweather while he was at large, but Romer was unshakable on his account of Caril's admission that she saw her family killed. Abruptly, the defense attorney shifted gears, asking about the day Caril signed the extradition waiver in Wyoming.

"She was advised of her rights, that she didn't have to come back voluntarily," Romer said, "that she could remain in jail there and at a later time be extradited."

"Was she advised that she could fight extradition?" McArthur asked.

"Yes, sir, she was."

"Was Caril ever told that when they got her to Nebraska, they were going to try to electrocute her in your presence [*sic*]?"

"No, sir," Romer said.

"Did she have any, oh, relative or attorney present during that interview, to your knowledge?"

"No, sir, she didn't."

McArthur moved back toward his seat. "I think that's all," he said.

On redirect, Scheele came back to the issue of the extradition waiver. "And was it carefully explained to her," he asked, "by myself and by County Attorney Dixon, just what was involved so far as extradition was concerned?"

McArthur bolted from his seat. "I'm going to object to this," he said, "as calling for a conclusion of the witness."

"It was opened up, Your Honor," Scheele fired back, turning to face Caril's defender. *"You* opened it up."

"But you are asking for a conclusion," McArthur replied, plainly angry, "when you ask to carefully explain what was involved without getting into the conversation."

"I'll withdraw the question," Scheele informed the court,

before Judge Spencer had a chance to rule on the objection. Retrieving a piece of paper from the prosecution table, he showed it to Romer, who identified it as the waiver Caril had signed.

"We offer in evidence Exhibit Number Twenty-Seven," he announced.

McArthur rose again, telling the bench, "I'd like to cross-examine as to foundation."

"You may," Judge Spencer said.

McArthur started rapid-firing questions at the witness. Where had the waiver come from? Who had written out the statement that Caril signed? Had she received a copy? Romer thought she had, and he believed Caril wrote the statement out herself, but he could not be positive. As to the waiver's origin, he drew a blank.

"I notice it recites 'To answer charges pending or yet to be filed against me,'" McArthur said. "Was anything said about what kind of charges were filed or yet to be filed?"

Romer was sure that murder had been mentioned as the leading charge, but he could not explain why it was missing from the statement on the waiver.

"And what is this about where she says, 'I exonerate authorities in Douglas, Wyoming, and in Nebraska here for any blame, compulsion, or interference in this connection'? What was the blame and compulsion and interference that they had used on her?"

Romer assured McArthur there was none, but he could not say why the legalese had been inserted in her statement.

"Sir," McArthur said, "to be fair, weren't they just trying to get something on—over—her signature so that she would never be able to assert the rights that were taken away at that place?"

"I don't believe so," Romer said.

McArthur seemed incredulous. "You don't think that; you think that this, a fourteen-year-old child in a state of shock, was treated fairly, do you?"

"I think she was."

McArthur then surprised the prosecution by withdrawing

his objection to the waiver, and the court adjourned for lunch.

Sheriff Earl Heflin, from Wyoming, was next on the witness stand, describing the removal of newspaper clippings from Caril's pocket when he booked her into jail, in Douglas. Scheele produced an envelope of clippings, and the sheriff readily identified them. Over an objection from McArthur, they were entered into evidence and passed among the jurors. All were clippings from the January 27 *Lincoln Star,* reporting the discovery of the Bartlett massacre, complete with photographs of Marion and Velda Bartlett, Betty Jean, and Charlie with Caril Ann. One of the articles contained a reference to "the slayings" that had taken place on Belmont Avenue.

Again, this time from Caril's own hand, came evidence that she had known about the murders of her family while she was on the run with Starkweather. There was no other logical conclusion for the photographs and stories she had clipped to carry with her on the road.

Everett Broening followed Sheriff Heflin to the stand, relating his discovery of Bob and Carol's bodies in The Cave. Again, Scheele offered up the crime scene photos, and they were admitted this time, over an objection from McArthur. Several of the jurors winced and grimaced, glancing almost furtively at Caril Ann, as they surveyed the victims sprawled in death.

When court adjourned that afternoon, a shaken Ninette Beaver cornered McArthur, quizzing him about the inconsistencies in Caril Ann's tale of ignorance about the Bartlett murders. Not to worry, she was told. The seeming glitch would be resolved when Caril testified, perhaps next week, or the week after. Beaver and her colleagues in the media would simply have to wait and see.

Court reconvened on Monday, November 3, but only for a quarter of an hour. Dale Fahrnbruch asked Judge Spencer for permission to add two more witnesses—Dale Smallcomb and Lee Lamson—to the prosecution's list. Their testimony would be critical, he said, concerning Caril Ann's "hostage" story and her chances to escape from Charlie Starkweather. McArthur instantly objected, noting that he didn't have a clue what either witness planned to say, and thus was not prepared to cross-examine them. Judge Spencer granted Fahrnbruch's motion, but allowed McArthur the remainder of the day to get himself prepared, and so court was adjourned.

Next morning, while the jury, press, and spectators sat waiting for a bombshell, Elmer Scheele instead produced a string of eight more scheduled witnesses, to finish laying the foundation of his case. Assistant Police Chief Eugene Masters was among them, describing the Bartlett home as "sort of a shack," referring to a note retrieved from Caril Ann's pocket, but the note was not produced in court. A grocer from the Belmont neighborhood stepped up to say that he had spotted Charlie in his store on January 24, one of the days when he supposedly was holding Caril Ann hostage at her home.

After the lunch break, Scheele called two of Charlie's relatives to testify that he had visited with them that same week, following the Bartlett massacre. He was alone both times, and had remained to chat for several hours—plainly giving Caril Ann ample time to flee the house, if she was so inclined. Rodney Starkweather described three visits to the Bartlett home, between January 22 and 27. On the first two visits—once alone, and once with Bob Von Busch—it had been Caril who sent him on his way; his final trip to Belmont Avenue, on Monday evening, had included the discovery of three corpses.

Officer Frank Soukup followed Rodney to the witness stand, relating his visit to the Bartlett home on January 25, responsive to the first complaint from Bob Von Busch. Caril Ann had answered to his knock.

"As soon as she opened the door," Soukup testified, "I asked her what the trouble was here. She said, 'Well, there isn't any trouble.' And I said, 'Well, we got a call that some people weren't allowed to enter the house. How come they couldn't come in?' She says, 'Well, I told them that my mother and father and little sister had the flu. My sister had a little baby, and she didn't want her to come in the house and catch the flu.'"

As for Caril's physical appearance, she had worn a nightgown under a kimono, with her hair in pin curls. Soukup came away with the impression that he had awakened her from sleep.

Surprise witness Dale Smallcomb was finally called to the stand after Soukup, but if the audience was looking for drama, they had waited in vain. Smallcomb described the January 27 visit to his service station by Charlie and Caril, when Starkweather had his Ford's transmission packed. Caril Ann had remained in the car while it was up on the rack, a matter of some twenty or thirty minutes, while Charlie, unarmed, had left her alone to wander around the station. She had not attempted to escape, call out for help, or otherwise alert the filling station's staff to her alleged predicament. On cross-examination, Smallcomb granted that Caril had looked tired, and acknowledged that he felt a certain air of menace from Charlie, but Smallcomb had been most concerned that he would try to rob the station.

Lee Lamson's testimony was a virtual echo of Smallcomb's, told from a slightly different perspective. He knew Starkweather from their school days, and it had been Lamson who hoisted Charlie's Ford on the service rack, packing his transmission while Caril sat in the car. A full half hour, give or take, and she had never said a word.

The rest of Tuesday's witnesses had also testified at Charlie's trial. Homer Tate and Marvin Krueger repeated their story of Charlie's flat tire and his ammunition purchase, but this time their testimony had a different twist. While Starkweather was waiting for his tire and buying shotgun shells, they said, Caril Ann had been next door at Brickey's, well beyond her so-called kidnapper's control.

On that sour note for the defense, at half past four, court was adjourned.

If Smallcomb and Lamson had failed to deliver the hoped-for bombshells, Judge Spencer made up for it on Wednesday morning, with an announcement that the prosecution had applied to bring Starkweather from the nearby prison, as a witness for the state. McArthur automatically objected to the move, but he was overruled.

Charlie would testify, as soon as they could get hm into court.

Meanwhile, Juanita Bell, the Brickey's waitress who had served Caril Ann on January 27, took the stand to testify. Caril had not spoken, other than to place her order, Bell explained, but neither had she acted like an ordinary customer. Rather, she seemed to stare at Bell the whole time she was waiting for her burgers. No, Juanita said on cross-examination from McArthur, she did *not* believe that Caril Ann had been trying to convey a silent plea for help. It didn't look that way at all.

Now it was Charlie's turn, the moment Caril's defense had dreaded and the prosecution had approached with all the care of experts tinkering with high explosives. No one could be sure what he would say, but from the tone of statements made since his arrest, McArthur and Caril Ann were fairly certain he was not about to help their case.

Ninette Beaver, ever vigilant for proof of Caril's innocence, reports that she seemed stricken when her onetime lover walked into the courtroom, briefly free of chains and shackles. She appeared to be trembling as she stared at Charlie, clutching the sleeve of Merril Reller's jacket, but was it an act, put on for the jury? If Caril Ann was frightened, the question remains: Was it Charlie that scared her, or what he would say on the stand?

Starkweather did not spare a glance for Caril as he swaggered to the witness chair. He seemed at ease, but spoke so softly in response to Elmer Scheele's direct examination that Judge Spencer ordered him to raise his voice.

Charlie complained about the tightness of his collar, and received permission from the bench to loosen it.

That done, Scheele led him through the grisly crime spree, one step at a time, beginning with the Bartlett massacre. Charlie repeated his familiar tale of being slapped by Velda Bartlett, lashing back at her, "defending" himself when Marion Bartlett charged into the room.

"Was Caril Fugate there when you did these things to Mr. and Mrs. Bartlett?" Scheele asked.

"I didn't see her when I shot Mr. Bartlett, no."

"But she was in the house?"

"Yes," Charlie said.

"And was she in the same room when you shot Mrs. Bartlett?"

"Yes."

"And was she in the same room when you threw the knife at Betty Jean?"

"Yes."

"Now then," Scheele said, "what did you do after all this happened there at the Bartlett home?"

"I cleaned it up," Charlie answered.

"When you were cleaning up, what was Caril Fugate doing?"

"Nothing," Charlie said. "Watching TV."

When the bodies were stowed in the outbuildings, Charlie testified, he had walked to the grocery store, leaving Caril in the house by herself. No, she wasn't tied up. On Wednesday, Charlie visited his aunt, again leaving Caril Ann alone and untied. The same was true on Friday, grocery shopping in the morning, visiting his aunt again that afternoon. There had been ample opportunity for Caril Ann to escape, if she had wanted to.

The rest of Charlie's testimony paralleled the statement Scheele had read into the record at his trial. According to his testimony, Caril had covered Bob Jensen and Carol King with the .410 shotgun during their last ride, and she had taken cash from Jensen's wallet. At the Ward house, Caril Ann sat alone in Jensen's car, again with the loaded shotgun, for twenty-odd minutes while Charlie went in and subdued the occupants. Inside the mansion, Charlie said, they had been separated much of the time, including a period while he slept. There were multiple telephones in the house, and Charlie himself had been unarmed "about half the day." En route to Wyoming, after the Ward massacre, Charlie had stopped for gas and gone off to the men's room, again unarmed, while Caril Ann remained in the car with *three* loaded weapons.

Judge Spencer interrupted Charlie at that point, to break for lunch, but it was much the same when court eventually reconvened. Scheele introduced a road map, and Charlie readily identified it as one he had carried during his flight from Lincoln. Opening the map, Scheele indicated several towns that had been circled with a pencil, and Starkweather read them off: Seward, York, Grand Island, Broken Bow, Dunning, Mullen, Alliance—following Highway 2 eastward, to the end of the line. Caril Ann had circled each town as they reached it, Charlie said. At no time, when they stopped for gas or food, had she attempted to escape.

"Your Honor," Scheele told the bench, "that completes the direct examination."

McArthur wanted time to study Charlie's several statements, prior to cross-examination, and the witness was excused, with orders to return on Thursday morning. Everybody in the courtroom watched him go, escorted by Sheriff Karnopp, until he passed through a side door and vanished from sight.

Scheele's next witness of the day was Dr. Vance Rogers, a Methodist minister and president of Nebraska Wesleyan University, who had been invited as a witness to Caril Ann's questioning by Dale Fahrnbruch, on February 1. Strangely, there was no transcript of the interrogation, but Dr. Rogers recalled Caril Ann as being cooperative, answering each question put to her without hesitation. On cross-examination from McArthur, Dr. Rogers granted that she had seemed frightened. None of her surviving relatives were present at the questioning, and he did not remember anybody mentioning a murder charge.

The crowd was back on Thursday morning, eager for another look at Charlie Starkweather. It was McArthur's job to shake the teenage killer's story, if he could, and thereby save his client's life.

"Charles," the attorney began, then hesitated, "do you prefer that I call you Charles, or Mr. Starkweather, or Chuck, or do you have—"

"It makes no difference," Charlie interrupted him.

McArthur stuck with "Charles." He led off the interrogation with some questions about Charlie's car, before he got around to murder at The Cave.

"When is the first time the thought of killing Robert Jensen entered your mind?"

"When he came up the steps," Charlie said.

McArthur focused on the details of the murder next. How many shots? How close together were they fired? How did the .22 pump action rifle work? How fast could Charlie pump and fire the weapon? How, exactly, did the victim fall?

Again, the lawyer shifted gears. "Charles, is it hard for you to see from where you are?" he asked.

"I can see," Charlie told him.

"Can you see Caril Fugate?"

"Yes."

"Do you wear glasses?" asked McArthur.

"Yes."

"And you could see better if you had them on?"

"Yes."

"I'm going to ask that he be permitted to wear them," McArthur said, addressing the bench.

"Your Honor," Charlie told the judge, "I don't feel like putting them on."

McArthur saw an opening. "Charles," he said, "would you rather not see what's going on here?"

"There ain't nobody in here that I want to see," Starkweather said.

McArthur went back to the murders, starting with the Bartletts. Why, he asked, had Charlie killed Marion Bartlett? Why Velda?

"Mr. McArthur," Charlie said, "in these murders, I wish not to talk about them."

"I can understand that," said McArthur. "I can understand that very well, but you realize that if there wasn't a reason, I wouldn't ask you."

More questions. Why had he killed Betty Jean? Robert Colvert? The Wards and Lillian Fencl? In Charlie's mind, each of the killings was justified.

"And has it been your position," McArthur asked, "and is it still your position that every time you killed anybody, the actual killing was when you were defending yourself?"

"Yes," Charlie said.

Charlie had been on the stand for two hours before McArthur got around to his statement of February 1, in which Starkweather said the Bartletts had been killed before Caril Ann came home from school. McArthur read off specific questions and answers, pausing after each one to confirm that Charlie's words had been recorded accurately. Charlie agreed that he has said those things to Elmer Scheele, but then he dropped his bomb.

"That's what I said, but it ain't true," he told the court. "That whole statement you're reading is a bunch of hogwash."

If McArthur was rattled by that, he hid it well, returning to his central theme, eliciting agreement from the witness that the printed statement was an accurate reflection of the story he had told on February 1, which Charlie now refuted as a pack of lies.

"What would you have done to Caril," McArthur asked, "if she had tried to warn anyone against you?"

"I wasn't worried about her talking," Charlie said. "I wasn't worried about what she did. She wasn't going to talk."

"Do you know what you would have done if she had?"

"Well," Charlie said, "I wasn't worried about her doing it, so I didn't think about it."

"And would that be true of when you went in the different filling stations?"

"She wasn't going to talk," Charlie repeated. "She was too worried about being caught."

McArthur tried to demonstrate that Charlie nursed a vicious grudge against his former love. The press had quoted Charlie, while his trial was going on, as saying that if he went to the chair, Caril should be sitting on his lap. Charlie denied the quote, but now McArthur threw it back at him and asked if he still felt that way.

"No I don't," Charlie answered. "Now I don't care if she lives or dies."

After the lunch break, Starkweather was shown the letter he had written to his parents from Wyoming, stating that Caril had no part in the murders. There was also Charlie's first confession, written at the Douglas jail, in which he said that he alone had killed the Bartletts, then deceived Caril with "a line they were somewhere." McArthur piled it on, returning to the February 1 confession, reading Charlie's long, detailed description of the massacre on Belmont Avenue.

"Now," the lawyer said, "will you answer whether those questions were answered and whether those questions were given as I have before recited?"

"Well," Charlie said, "like I told you this morning, most—parts of that statement is a bunch of hogwash."

"That isn't my question, sir."

"I told you this morning I couldn't remember the answers."

Finally, like pulling teeth, McArthur won a small concession from the witness, Charlie willing to admit that he had told Bill Romer that Caril Ann had no part in the string of violent deaths.

"I said it," Charlie granted.

"I believe that's all."

Not quite, however. Elmer Scheele came back at Charlie on the redirect examination, driving home his basic point about the Bartlett murders.

"Now, Charles," the prosecutor said, "why did you not tell the entire truth to me when I asked you questions about those matters?"

"I told you that once before," Charlie answered.

"Well, will you tell me now?"

"I was protecting Caril Fugate."

What about the letter taken from his pocket in Wyoming? Charlie testified that they had written it together, in the firm belief that the police would kill them both, so there had been no need for lies.

McArthur tried to patch the damage up on recross, but the redhead stonewalled him, refusing to be swayed by argument or innuendo. Caril had been an equal partner in the murder spree, he said, and he would not protect her anymore.

At 4:00 P.M., the sheriff led Charlie away, back to his cage. Scheele and McArthur managed to agree on a motion for early adjournment, and Judge Spencer concurred with a rap of his gavel, sending them home for the night.

Friday's testimony lacked the drama of Charlie's two days on the stand, but it continued hammering away at Caril Ann's defense. Gertrude Karnopp was the star of the morning, describing her conversation with Caril on the drive back from Gering, to Lincoln.

"The first words that were said to me about the events during that time," Mrs. Karnopp said, "was when Caril asked me, 'Are my folks dead?' And I didn't answer immediately. And she said, 'Who killed them?' And I believe my answer was, 'Don't you know, Caril?' And she told me that the first that she had known about it was when Mrs. Warick, the Scotts Bluff County sheriff's wife, had told her in the jail in Gering. She talked about her family at various times during the day, and she mentioned that she didn't like her stepfather very well, that he was very strict with them. . . . And she also told about one time, she started talking about a fight that had taken place at their home when Charles came in and her mother was washing, and they had gotten into a fight, and then Charles said some bad things and her mother said some bad things is the way she put it, and Charles grabbed at her little sister, as I remember her saying it, and then she stopped talking about this fight. She also showed me some pictures that she had of her mother and father and her little sister."

Scheele produced some clippings from the newspaper and showed them to his witness. Mrs. Karnopp readily identified them as the pictures Caril Ann was carrying.

"What else did she say?" Scheele inquired.

"She talked about her sister Barbara," said Mrs. Karnopp. "She also at one time said that the papers said that those three bodies that were found where they were shot, but they weren't shot outside, they were shot in the house. . . . I asked her which three bodies she meant. She waited a moment, and she says, 'Mr. Meyer's body was shot in the house and drug out there,' and then she refused to talk to me."

"What was her conduct during the course of the trip?" Scheele asked. "Can you describe how she acted and behaved?"

"Well," Mrs. Karnopp answered, "when we first got in the car she seemed to me to be sullen and pouty, and then she, after about a half hour or so, she talked, and talked freely and willingly, seemed to visit, told things. And then, I think it was shortly after we'd left Hastings that she cried for a little bit, and I started talking about school and different things, and she seemed to be all right the rest of the way."

By the time their caravan had reached the prison, to deposit Charlie, Caril Ann had been "waving and smiling" at reporters. In parting, Mrs. Karnopp said, the girl had "told about writing a note or letter of some kind and said it should be in her blue jacket."

The note again. It was supposed to be Caril's "proof" that she was Charlie's hostage all along, a desperate plea for help that she had written out, then failed to leave at any of their many stops along the way. McArthur tried to resurrect the phantom correspondence later in the day, when Sheriff Karnopp took the witness stand.

"Now, Sheriff Heflin said that he found a note on Starkweather," Caril's attorney said, "and, I believe, on Caril Ann, and mailed them both to you. Did you ever receive the note that was found on Caril Ann?"

"I never received a note from Sheriff Heflin," Karnopp answered, slamming that door in McArthur's face.

The remainder of Friday's testimony consisted of foundational evidence for the introduction of Caril's 166-page unsigned statement to Dale Fahrnbruch, recorded on February 1. Three witness to the interrogation were presented, including Assistant Police Chief Eugene Masters, psychiatrist Edwin Coats, and stenographer Audrey Wheeler. None agreed with the earlier assessment by Dr. Vance Rogers that Caril Ann was "terribly frightened" during the interrogation. In fact, they said, she had seemed perfectly all right.

Before adjourning for the day, Judge Spencer polled the jurors for their opinion on working next Tuesday, Armistice Day, and the panel voted to stay home. After the jurors were excused, McArthur rose and made a motion for a mistrial, citing Charlie Starkweather's refusal to answer certain questions during cross-examination. His stubbornness amounted to a prejudicial error, the defense attorney said, and "the only way to correct it would be to declare a mistrial and start over again."

Judge Spencer disagreed. At any time, he pointed out, McArthur could have asked the court to require specific answers. Had he done so?

No, McArthur grudgingly admitted, he had not.

Motion denied.

Monday morning, the tenth, found Audrey Wheeler back on the witness stand, with her transcript of Caril Ann's statement, requested by McArthur in preference to letting the witness testify from memory.

"Who was present at that time?" asked Scheele.

"Mrs. Karnopp, Dr. Coats, Mr. Fahrnbruch, and myself," the witness said.

"And during the course of that conversation did Mr. Fahrnbruch make any explanations to her?"

"Yes, he did," Wheeler replied. "He first explained to her that she would be taken to the county attorney's office that afternoon, at which time her father and her sister would be present and she would be given an opportunity to visit with them before she was taken over to the county court for arraignment. . . . [H]e told her that this was a very serious charge; she said she understood that. He told her that she would be taken to county court and arraigned, explained the charges that would be filed against her, which would be first-degree murder and murder committed in the perpetration of a crime. He asked her if she understood that, and she said she did. He then told her, asked her, if she knew that at the time these things were going on that they were wrong, and she said she did."

Dale Fahrnbruch had advised Caril of her right to have a lawyer, Wheeler said. Caril Ann also acknowledged that Scheele himself had told her the same thing, before she left Wyoming.

"Did she say whether or not she had asked me or anyone else to provide an attorney for her?" Scheele pressed on.

"She said no, she had not."

McArthur rose to cross-examine. "Miss Wheeler," he began, "wouldn't you say that the way you have related this conversation is quite misleading?"

"I don't understand what you mean by misleading."

McArthur asked the witness to check her transcript, while he read aloud from his own copy, covering the exchange she had just described.

"By Mr. Fahrnbruch, 'And did Mr. Scheele explain to you, and did he explain to you in Wyoming, did he not, that you could have a lawyer if you wanted one?' And the answer was 'Yes.' And the very next question, 'And you told him at that time that you did not want a lawyer?' And the answer, 'No, I never. I didn't know what he meant at that time by that. I thought he meant by the district attorney.' And the next question and answer [*sic*], 'Did you want a lawyer at that time?' And the answer, 'Yes.' And the next question and answer [*sic*], 'And you want a lawyer now, is that right?' And the answer, 'Yes, but who would take it?' "

Wheeler granted that McArthur's reading of the transcript was correct, a point for the defense, but Caril Ann's statement was admitted into evidence regardless, over the objections of her lawyer. Scheele used up the remainder of the day, reading the transcript in its entirety, and while much of it paralleled Starkweather's earlier statements, including repeated claims of innocence from Caril Ann, it also featured the clumsy lie that she "didn't see" the newspaper clippings police had removed from her pocket. Her alleged SOS message—*Help. Police. Don't ignore.*—was also mentioned in passing, with Caril's statement that it "should be" in the pocket of a coat retrieved from Lauer Ward's stolen Packard. At that, she was allowed to have the final word before the holiday.

> FAHRNBRUCH: Now is there anything else, Caril, that you know of about any of the cases, the Colvert case, the Meyer case, the Jensen case, the Carol King case, the Mr. and Mrs. Ward or the maid case, that you haven't told me about?
>
> FUGATE: Yes. I didn't know he was going to kill any of them.

The state rested its case on Wednesday morning, November 12, and John McArthur called his client as the first defense witness. His early questions tried to cast Caril Ann in the role of a normal eighth-grade girl who hoped to be a nurse someday, eager to be helpful in confinement at the state hospital, but even sympathetic observer Ninette Beaver was forced to admit the contradiction between Caril Ann's words and her defiant attitude.

"That was what the words said," Beaver wrote, almost twenty years later, in a book-length plea for Caril's release from prison. "But they were said in a rapid-fire diction that contradicted them as they came out of her mouth. The voice was not what a child's voice was expected to be."

Caril Ann told her attorney she was "scared to death" of Charlie on the witness stand, and then perused some snapshots of her family taken before the massacre, all smiling, laughing, seemingly at ease with one another. It was difficult to reconcile the photographs with what had happened on the afternoon of January 22.

McArthur asked about the day when Caril Ann claimed that she had broken up with Charlie. "That would be the nineteenth day of January," he reminded her. "Tell us about that. What happened?"

"He came down," Caril said, "and he came in the house, and we were doing the washing, and he started spouting off about different things and accusing me of going out with other boys, saying nasty things, and I told him to leave and not to come back and I didn't want to ever see him again. And my mother was out in the kitchen, and so was my little sister. I went out in the kitchen and I told my mother that I told him to go away, and she told him to go away. And his face turned red, and he got mad about it, and he was hitting his hand with his fist. And he asked me if I never wanted to see him again, and I said, yes, I never wanted to see him again. And he says, 'All right,' and hung around for a few more minutes, and he went out the door and slammed it."

"Caril," McArthur asked, "before that time, what did Charles mainly talk about?"

"He talked mainly about, he was a big sheriff and all that, he was always telling stories," she replied. "He'd say, oh, just tell little stories about being sheriff and how many Indians he caught and everything."

From Wild West fantasies, McArthur shifted to the central issue of the case against Caril Ann. After their car bogged down the second time, at August Meyer's place, she had been carrying "my father's gun that [Charlie] hit the dog with." Starkweather had been packing Meyer's .22, at least one knife, and Velda Bartlett's empty .32 revolver, hanging on to Caril Ann's arm.

"I was tired, and scared, and nervous," she maintained, when her attorney asked how she had felt. "And I was scared to death of him."

Why was she carrying a gun?

"After he hit the dog with it," she said, "he told me I was to carry it until he could get it fixed. He said it broke something after he had hit Mr. Meyer's dog with it."

Another alibi of sorts. She had a loaded gun, but now, for the first time, claimed that she thought it was *broken,* unable to fire.

As Robert Jensen's car approached them in the dark, Caril told the court, "[Starkweather] said he was going to flag him down, for me not to say anything, and for me to shut up, and if I did say anything, it would be too bad." On the drive back toward Bennett, Caril said, "I was thinking he was going to kill me, because he had killed Mr. Meyer."

No mention of the fact that she had earlier expressed an urge to kill Meyer on her own, because he had been inconsiderate enough to let the rain fall on his unpaved driveway prior to their arrival at the farm.

The robbery of Robert Jensen was recounted with a twist: It wasn't Caril's idea to take his wallet, after all; she did it reluctantly, on Charlie's command. "I didn't do it at first," she insisted. "I was scared. . . . Robert Jensen said, 'Do what he says so no one will get hurt,' and I was shaking and I didn't want to do it, and he screamed at me again, and told me to take it out, and I did."

"Who screamed at you?" McArthur asked.

"Charles Starkweather."

How was Charlie looking, at that time?

"He was shaking and nervous," Caril said, "and his face

looked like it just came out of a fight. . . . [I]t was angry and mean and all wrinkled up."

Each step of the way from then on, Caril maintained, she had been Charlie's hostage and puppet. She pointed the shotgun at Carol King and "whispered" for King to get out of the car because Charlie had ordered it. She waited in the car "maybe ten minutes," while Starkweather marched his other captives to The Cave, and then heard gunshots.

"What were you doing during those ten minutes?" asked McArthur.

"Shaking."

"When you heard the shots, what did you do?"

"I started crying, because I thought I knew what he had done."

"Caril," her attorney pressed on, "why didn't you jump out and run away?"

"I couldn't move after I heard the shots. I couldn't move," she insisted. "I was froze stiff."

In Caril Ann's version, though, she *had* made several attempts to save herself. Bob Jensen's books were thrown out of the Ford "to leave a trail." She also had a "white note," written at Dale Smallcomb's filling station, but she never had a chance to pass it on—not in the diner, when she was alone with Juanita Bell; not in the Ward house; not at any of their other stops between the twenty-seventh and the twenty-ninth of January.

"Why didn't you jump out and run?" McArthur asked again.

"Because he had the knife with him," Caril said.

"Did you want to get away, Caril?"

"Yes, I did."

"Was there any time at all that you were with Charles that you did not want to get away?"

"No, sir."

"You always wanted to get loose, didn't you?" McArthur asked.

"Yes, sir, but he always told me that if I ever got loose my family would be killed, and it would be my fault."

Caril Ann complained that she was tired, as the direct examination started winding down. McArthur's last few questions drew responses of "I don't remember," and he gave up for the moment. Caril Ann was excused, to be recalled for further questions and Scheele's cross-examination at a later time.

Next up for the defense was Dr. Erwin Zeman, to describe the injuries sustained by Carol King, including several stab wounds to the genitals. The implication—that another female would be psychologically incapable of such a crime—was readily apparent, if historically inaccurate. Once Dr. Zeman was excused, McArthur introduced the testimony Dr. John O'Hearne had given during Charlie's trial, maintaining that Starkweather was insane, and thus unworthy of belief. It was 4:33 P.M. when he stopped reading from the transcript, and court was adjourned for the day.

On Thursday morning, Elmer Scheele read off his cross-examination of O'Hearne from Charlie's trial; McArthur then got up to read the redirect from Clement Gaughan, Scheele responding with the transcript of his recross. It was a bizarre performance, with the witness back in Kansas City, and it left some of the jurors wearing dazed expressions, yawning cautiously behind raised hands.

With the recitals finished, John McArthur summoned Alice Ward to testify that Lauer and Clara Ward had been healthy, active, intelligent people. Two more witnesses said the same for Robert Colvert: smart, strong, able-bodied. None of it was relevant to Robert Jensen's death, but the defense was clearly trying to suggest that if three sturdy adults could not save themselves from Charlie Starkweather, what chance did fourteen-year-old Caril Ann Fugate have? Jurors were not reminded that the murder victims had been guarded constantly, without an arsenal of loaded weapons close at hand, one of them bound, the others gunned down by surprise.

From his attempt to paint Caril as a helpless weakling, the attorney switched to a parade of witnesses who would describe her as a cheerful, well-adjusted child from a happy, hardworking family, who earned her pocket money babysitting for the neighbors. Pansy Street did what she could for her granddaughter, describing her first visit to Belmont Avenue on January 27.

"And what did you do when you got out there?" McArthur asked.

"I—well, now, I don't know whether I told the taxi to wait or not," Mrs. Street replied. "But anyhow he was in the drive, and I went up to the house, and I didn't even knock, I didn't get clear up to the screen door, that I know, and the door was opened. Now, I don't remember by who or when or how. . . . I seen Caril standing, oh, about two feet back in the—which we would call the dining room. . . . She looked awfully white to me. . . . I think she stared right at me, stared terribly hard right at me. . . . She said, 'Go away, Grandma, go home, Grandmom, oh, Grannie, go away,' and—Well, all the time that she was talking to me she kept stepping back in the middle of the dining room, which is a long room. They have a gas heater, and she kept stepping back towards the gas heater. . . . I was trying to see whether she was crying or not, I can't remember whether she was crying or not, but I noticed especially, she put her hand up over her mouth, and as she stepped back toward that gas heater, it looked like, oh, she moved her fingers some way like they were pointing over in the corner, it looked at that time like she was."

That must have come as a surprise to the police, since Mrs. Street had offered no such statements in her various complaints. In hindsight, though, it is entirely understandable that she might fudge her memory a bit to save her granddaughter from the electric chair.

Urged on by John McArthur, Mrs. Street described herself "screaming" for Velda to speak up or come to the door, but the house remained silent. Finally, she had threatened to return with a search warrant, directing her cab to police headquarters, where two officers were assigned to investigate.

"Do you know whether it was Detectives Hansen and Fischer?" McArthur asked.

"Well, all I know," the witness said, "one of them was bald-headed and he wasn't very nice."

"That would be Fischer," the attorney quipped, evoking laughter from the gallery and a warning rap from Judge Spencer's gavel.

Their search of the Bartlett home was uneventful and unsatisfying. Velda's bed had been "too clean for three people to be sick in it," but the detectives weren't impressed. On their drive back to the station house, one had advised her that, if he were Mrs. Street, "I would go home and I wouldn't stick my nose in my married kids' affairs if they didn't want me around."

Friday's lead witness was Hazel Heflin, wife of the sheriff in Douglas, Wyoming, who had received Caril Ann into custody from Bill Romer, the day of her capture. An ideal defense witness, Mrs. Heflin described Caril as shaky and tearful, fidgeting with "a little piece of string she picked at all the time." Before she was sedated by a local doctor, Mrs. Heflin said, "She cried and screamed for her mother and little half-sister and wondered why they didn't call, and I said the phones are so busy now they couldn't call anyway. She said, 'Well, maybe I can call a little later,' and I said, 'Perhaps you can.'"

Caril's sister Barbara and husband Bob Von Busch came next, describing the Bartlett family as a cohesive unit wherein everyone was happy, and the several members all got along famously. Barbara recalled her sister's choice of words on Saturday, the twenty-fifth of January, urging her to leave the house on Belmont Avenue "so Mother don't get hurt." Bob confirmed the account, adding details of his five-year friendship with Charlie Starkweather, disrupted by his plans to marry Barbara. At one point, Von Busch testified, Charlie had tried to turn his fiancée against him to prevent the marriage.

A next-door neighbor of the Bartletts followed Barb and Bob, describing how she had come home from work at four o'clock on January 22 and was there for the remainder of the day. She had heard nothing in the way of gunshots, screams, or other sounds of combat emanating from the Bartlett home.

With that, McArthur brought Caril Ann back to the witness stand, handling her like a Fabergé egg, receiving stone-faced answers in return. No matter how her sympathizers piled on adjectives—"tiny," "petite," "pale as a ghost"—she came across as one tough customer, despite her claims of being terrorized by Charlie Starkweather.

That said, Friday's testimony was more of the same, Caril Ann explaining that every move she made with Charlie, between January 22 and their capture on January 29, was a result of sheer soul-numbing fear. She "couldn't hardly move" when August Meyer was shot, but she had tossed his hat into the outhouse with his body, and had left the homestead carrying a loaded gun. When Howard Genuchi towed their car out of the mud, Caril kept her mouth shut out of fear for her missing relatives, convinced that Genuchi would die if she asked him for help.

"Where—do you remember where the next place was where Charles drove?" McArthur asked.

"I believe it might have been to a filling station," Caril replied.

Judge Spencer interrupted the exchange, asking McArthur, "Have you reached a place?"

"I think we have," the lawyer said.

The jurors had another weekend coming up, and Caril Ann went back to her cell.

She was back on the stand Monday morning, McArthur leading her through a recital of all the things she had been forced to do against her will, on Charlie's orders: buying hamburgers at Brickey's; pointing a loaded gun at Lillian Fencl; playing lookout and alerting Starkweather when Lauer Ward came home; bringing a second gun to Charlie while he killed Merle Collison. There was no mention of her sex life, though McArthur could presumably have called it rape.

She had been terrified, of course, but Caril still claimed that she had tried to warn police, her relatives—the world, in fact—that Charlie Starkweather had gone off the deep end. She had dropped broad hints to her sister on the afternoon of Saturday, the twenty-fifth, and when police stopped by that night, Caril said, she tried again.

"Did you do anything or try to give this—to tip the policeman off or warn him or anything that way?" McArthur asked.

"Yes, sir."

"What did you do?"

"I said some nasty things about my brother-in-law," Caril replied. "If the policeman had checked back with my brother-in-law, they [sic] would have known that something was wrong, because I never said anything nasty about my brother-in-law. . . . I knew if the police would tell Bob what I had said, that Bob would have knowed that something was wrong."

Another clue, Caril Ann explained, had been the "sick note," which she signed "Miss Bartlett."

"Now, who is Miss Bartlett?" McArthur asked patiently, taking his time.

"Well, my little sister can't write, but she's Miss Bartlett," Caril said. "Whoever would read that note would know that my sister could never write and my mother would never sign the note 'Miss Bartlett.'"

McArthur finished his direct examination in time for lunch, and it was Elmer Scheele's turn with the witness when court reconvened, two hours later. He met immediate resistance, Caril Ann working up a head of steam as Scheele began his questions with the matter of her extradition from Wyoming.

"Caril," he said, "do you recall first meeting me out in Douglas, Wyoming, in January?"

"No, sir," she answered stubbornly, "I don't."

"Do you recall having a conversation with me there in the kitchen of the sheriff's house?"

"No, I don't." Caril Ann said, deliberately forgetting that she had described that very conversation during her direct examination by McArthur, quoting what she said to Scheele from memory, allegedly verbatim.

"And do you remember," Scheele pressed on, "that it was explained to you the procedure that could be gone through to extradite you to go back to the state of Nebraska to face trial?"

"I was told," she said, contradicting herself, "that I could go back of my own free will or else have the waiver and go back with the law."

In fact, as Scheele kept grilling her, Caril Ann *did* manage to recall that she had been informed she was entitled to an extradition hearing, with a lawyer, if she wanted one.

"And you were also told that if you wanted to, you could waive the extradition proceeding and go back with Nebraska authorities voluntarily, were you not?"

"Yes, sir."

"And didn't you decide yourself that you preferred to go back voluntarily," Scheele asked, "without having the hearing before the governor of Wyoming?"

"I was told," Caril said, "that I could either have it, go back freely and voluntarily, or else I could go back against my will."

Caril made it sound as if she had been promised freedom in Nebraska, but the prosecutor wasn't buying it. "No," he corrected her, "that you would have a hearing before the governor of Wyoming, and he would determine whether you would be sent back; wasn't it explained that way?"

"It was explained the way I said," Caril Ann insisted,

digging in her heels, "that I could either go back on my own or go back with them."

"At any rate," Scheele said, sidestepping the semantic snarl, "did you come back to Nebraska voluntarily and willingly?"

"Yes."

Caril's anger was apparent as Scheele started breaking down her hostage story, pointing out repeated instances when she could easily have run away from Charlie Starkweather. There is no doubt that Caril's defiance hurt her with the jury, playing dumb and making Scheele repeat each question several times to get a simple "yes" or "no."

"Did you and Charles Starkweather go to the 'old lady's' house after you left the Bartletts' on Monday?" Scheele asked.

"I don't exactly remember."

"You stayed out in the car?"

"He told me to stay there and not to leave," Caril said.

"But did you stay in the car?"

"And he said if I did I'd get shot."

"But *did* you stay in the car while he was in the garage?" Scheele asked.

"He told me my family was in the house, and if I tried anything they'd get hurt."

"But do you understand my question: Did you remain in the car during the time that he was back in the garage?"

"Yes, sir."

"And then," Scheele went on, "during that time that you were sitting out there in the car, at that time you thought that's the very place where your family was, didn't you?"

"Yes, sir."

"Did you do anything or make any effort to go to the house while he was out in the garage?"

"I didn't want my family to be hurt, no."

"But *did* you make any effort to do that?"

"No, sir."

At Smallcomb's service station, Caril Ann grudgingly admitted that Charlie was unarmed when he left the car, but

she "couldn't remember" where his gun was—namely, in
the Ford with her, up on the service rack. She initially
denied entering Brickey's Café, then reversed herself and
admitted going in alone, because "he told me to." In fact, if
Caril Ann was believed, her every move from January 22 to
29—including everything she did alone or in the company
of others, with her so-called captor nowhere to be found—
was dictated by Charlie Starkweather. Caril Ann's belliger-
ence was such that her attorney must have felt relief at 4:20
P.M., when court was recessed for the day.

Tuesday would bring no respite from the prosecutor's
questions, though. "When was the first time, Caril," Scheele
asked, "that you knew anything about any gang that Chuck
was supposed to be running around with?"

"The first time I was there," she told him. "Tuesday."

"Nothing had ever been mentioned about that before?"

"Yes, sir," Caril replied, changing her story. "He mentioned it on Sunday, when I broke up with him."

"Had he ever mentioned it before that?"

"Yes, sir." Changing once again, before the jury's eyes.
"He mentioned it a lot of times . . . ever since we'd been
together."

"And yet you continued to go with him?"

"Well, he just mentioned certain things about them,"
Caril said, hedging her bets. "He'd been with them and
joined them, and he was the leader of them."

Monday's pattern repeated itself, Caril balking at each
question, feigning confusion, finally conceding Scheele's
points in a peevish, pouty tone. Reluctantly, she identified
her signature with Charlie's, in the passbook for their joint
bank account. Yes, that was her purse with the snapshots in
it, showing Charlie, his old Ford, his brothers.

"And even after you left the Wards' home," Scheele went
on, "while you were on the way to Wyoming, did you tell
Chuck Starkweather that you loved him?"

"Yes, I did," Caril said. "I was afraid he was going to kill
me."

"And did you kiss him?"

"No, sir," Caril replied.

"You never did that?"

"No, sir; he kissed me."

"He kissed *you?"*

"Yes, sir."

"I believe that's all," Scheele said, leaving the jurors with a bad taste in their mouths.

A few rebuttal witnesses were called—Dr. Edwin Coats, insisting that Charlie was disturbed, but not insane; Wyoming prosecutor William Dixon confirming that he had explained the extradition procedure to Caril in detail—before the state rested its case. It was five minutes to noon when Judge Spencer recessed for the day.

McArthur had first shot at closing arguments on Wednesday the nineteenth, repeating his assertion from day one that Caril's many attempts to warn police and members of her family about Charles Starkweather had been ignored or sadly misinterpreted. Whatever she had done—from buying food to looting Robert Jensen's wallet to pointing loaded guns at other victims in the murder spree—she had been following Starkweather's orders. Each move she made, from staring at Juanita Bell to passing Charles a second gun so he could finish off Merle Collison, should be interpreted to Caril Ann's benefit. As for the vanished note, she had not passed it on or run away from Charles, much less used any one of several guns they carried to disarm or kill her captor, since she feared that Charlie's nonexistent gang would harm her vanished relatives. McArthur challenged jurors to select one instance when Caril Ann could have escaped from Starkweather, much less saved any of his victims from untimely death.

It would be Elmer Scheele who took that challenge, though. In his reply to the defense remarks, he would not list each time that Charlie left Caril Ann alone, unsupervised, frequently armed. The jurors would remember those occasions, Scheele declared, and only the most obvious example should suffice to prove his point. On January 25, two armed policemen, trained for handling violent criminals and helping those in danger, had turned up on Caril Ann's doorstep. Charlie, by her own admission under oath, had been asleep when they arrived, but Caril had gone to wake him up and warn him that the cops were there. Then, while he huddled in the bedroom, out of earshot, Caril had missed another chance to whisper a request for help, lied to protect him, sent the two patrolmen on their way.

It was unprecedented, Scheele acknowledged, to convict an eighth-grade girl of murder one, but he did not request a death sentence, despite the fact that Caril's age was irrelevant.

"Even fourteen-year-old girls," he told the court, "must realize they cannot go on eight-day murder sprees. We have leaned over backward to give this girl a fair trial. Now, ladies and gentlemen, the time has come when she must face the consequences of her conduct. This fourteen-year-old girl is guilty of first-degree murder as charged. We must convince persons of all ages they will be caught, tried, and punished if they break the law. I ask you to bring back the verdict of guilty of first-degree murder for the robbery-slaying of Robert Jensen."

McArthur, as Caril Ann's defender, had the last word coming, and he took his time. Caril was a scapegoat, he insisted, bearing the weight of community anger inspired by police negligence in the Starkweather case. Without that public outrage, building since the unsolved Colvert murder in December 1957, reasonable men and women would immediately see that Caril was innocent, a helpless child who had been "putty in Starkweather's hands." The prosecutor's office had deceived Caril, tricked her into waiving extradition in Wyoming, into making statements that described activities without investigating motives. Scheele and company had cashed in on her innocence and used it as a weapon, said McArthur, while they built their case around the testimony of "a madman." Even Charlie Starkweather, vindictive and deranged, placed Caril 150 feet away from

Robert Jensen when the fatal shots were fired. Caril Ann was innocent, McArthur said, and should be freed to join surviving members of her shattered family.

As in Starkweather's case, Judge Spencer sent the jurors home that night with a reminder that they would begin deliberations in the morning, and that they would be sequestered until they had reached a verdict.

Next morning, Spencer took the best part of an hour to instruct the jury. Verdicts were required on two distinct and separate charges: first-degree murder and murder perpetrated during the commission of a robbery. Caril Ann could be convicted or acquitted on either charge, and on the first count, jurors also had an option of convicting her for second-degree murder—again, without premeditation. Judge Spencer reminded the panel that Caril Ann was "not on trial for failing to run away from Starkweather, for failing to report such crimes as he may have committed, or for failing to prevent such crimes." Such negligence on her part, willful or otherwise, would be "relevant only for the purpose of determining the state of her mind at the time Starkweather killed Jensen."

With a nod to the defense, Judge Spencer also cautioned jurors that Caril Ann should be acquitted on both counts if they determined that she had accompanied Charlie under duress, since mere presence at a murder scene does not translate to culpability. As for Starkweather himself, Spencer went on, "Extreme care and caution should be used in weighing his testimony. You will scrutinize it closely in the light of all the other evidence in the case and you will give it such weight as you may think it is entitled to have, keeping in mind the credibility of such a witness."

It was the best McArthur and Caril Ann could hope for, under the circumstances, as the jury retired to deliberate at 10:01 A.M. Eleven hours and forty minutes later, when the panel retired to the Lincoln Hotel, there was still no verdict in sight.

So far, deliberations had been rocky. Jurors had attacked

the problem backward, considering potential sentences before they argued guilt or innocence, and finally agreed that Caril should go to jail for life, instead of to death row, if they decided she was guilty. She could thank her sex and tender years for that, but otherwise, the jurors were not much impressed with Caril's performance on the witness stand. The terse replies, her "snippy" attitude, and obvious evasions under cross-examination, stripped away whatever sympathy the panel may have felt for her predicament. Aside from anger at the state, indeed, Caril's only demonstration of emotion in the trial had been apparent fear when Charlie took the stand, but it was difficult to judge if she was frightened of his trigger finger or his tongue.

It took the jury two more hours on Friday morning to decide, convicting Caril Ann on the second count and recommending life imprisonment. Announcement of the verdict cracked her cold mask for the first time since the trial began.

"No!" she cried out, as sentence was pronounced. "I'd rather be executed!" Caril's attorneys tried to calm her, but her voice could still be heard above the babble in the court. "Someday," she said, "they're going to find out they made a mistake."

Perhaps, but no one thought so at the time. Caril Ann was on her way to the Nebraska Center for Women at York, some fifty miles due west of Lincoln. She had passed it once before, when she was on the run with Charlie, and had marked it on his road map, killing time.

19

A Handful of Sand

The rest was anticlimax. On November 29, McArthur sought a new trial for Caril Ann, alleging seventy-one separate errors in the original proceeding. Worst of all, he said, one of the jurors—H. A. Walenta—had made a one-dollar bet on whether Caril would get the chair because of public outrage in the case.

Scheele and McArthur stood before Judge Spencer on Saturday, December 13, to argue the merits of McArthur's complaints. The prosecutor called Walenta's bet—which had been made two days before the trial began—"a most unfortunate occurrence," but denied that it had played a role in Caril's conviction. "I would have joined Mr. McArthur in a motion for a new trial," Scheele told Spencer, "if the jury had voted the death penalty."

Caril Ann was present one week later, when the judge aired his decision. Betting on the final sentence in a case, he said, "was reprehensible and cannot be condoned. But the question is whether or not Caril received a fair trial." In fact, Spencer declared, juror Walenta had been questioned fully by both sides, and the defense had not rejected him for cause. There was no evidence that his one-dollar bet, however ill-advised, had influenced the jury's vote in any way. Accordingly, the motion for a new trial was denied.

Appeals were underway for both defendants, one set of lawyers hoping to win Caril Ann's freedom, the other swimming upstream in an effort to save Charlie's life. His first execution date had already passed, pending a decision on Clem Gaughan's motion for a new trial, and when that was denied, Charlie's case went to the state supreme court. There, on December 19, his death sentence was affirmed, with a new execution date set for March 27, 1959. Seven weeks later, on February 6, the same court refused to suspend Caril Ann's sentence of "natural life."

Charlie's next logical step would have been an appeal to the federal courts, a move that cost about $10,000 in those bygone days, and since his family did not have the cash to spare, Starkweather came up with another plan. He wrote a letter to Judge Spencer, stating that he felt attorneys Matschullat and Gaughan had improperly presented his defense. He was dispensing with their services, and would proceed with any further legal action on his own.

The court agreed.

Starkweather's second letter went to the Nebraska Board of Pardons. Created back in 1920, consisting of the governor, secretary of state, and the state attorney general, the board had commuted only four death sentences in almost sixty years. The *good* news was that only nine condemned defendants had applied for clemency in all that time, which, on the surface anyway, gave Starkweather the next thing to a fifty-fifty chance.

In fact, his letter won him a reprieve. The board stayed Charlie's execution and announced that he would be allowed to plead his case at a public hearing on Tuesday, April 21.

While Charlie waited, he was far from lonely. There were visits from his mother, prison chaplain Robert Klein,

Deputy Warden John Greenholtz, James Reinhardt, and Marjorie Marlette, from the *Lincoln Journal*. There was no death row, per se, at the Nebraska penitentiary, so Charlie kept his eight-by-twelve-foot private quarters in the prison hospital. There was a TV in the corridor, and his requests for writing implements or art supplies were usually approved.

From Charlie's window, he occasionally spotted groups of visitors on guided tours of the prison, and his ego told him they were there for *him*. He asked one guard why none of those who came to call were ever shown his cell, and Charlie seemed depressed when he was told the tours had been going on for years.

Aside from legal business, Charlie's prison letters went to members of his family. His brother Greg, then eight years old, was told to read the Bible and "be nice to mom and dad." A letter to his parents, touched up by the *Journal* prior to publication, read in part:

> Holding on to my life is like trying to hold a handful of sand. If death is still inevitable, God will triumph. Man may take my life, but my soul belongs to Him.
>
> All my hopes now are of staying alive and repenting for the wrongs I have committed. Killing is a terrible sin against God and man. I hope that someday killing and the taking of human life, even in war, will only be a terrible memory.

He was willing to keep that memory fresh, however, by writing his autobiography. In fact, aside from a vague wish "to please his mother," writing was the only reason Charlie ever gave James Reinhardt for his efforts to avoid the chair. If he were only given half a chance, Starkweather thought that he could "get along fine in the prison," and that "murderers, especially, would like me." His religious conversion, meanwhile, was haphazard at best. Charlie maintained that "Jesus had made me sorry that I killed them people," but his remorse was always tempered with an understanding that "If they'd a done what I tolded them, I wouldn't a killed them."

His approach to writing was equally erratic, reflecting Charlie's personality and poor grasp of the English language. Counting on an audience of millions, he could barely frame a sentence, and his spelling was enough to leave a copy editor in tears, wild flights of melodrama strung together with clichés, sprawling over some two-hundred pages. It was clearly good business, rather than profound writing, which enabled Marjorie Marlette to sell part of Charlie's manuscript to *Parade* magazine for $1,000. The piece was published on March 15, with Marlette later complaining that it was "edited to the point it became flat."

Why did Charlie write? He claimed that it was done "so others won't make the same mistake," but James Reinhardt saw ego at work, Starkweather laboring to guarantee his place in history. Marjorie Marlette, meanwhile, had a different take. "Like many offenders," she later told reporter William Allen, "Charlie saw his book as a way of atoning, of making something good come out of the wrongs he had committed." She also questioned Reinhardt's personality assessments of the inmate, telling Allen, "I always felt that Charlie was experiencing a remorse so deep and hopeless that he felt he might as well go along with Reinhardt's perceptions of him as not." In her eyes, Starkweather "was reacting to leads the criminologist gave him, rather than expressing his own feelings."

Guy Starkweather, meanwhile, was showing symptoms of addiction to publicity familiar from our own era of "trash TV" and supermarket tabloids. When he came to visit Charlie, Guy would make time, afterward, to hang around and introduce himself to other visitors, making sure they understood that he was "Charlie Starkweather's father." Once, he asked permission to get Charlie's signature on little strips of paper, which he planned to sell; another time, he wanted locks of Charlie's hair, for the same purpose. Each time, John Greenholtz told him that the money-making schemes were inappropriate.

Governor Ralph Brooks was sidelined with a bout of influenza on April 21, but Charlie still got to plead his case before Secretary of State Frank Marsh and Attorney General C. S. Beck. The public hearing was conducted in a conference room at the state prison, with Mayor Sterling Glover from Bennett leading a delegation of twenty angry residents to oppose Charlie's plea for leniency, supported by attorney Edwin C. Perry, from Lincoln. Days earlier, a town meeting in Bennett had produced an anti-clemency petition bearing some 150 signatures, which was presented to the two-man pardon's board.

Guy and Helen Starkweather were also standing by, as Charlie made his plea for life imprisonment. He had repented for his crimes, the killer said, and he would bring his victims back to life if that were possible. Before the rampage, he was not concerned with human life, but that had changed, "mostly by reading the Bible." As for his lawyers, Charlie said, "I honestly believe if I was represented right, I would've gotten life." He didn't trust attorneys now, but thought the two board members would be "honest and open-minded."

Frank Marsh asked Charlie if he had enjoyed the international publicity his crime spree had received, but Charlie wasn't falling into *that* trap.

"Anybody that wants it can have it," he replied.

Beck, for his part, was more interested in finding out if Charlie's mental state had changed since his arrest.

The redhead frowned. "You mean, am I going nuts or something?" he asked.

"Yes," Beck replied.

Starkweather scowled and answered, "No."

Was there anything else, Beck asked, that he would like to say?

Charlie considered it, but let it go with the remark that there were indeed "some things I'd like to say, but I just can't."

Starkweather's parents also had a chance to testify, Helen agreeing with her son that he had not been represented properly at trial. Attorneys Matschullat and Gaughan, she maintained, kept asking her to testify that Charlie was "peculiar," in support of their insanity defense. "From the beginning," Helen testified, "they seemed to be against us." Guy, for his part, thought that Charlie should be treated just like Caril Ann. "There also was another party in on this spree," he reminded the board, "and if the other party is given life, why shouldn't he be given life?"

Charlie's last witness was Ferris Fitzpatrick, an opponent of capital punishment who had flown in from Michigan to plead for Charlie's life. Beck cut him off when he digressed from Charlie's case and started to discuss the death penalty in general terms.

Ed Perry wrapped it up for the opposition, reminding the board of Charlie's heinous crimes, reporting that the citizens of Bennett found his death sentence "eminently correct." If Charlie was allowed to live, he said, there was the threat of "possible escape and continuation of further murders due to his established and clear disregard for human lives." Summing up, Perry declared, "Nothing has been brought to light to indicate that Charles Starkweather can ever become a useful or safe citizen. If there was ever a situation in which capital punishment was justified, this is certainly such a situation."

Five witnesses had been disposed of in forty-four minutes, and the board members needed only five more minutes to reach their decision, behind closed doors. At 10:50 A.M., administrative assistant Loretta Walker returned with the verdict: Charlie's petition for clemency was denied, May 22 fixed as his new execution date.

Following the announcement, prison officers escorted

Mrs. Walker to the hospital, where she broke the news to Starkweather.

"I half-expected it," he said, and turned away.

Another new-trial motion brought Caril back to Lincoln in early May. Caril testified that shortly after she was brought back from Wyoming, someone at the mental hospital—she couldn't quite remember who—had told her Charlie was asking to see her. Caril had told the person she was "scared to death and didn't want to see him." Driving home the point, she sent Charlie a note.

> Chuck. I don't want to sea you. Because I might do something I would be sorry for later on.
>   Caril Fugate

Sheriff Karnopp was the only other witness in the brief proceeding, testifying that he had visited Caril in response to Charlie's repeated pleas for a meeting, and that he had asked for her to write the note.

"She said that she didn't want to see him," Karnopp told the court, "and I asked her if she wouldn't write that, so that I could take it and show it to Chuck, so that he wouldn't think that I was lying to him if I came back and said she said no."

John McArthur seemed to smell a conspiracy behind the note. "Mr. Karnopp," he asked, "were you anxious to curry the favor of Charles Starkweather?"

"Not particularly," Karnopp answered. "No, sir."

"What was your reason for going to so much trouble at his request?" McArthur asked.

"Well, you know," the sheriff said, "I kind of believe in treating them the way I like to be treated, even though they are criminals."

"Well," McArthur pressed on, "Charles had asked repeatedly to see Caril Ann, had he not?"

"He had," Karnopp agreed.

"And you brought him a note from Caril Ann saying that she didn't want to see him, didn't you?"

"That's right."

"You knew, of course," McArthur said, "that the effect of that would be to turn Charles Starkweather against her, did you not?"

"I never gave that any thought, no, sir. I don't know that it did."

"As I understand it," the attorney said, "Mr. Starkweather signed his statement after you had shown him the note, Exhibit Sixteen?"

"Yes, it was after that," said Karnopp.

"Then, upon reading the note from Caril Fugate that she didn't want to see him, he signed this statement which incriminated her. Is that the way it worked?"

"Well," Karnopp said, "he signed the statement."

"Did he refuse to sign such a statement until you proved to him that Caril Ann didn't want to have anything to do with him?"

"That wasn't mentioned at all," the sheriff said. "No, sir."

"How did it happen," McArthur demanded, "that he read the note first and signed the statement afterward?"

"Because," Karnopp said, "I had the note and I wanted him to see it so he wouldn't think that I had lied to him about her wanting to see him."

"Why hadn't he signed the statement *before* you showed him the note?" McArthur asked. "Do you know that?"

"I don't believe it was ready."

On redirect, Elmer Scheele led Karnopp through a chronology of the mechanics surrounding Charlie's statement, recorded on a Saturday, transcribed and typed for his review on Sunday afternoon.

"And upon receiving the completed written— typewritten statement, unsigned," Scheele said, "then is when you and I returned to the penitentiary and that's when you delivered the note to Starkweather?"

"That's right," Karnopp said.

"And then, we commenced with the reading of the statement, he making corrections and signing each volume as it was read?"

"That's correct."

"And the obtaining of this note had no connection whatsoever with the obtaining of this statement?"

"Not any whatsoever," Karnopp agreed.

"As a matter of fact," Scheele went on, "you checked with me before making the visit to the state hospital?"

"I did, yes, sir."

"And it was done with my knowledge and consent?"

"It was."

"That's all."

McArthur rose on recross, making one last attempt to sketch a dire conspiracy against his client. "You say that you talked to Mr. Scheele before going to see Caril Ann about this note?" he asked.

"I did, sir," Karnopp answered.

"Did you contact Caril Ann's attorney before doing that?"

"No, sir."

"You did not?"

"No, sir."

"Did you give Caril Ann a copy of that note?"

"A copy of it?" Karnopp seemed confused.

"Yes."

"No, I didn't. There was no copy," Karnopp said, "just the original."

Judge Spencer chose that moment to ask Scheele, "Did Caril Ann have an attorney at that time?"

"No," McArthur answered.

"I don't believe she had an attorney at that time," Karnopp agreed. "That was the day after she was brought back from Wyoming."

"Wasn't that," McArthur said, "after the time that Bill Blue had been out there a couple of times and interviewed her at the state hospital?"

"No," Karnopp said. "I don't believe that he had at that time. I think Mr. Blue came into the picture on Monday."

"On the Monday following?"

"That's right."

"And have you made other trips and done other favors for Mr. Starkweather," McArthur asked, "besides getting this letter from Caril Ann?"

Scheele objected to McArthur's turn of phrase, but he was overruled. "You may answer," the judge told Sheriff Karnopp.

"That's the only request he ever made of me."

"And this is the only thing of this type that you have done for him?"

"Yes, sir."

"And in reality," McArthur said, "wasn't that done for the use of the state in the prosecution of Caril Fugate?"

"I told you what I did it for," the sheriff replied, "and it's in the record."

"Very well," McArthur said, clearly skeptical. "That's all, thank you."

Judge Spencer thought about the problem for a while, then called Caril back to court on May 19. The motion for a new trial was denied, McArthur telling newsmen that he planned to take it up with the state supreme court.

Before he had that chance, though, Caril would follow Charlie's example by taking matters into her own hands. Two days after Judge Spencer's ruling, on May 21, she fired off a telegram to the White House, addressed to President Dwight Eisenhower.

I AM NOW FIFTEEN YEARS OLD STOP ABOUT A YEAR AND ONE HALF AGO ON A DAY WHEN I WAS IN PUBLIC SCHOOL, NINETEEN YEAR OLD STARK-WEATHER WHOM I HAD TOLD SEVERAL DAYS BEFORE IN FRONT OF MY MOTHER NEVER TO SEE ME AGAIN WENT INTO MY HOME AND KILLED MY TWO YEAR OLD BABY SISTER, MOTHER AND STEPFATHER STOP STARKWEATHER FIRST CONFESSED I HAD NOTHING

TO DO WITH HIS MURDERS WHICH IS TRUE STOP
LATER HE CHANGED HIS STORY AND SAID I HELPED
HIM DO HIS MURDERS WHICH IS NOT TRUE STOP HE
FORCED ME TO GO WITH HIM AGAINST MY WILL
STARKWEATHER WILL BE EXECUTED TOMORROW
STOP I HAVE BEEN DENIED BY GOVERNOR BROOKS A
REQUEST TO SEE HIM AND SEE IF HE WILL TELL THE
TRUTH IN FRONT OF A MINISTER OR SOME ONE ELSE
WHO WOULD BE FAIR BEFORE HE IS EXECUTED STOP I
KNOW OF NO ONE ELSE TO TURN TO BECAUSE ALL OF
MY FAMILY I WAS LIVING WITH HE KILLED STOP I
KNOW YOU ARE VERY BUSY BUT PLEASE HELP ME IN
ANY WAY YOU CAN THANK YOU

CARIL ANN FUGATE

Eisenhower's special counsel, David W. Kendall, made some phone calls and replied to Caril as best he could. "The Starkweather case is entirely a state matter," he wrote. "The President has no authority in any way to comply with your request."

The day before Caril's telegram to Eisenhower, Charlie suffered another setback. On May 20, Governor Brooks denied a stay of execution requested on Caril Ann's behalf, while her lawyers continued their efforts to make Charlie "tell the truth." Starkweather was in line to die at 6:00 A.M. on Friday the twenty-second, just two days down the road.

The night before his scheduled send-off, Charlie gorged himself on steak, french fries and corn, buttered toast, a salad topped with mayonnaise, and apple pie à la mode, washed down with coffee and two bottles of Coca-Cola. A prison barber shaved the crown of Charlie's head and a six-inch strip on one calf, to make a decent ground for the electrodes. No one will ever know what Charlie dreamed that night, but he was dozing fitfully at 4:22 A.M., when a member of the warden's staff arrived to wake him up.

It was a stay of execution, granted by federal district judge

Richard Robinson, in Omaha. Guy Starkweather had made a call, belatedly, to ask if Charlie could pursue appeals of his conviction in the federal courts. His son was being rushed to death without a lawyer, Guy complained, omitting the fact that Charlie had fired his counsel in defiance of the trial court's best advice. Judge Robinson was interested enough to put the execution on hold, but it was merely a breather, nothing more.

At that, it was too much for some. Syndicated columnist Robert Ruark spoke for thousands of furious Nebraskans, as he raged at the delay in print.

> Something—I use the word advisedly—named Charles Starkweather has been granted a stay of execution for a fit of whimsy in which he managed to kill by gun and knife exactly 11 persons. You cannot blame the little monster's father for trying everything to save the little monster with the street corner haircut and the bed-room-eyes-cum-droopy-cigaret. . . . Anything with a face like Starkweather's literally belongs in a bottle in a medical museum. But creep that he is, I claim that undue cruelty in the name of law has been administered to Charles Starkweather. . . . An eleventh-hour reprieve, which gives him two more weeks of torment, is not nice even for a mad dog.

Three more attorneys were appointed to perfect the lame appeal, but they were being sent to battle without weapons. Charlie's first defense team had done everything it could to save his life, despite obstructionism from their client and his family. The fact that he had fired them for their trouble, to pursue some half-baked mission of his own, was not enough to qualify for a new trial or commutation of the death sentence. A three-judge panel spurned the motion and set Charlie's final execution date for Friday, June 12.

It looked like curtains, but the drama wasn't over yet.

Attorney James J. Laughlin, out of Washington, D.C., approached Guy Starkweather and offered to prepare a writ of habeas corpus, arguing that Charlie was illegally confined. The flamboyant sixty-one-year-old, who had defended "Axis Sally" at her 1949 sedition trial, announced that he was taking Charlie's case free of charge, in the interest of justice. He had plans, said Laughlin, that would stall the redhead's date with death for years.

At first, it seemed that he was onto something. In Washington, on June 10, U.S. Supreme Court Justice Charles Evans Whittaker granted another stay of execution, giving Laughlin one week to submit a petition for full review by the court. Starkweather's lawyer made the deadline, claiming once again that Charlie had been denied effective counsel before his trial, adding the complaint that inflammatory evidence of ten irrelevant murders had been wrongfully admitted by Judge Spencer in the Jensen case.

But it was all in vain.

On Monday, June 22, the Supreme Court issued a routine order refusing to review Starkweather's case. The vote was unanimous, and Justice Whittaker followed up a day later by denying Laughlin's request for another stay of execution.

There would be no more delays.

With less than two days left to live, Charlie submitted to a final interview of sorts. The questions were generic, and his written answers were predictable clichés, but they deserve inclusion here, if only as a sample of Starkweather's evolution from inarticulate triggerman to jailhouse philosopher.

Q: What is the most important message you want to tell people in the United States at this time in the way of advice to other kids after your experience?

A: Any advice to the young people today is to go to school, and attend Sunday school, and church every Sunday. Go to church and receive the Lord Jesus Christ as your own personal Savior. Our God is a kind God, he'll forgive, and accept you as one of his even if your heart is black and heavy with sin. With God there be peace within your soul, and in Heaven eternal life will be in your hands through all eternity. You can feed the mind with knowledge, and the body with food, but don't forget the soul; feed it with the love and the words of the Lord. So I advise young and old to attend their church of God and worship the Lord Jesus Christ, and pray that we can maintain the Christian faith that holds together the trust, the truth, the love, and the righteousness of the American people, and the people of the world. . . .

Public repentance aside, Charlie was still being Charlie on June 24, his last full day of life. That morning, Warner Smith, a member of the Lions Club from Beatrice, Nebraska, asked Charlie if he would donate his eyes to the club's eye bank. It seemed a curious request, considering his well-known vision problems, and Starkweather was fresh out of Christian charity.

"Why should I?" he replied. "Nobody ever gave me anything. Why should I do anything for anyone else?"

As his appointment with the Reaper drew inexorably nearer, Charlie seemed to lose some of his edge. At one point, he told Mike Shimerda, one of the rare guards who had befriended him, "Don't worry about me, Mike. I died the last time. They can't kill me again." A short time later, though, in conversation with his mother, he was weakening. "I don't feel right," Starkweather said. "I was okay the last time. I was ready. But now I'm all mixed up."

Mixed up or not, Guy and Helen knew their boy was running out of time. That afternoon, they filed another petition at the local courthouse, over Charlie's signature, seeking a new trial on grounds that (a) Investigator Harold Robinson had "intimidated witnesses and procured false evidence" during his review of the manhunt; (b) Charlie claimed Nebraska had somehow prevented him from fighting extradition from Wyoming; (c) "false testimony" had been given at his trial; (d) Charlie had been "misled into signing conflicting and contradictory statements; (e) the death sentence was a "result of great pressure"; and (f) Caril Fugate had been wrongfully advised by prosecutors not to testify at Charlie's trial, thus robbing Charlie's lawyers of a chance to question her.

The desperate petition was rejected, with an order for the execution to proceed at midnight.

As darkness fell outside the prison, teenagers from Lincoln and surrounding towns began parading past the prison, some of them defiantly drinking beer, while others stuck to Coke or Pepsi, music blaring from their radios. Some of the boys with cars brought girls along to watch the show; those who arrived on foot were mostly lone wolves, sometimes straggling in by twos or threes. A team of prison guards was stationed on the street outside, to keep them moving, but it didn't seem to do much good, a group of fifty-odd observers sticking to the death watch, circling, always coming back. It was impossible to tell if they were enemies or fans of Charlie's, but they were determined to remain and see it through.

Inside, Starkweather's family said good-bye to him at half past ten and left him with the prison chaplain. Charlie had been painting through the afternoon, with oils provided by Deputy Warden Greenholtz, working on a battle scene. The painting was unfinished when he gave up on it, faceless soldiers standing on the field of death. Charlie reserved his final moments for the chaplain, clinging to a plastic cross that Klein had given him to carry on his last walk, to the chair.

At 11:30 P.M., seventy-five-year-old Dr. B. A. Finkle, standing by to pronounce Charlie dead, himself collapsed and died of heart failure outside the warden's office. The ambulance reserved for Charlie carried him away, while urgent phone calls brought another vehicle and a replacement—Dr. P. E. Getscher—to the penitentiary. It was a glitch, but there would be no postponements.

Charlie got another visit from the now familiar prison

barber, touching up the bald spots on his crown and calf. He seemed relaxed, all things considered, and he did not struggle when the escort team arrived at five minutes to midnight. Chaplain Klein was with him as he left his cell, intoning Charlie's favorite Bible text. It was the twenty-third psalm.

The Lord is my shepherd . . .

Nebraska's death chamber was in the basement, not unlike The Cave where Bob Jensen and Carol King had died, except that it was clean and brightly lit, with thirty-five witnesses lined up to watch Charlie die. State law permitted the condemned to choose three witnesses, but Charlie had declined. The thirty-five, including twenty newsmen, had been chosen from a list of more than sixty applicants who had requested ringside seats.

Yea, though I walk through the valley of the shadow of death . . .

The crowd of teenagers outside the penitentiary was growing, mostly stationary now, and waiting for the lights to dim. Police were summoned to disperse them, just in case.

I will fear no evil . . .

Charlie dredged up a smile for the audience as he entered the chamber, offering no resistance as he was marched to the chair. A blue curtain was drawn around the chair itself, as if to spare the witnesses who were about to watch him fry from seeing Charlie buckled down. A partial leather mask secured the main electrode to his scalp, but it did not prevent his speaking as the straps were fastened to his chest and arms.

"They're too loose," he complained. "Can you make them a little tighter?"

When the adjustment had been made, the curtain was drawn back to give the witnesses an unobstructed view. They could not see the executioner—an electrician brought in from another state, earning two hundred dollars plus expenses for his work that night—but Charlie was the star, in any case. Strapped down, wearing the headpiece that resembled an old-fashioned football helmet, he might have made a comic figure under different circumstances.

Deputy Warden Greenholtz stepped forward, eyes brimming with tears over the death of Dr. Finkle, and asked if Charlie had any last words for the crowd. Starkweather seemed to think about it for a moment, finally shaking his head in an emphatic negative.

Off-stage, the executioner was waiting for his signal. When it came, he threw the switch three times, each closure of the circuit slamming 2,200 volts through Charlie's brain and body. When the current struck, he lurched against the leather straps that held him, body twitching, cooking from the inside out.

Dr. Getscher pronounced Charlie dead at 12:04 A.M., and prison guards came in to lead the witnesses away. Starkweather's parents heard the news on radio, at Helen's mother's house.

Charlie was twenty years and two months old.

Epilogue

"Only My Story Will Live"

Starkweather's execution scuttled any fleeting hope that he would change his tune again, belatedly, and somehow rise to Caril Ann's defense. She was inside for the duration, and she spent her first eight months as inmate number 1427 in virtual solitary confinement, sheltered by the administration because of her age and notoriety. The potent combination made her vulnerable, both to reputation seekers and the same-sex predators who may be found in every lockup on the planet.

Caril Ann was not entirely cell-bound, though. She was released to shower (solo) or visit the warden's office from time to time, and chapel was mandatory for all inmates. In Caril's case, so was school, and she applied herself with unaccustomed diligence, now that her options were reduced to zero. In the joint, she finished high school, learned to type, and finally surprised her keepers by becoming an accomplished public speaker. Over time, the leash would be played out enough for her to speak at public gatherings, discussing prison topics under the umbrella of a program known as "Operation Outlet." And she never lost sight of her goal, which was to win her freedom back.

But to accomplish that, she would need dedicated friends.

One such was James McArthur, son of Caril's defense attorney. He had watched her trial and shared his father's firm belief in Caril Ann's innocence. In 1963, he entered law school, following his father's footsteps. One of his professors, Dale Broeder, had been briefly involved with the case in its early days, before Caril Ann was cleared for trial as an adult, and he enjoyed discussing the fine points with young McArthur, outside class.

In June of 1964, McArthur and son were encouraged by the U.S. Supreme Court's ruling in the case of *Escobedo v. Illinois.* A chronic felon, Danny Escobedo, had confessed his latest crime before a formal charge was filed, and was convicted on the basis of his statement. The significance to Caril Ann's case: Detectives had ignored his plea for an attorney until they were finished grilling him and had the signed confession in their hands. In Washington, the high court voided his conviction on grounds that the constitutional right to counsel applied from the moment of arrest, not formal accusation of a crime.

Caril Ann turned twenty-one a month after *Escobedo* was decided, her attorneys celebrating the occasion with a petition for habeas corpus filed with the federal district court. Judge Robert Van Pelt agreed with McArthur and Merril Reller that *Escobedo* should apply retroactively to Caril Ann's case, but the state was entitled to appeal, and Nebraska legislators were not idle in the meantime. A new law, dubbed the Post-Conviction Act, required inmates to exhaust all legal remedies at the state level, before carrying appeals to the federal court system. The law had not existed when McArthur and Reller filed their federal petition, but it stopped them in their tracks.

Back to square one.

In July 1965, McArthur filed a "show cause" motion, asking the state to explain why Caril should not be freed on bail. The *Escobedo* ruling entitled her to a new trial, in his opinion, and he accused the state of deliberately stalling, denying his client due process. When Lancaster County's attorney responded in August, his tone was dismissive. Caril Ann was ineligible for bail, he argued, since McArthur's authority for a new-trial petition was "too vague and indefinite" to rate a hearing.

That December, John McArthur saw two more petitions for a new trial rejected at the county level. Five days before Christmas, he announced his intent to seek relief from the state supreme court, but further stumbling blocks had been thrown in his way. A supplemental ruling in the *Escobedo* case eliminated retroactive applications, but Nebraska's state supreme court held the door of hope ajar for Caril, remanding her case to Lancaster County for an evidentiary hearing "upon evidence other than that which appears in the record."

On Monday, February 27, 1967, Caril was driven back to Lincoln for her hearing, focused chiefly on the voluntary nature of the statements she had made before her trial. Judge William Hastings was in charge of the proceedings, which consumed four days. Caril Ann was first to testify, alleging (for the first time on the public record) that she had observed shock treatments while she was confined at the state hospital, and had believed that she was "next in line" if she did not cooperate by talking to her prosecutors. On cross-examination, County Attorney Paul Douglas attacked Caril's shaky credibility, effectively demolishing her latest bid for sympathy.

"You said you saw shock treatments?" he inquired.

"Yes," Caril replied.

"When was the first time?"

"I don't remember."

"Could it have been a month before you saw the first one?"

"I don't remember how long it was," Caril insisted.

"Could it have been five days?"

"All the days ran together."

"Was it in the first ten days? Could it have been thirty days?"

"I didn't count the days!" she snapped at him. "I don't know how many days passed."

Another angle of attack. Had anybody threatened Caril before she gave her statements to Dale Fahrnbruch?

"An out and outright threat, no," she conceded.

What about promises of leniency?

Caril told the court that she "was under the impression I could leave" if she testified against Charlie in court.

"Who left you with that impression?" Douglas asked.

"It was just an impression."

State witnesses included Dale Fahrnbruch (now in private practice), stenographer Audrey Wheeler, District Judge Herbert Ronin, Elmer Scheele (himself a county judge, by then), and Harry Spencer (who had since advanced to a seat on the state supreme court). All five agreed that Caril Ann's civil rights had not been violated or abridged in any way. Judge Hastings saw it their way, and his ruling of March 2 held that Caril was not entitled to relief under the Post-Conviction Act.

A day later, John McArthur filed the obligatory motion to vacate that ruling and order a new trial. Judge Hastings rejected the motion on March 8, and McArthur bounced back on the ninth with notice of intent to appeal before the state supreme court. It had taken him nearly three years, but he was edging back into position for a federal appeal.

It was December 1967 before the Nebraska Supreme Court heard Caril Ann's appeal on the new-trial motion, and the district court's decision was affirmed. Four days later, the defense team filed its second petition for habeas corpus in federal district court, but there would be no repetition of the easy victory with Judge Van Pelt from 1964. This time around, both federal judges in Nebraska saw fit to disqualify themselves, and it was January 1970 before Judge Elmo Hunter was imported from Missouri to hear Caril's case. A new evidentiary hearing was scheduled for February 6, and while Caril Ann felt confident in the wake of her testimony, the results were disappointing. Three months later, to the day, her motion for a writ of habeas corpus was denied.

The next rung of the federal ladder was the U.S. Circuit Court of Appeals, where the McArthurs (minus Merril Reller, who had died in August 1968, while on vacation in Australia) argued Caril's case on December 14, 1970. More than a year later, on December 30, 1971, a three-judge panel rejected her plea by a vote of two to one. Caril Ann's defenders countered with a motion for a hearing by the complete nine-man panel, and while the motion was granted, Caril's appeal was once again denied, on February 7, 1972.

Two months later, James McArthur played his final card, applying for review by the Supreme Court of the United States. The early optimism spawned by *Escobedo* had evaporated over eight long years of uphill slogging through the state and federal courts, but there was one thing to be said for Caril Ann's last appeal.

Whichever way it went, the issue would be settled, once and for all.

While she was waiting for that last hand to be dealt and played, Caril Ann was pleasantly distracted by the media. NBC News was preparing a documentary on her life, titled "Growing Up in Prison," with Caril's friend Ninette Beaver in charge of the interviews. That spring, lead cameraman Scott Berner found Caril cheerful, poised, and helpful to a fault. "You'd think she'd been doing it all her life," he told Beaver. "I wish some of our high-priced talent were as easy to work with."

On camera, Caril Ann came off sounding self-assured. "Through counseling," she told the world, "I found out two things. One, I am Caril Fugate, and it doesn't leave a bitter taste in my mouth. For years, it used to. . . . The other one, I found out that I'm a child of God and that no matter what happens, no matter what *happened,* in the sight of God it's over. And I think those two things, side by side, have helped me come a long way."

The hectic memories of Charlie Starkweather would always haunt her, Caril Ann said, but nowadays she tried to keep them locked away "behind a little door," reminding herself that "the past is over and there's nothing I can do." As for the slaughtered victims, "I'm deeply sorry that it happened. There was really no way that I could stop it. He was a madman, and you know, the thing of it is that people don't realize that I lost *my* family, too."

To many viewers in Nebraska, it would seem a lame defense, evoking echoes of the joke about a lad who murdered both his parents, then sought leniency in court because he was an orphan.

To their credit, Beaver and company did not limit their interviews to Caril Ann. Controversial juror H. A. Walenta was captured on film, explaining that Caril's persistent refusal to run away from Charlie Starkweather had doomed her in the jury's eyes. It would require "a miracle," he thought, to overturn the verdict on appeal. Victor Walker, Nebraska's director of prisons, acknowledged that Caril had made "very good progress" at York, avoiding any conflicts with authority since her conviction, taking full advantage of the institution's rehabilitation programs. Governor James Exon was cagey, telling Beaver, "I have not seen a great amount of opposition—nor have I heard of it—to Caril Ann Fugate returning to society when the professionals think she is ready to return."

Of course, there *was* opposition, clearly expressed by Bob Jensen's mother when NBC's cameras got around to recording her side of the story. "The thing that struck me most about [Caril], then and now," she told Beaver, "was her very, very cold eyes—the unfeeling look that she would have."

What about the fourteen years Caril Ann had spent in jail?

"All right," Mrs. Jensen replied, "you've paid a few years.

We'll just forget about it all. It was in the past. But you *can't* forget about it. . . . Bob and Carol are as real to me as if it happened last night or yesterday. I don't think she has paid for what she did. I don't think she can ever pay for what she did. And I think it would be—I don't quite know how to word it—a miscarriage of justice for the ones that were taken for her to be released and have a good life from now on. Their life was taken from them right at the very prime."

The documentary was aired on August 29 and backfired on Caril in an unexpected way, compelling her to drop out of the prison's "Operation Outlet" program. Before the broadcast, she would later say, she thought the audiences she addressed were interested in her message; some, indeed, had never known exactly who she was. But after "Growing Up in Prison," she was a celebrity again, concerned that people came to hear her speak from curiosity about her case, more than the message she was trying to convey.

On October 10, 1972, the U.S. Supreme Court voted eight to one—with Justice William O. Douglas as the lone dissenter—to reject Caril's petition for a writ of certiorari. It was the end of the road for judicial appeals, but Caril Ann had still not exhausted her options.

Her next step was an application for parole, filed with the state parole board. In Nebraska, as most other states, "life" in prison rarely meant *life*, but Caril and her defenders were taking a gamble, approaching the board so soon after her TV appearance and rejection by the nation's highest court. John Greenholtz was the chairman of the board, by then; his two companions on the panel were septuagenarian Harold Smith—formerly a captain with the Nebraska Highway Safety Patrol and a witness at Charlie's trial—and forty-something Edward Rowley, an educational administrator who had worked extensively with juvenile offenders.

It was June 6, 1973, when the three-man board paid a visit to York, interviewing twelve applicants for parole. Caril Ann was last in line to speak, appearing nervous, but she scored enough points with her spotless prison record for the board to grant her a public hearing, scheduled for August 22, at the state prison in Lincoln. The outcome of that hearing would not, however, determine the issue of Caril's freedom. Under Nebraska law, a two-step process was required to put a lifer back in circulation on the street. Before parole could even be considered, the Nebraska Board of Pardons had to commute a "life" sentence to a finite term of years, from which a possible parole date could be calculated. Caril's performance at the Lincoln penitentiary, in August, would determine whether the parole board recommended commutation to the pardons board, in which case she would have to wait for a decision from *that* body to decide her fate. If the parole board turned her down, at least another year would have to pass before she tried again.

On the appointed Wednesday, Caril was transported to Lincoln, to the same institution where Charlie had been put to death. Reporters were waiting well before the hearing's scheduled commencement time, at 8:15 A.M., anticipating fireworks when Nebraska's most notorious female inmate made her bid for freedom. Still, of thirty-seven scheduled witnesses besides Caril Ann, only five had turned up to oppose her release.

Caril's rooting section was led by James McArthur, describing her "positive outlook" and the "affirmative attitude on her part that she was actually looking forward to doing something." The recent documentary aside, McArthur cited Caril's "extremely reluctant" attitude toward publicity, suggesting a desire "to more or less melt back into private life and no longer be a public figure." Above all else, he said, Caril clung to hope.

Nebraska's director of prisons, Victor Walker, was the next to speak in Caril's defense, distinguishing her case from those of most female inmates who "have a tendency in prison to sit back and let the world go by." Caril, on the contrary, had been working overtime to better herself. "In this respect," he said, "if anyone by their behavior and by their cooperation has earned consideration, Caril has." Walker agreed with the suggestion of one board member that Caril was "just as ready now as she'll ever be, and any further incarceration would be more or less useless."

Like Charlie, Caril Ann had been "born again," joining the Church of the Nazarene, and twenty members of the congregation drove from York that morning, led by Rev. William Shipman and his wife, to speak on her behalf. Four other witnesses had never met Caril personally, but they advocated her release on general principles. One such, Ed Neil from Omaha, had grown acquainted with a number of ex-convicts in his work for Goodwill Industries. "After about so long," he told the board, "a person reaches a saturation point of reform. A person can absorb no more, and the only way you can prove rehabilitation is by letting one out."

Charlotte Fox, by contrast, *had* known Caril Ann, but long ago, when both of them were adolescent baby-sitters in the run-down Belmont neighborhood. She had not seen Caril Ann since 1958, but that did not prevent her forming an opinion on the case. "I think she's done enough time," Charlotte told the board, "and she should be able to get out and prove herself, because she has done a lot of good down at York. I saw the TV media they had on her."

"Have you visited her at York?" asked Harold Smith.

"No," Charlotte admitted, "I never have. Never had the chance to visit with her, but I knew her when she was young." Anonymous neighbors in Lincoln, she said, shared the same opinion. "She's been in there long enough."

Robert Mann and his wife had driven all the way from Michigan to testify on Caril's behalf. Greenholtz inquired about their interest in the case, and Mann replied, "Since the television documentary of about a year ago, about Miss Fugate, my wife and I have been concerned as to how the state will hopefully direct her future. From what we gathered, observing the presentation, Miss Fugate's record at York is self-explanatory. . . . I feel personally that Caril Fugate needs the opportunity to prove herself a responsible individual."

Unlike Charlotte Fox, the Manns *had* visited Caril Ann at

York, not once but several times, using Robert's vacations for interstate treks to the prison. They considered Caril a friend and had no doubt that she should be released.

Neither did Bill Gillard, a state prison employee who was also chairman of a group committed to penal reform. Gillard had corresponded with Caril Ann, but they had never met. As with the Manns and Caril's old baby-sitting crony, Gillard's interest in the case had been inspired by the August 1972 documentary. Based upon that sympathetic presentation, Gillard was convinced that Caril deserved another chance.

Some witnesses, however, had been less than charmed by Caril's appearance on TV. The first to speak was Yvonne King, Carol King's sister-in-law, and it was clear from the beginning of her testimony that board chairman Greenholtz was already leaning toward clemency.

"Do you feel, ma'am," he asked "that Caril should not be released?"

"That's right."

"Have you considered the length of time she's served in the institution? The contributions that she has made since she's been incarcerated? Taken into consideration her age when this tragic event occurred?"

"Yes, I've thought about that," the witness replied.

"Her age now?"

"That don't bring Carol King and Bobby Jensen back."

Yvonne made it clear that she believed a jail sentence of "natural life" should mean exactly that: imprisonment until the inmate died in custody. Greenholtz acknowledged the suffering of Caril and Charlie's victims, allowing that Yvonne had "every right to be here" and express her opposition to parole, but he was obviously more concerned by the fact that "Caril has served half her life in the institution."

Wayne King followed his wife to the witness chair, adding his negative vote to the tally, if anyone was truly keeping score.

"We know the grief your family has suffered as a result of

this," Greenholtz said. "Do you think that probably *someday* she should be released?"

"No, I don't," King replied.

"You feel," Ed Rowley interrupted, "she should be incarcerated for the balance of her natural life?"

"I feel," Wayne said, "she was old enough at the time. She knew what she was doing, and no matter what she does now, I don't feel it gives her the right to be able to be out."

It was the same when Carol King's mother took the stand. Mable King Swale believed that the jurors who sentenced Caril Ann to "natural life" knew what they were doing and meant what they said. No matter how John Greenholtz tried to win her over, spelling out the various restrictions of parole, he was unable to convert Carol's mother to the cause of clemency.

"You realize," the chairman said, "she has certain freedoms now, due to the time she's been there. She's a trusty."

"Yes, I know that."

"She gets out into the community," he continued. "She attends church very regularly."

"I do that, too," Mable said. "Regularly. That doesn't make me a Christian, either, entirely."

"Our philosophy," said Greenholtz, giving up and laying his cards on the table, "is that people are sent to institutions *as* punishment, not *for* punishment. It *is* punishment. But you have to realize that punishment should have an end someday in a person's life, otherwise it becomes a slow, expensive, inhumane method of execution. Then, our whole system of corrections becomes useless, pointless. We could fill up our institutions with people who have to serve their maximum terms; then we would have people who would tend to become animalistic. They would lose all sense of hope."

"Well," said Mable, unconvinced, "she didn't give her victims a chance."

Pauline Jensen was next on the hot seat, speaking out on behalf of her murdered son. Greenholtz commiserated with her "tragic loss," but he delayed the reading of her prepared statement to inject another plea for mercy. Caril Ann was "a different person altogether" in the chairman's view, and if paroled, she would "always have a string tied to her; she'll have to be responsible to people." (In fact, as Greenholtz had to know, Nebraska's average lifer on parole was freed of all restrictions after four or five years on the street.) He lamented Caril Ann's early time in solitary, and noted once more that she had earned her diploma in prison, though forced to admit that "with an eighth-grade education it wasn't too hard for her."

The witness wasn't buying it. She had prepared a statement, and she meant to read it to the board members, regardless of their attitude.

"I definitely oppose parole for Caril Fugate," Mrs. Jensen began, "not because I don't believe in rehabilitation or parole, but because I feel the degree of punishment should fit the crime. And, considering the brutal way Caril Fugate and Charles Starkweather murdered the eleven victims, punishment has been very slight. I feel that people who kill someone in the heat of anger should be treated quite differently than those who go on a murder spree for their thrills. I think, considering the magnitude of these horrible crimes, life imprisonment would be neither cruel or inhumane punishment. She could never pay for the horrible things she has done, but she has surely forfeited any right to be part of society in general. It seems more compassion is always dealt to the criminal, and the victims and their loved ones aren't really considered. Nor is society in general. I would question whether a person who could watch such crimes—let alone participate in them—could ever really be rehabilitated so they would be safe to be returned to society. Even if this could be accomplished, she was sentenced to serve all of her natural life in prison by a jury trial and a fine judge, now deceased, and I sincerely feel they meant for her sentence to be carried out and upheld as determined by the courts. And life imprisonment should mean just that—life imprisonment."

Turning to the famous TV presentation, Mrs. Jensen said,

"I could hardly understand the way Caril Fugate answered questions over the documentary. Her answers were so distorted from facts and proofs released at her trial. She mentioned not having a family. Had she forgotten *why* she was without them? And her baby sister? [Lauer] Ward's son also grew up without his parents, but not by choice.

"Some think she should be given the chance to prove her worth to society. However, because of her, four young people—including her baby sister—had no chance to prove themselves. I suppose a mother's opinion would not carry very much weight; but I think that anyone who knew our Carol and Bob would define them as decent, loving children whose main thoughts were of helping others, which they were trying to do when murdered by Caril Fugate and Starkweather, and bring happiness and love to their families."

Greenholtz requested a copy of the statement for his files, as if it would be granted more attention later, and the witness was excused.

The fifth and final witness speaking out in opposition to Caril Ann's parole was Henry W. Wald, of Lincoln, yet another total stranger to the case. He agreed with the Kings and Mrs. Jensen that "life" should mean *life,* reminding the board that Caril Ann's sentence had already been reviewed and upheld by "every court in the United States." Nor did incarceration for a term of fifteen years, in Wald's opinion, cover Caril's complicity in ten premeditated homicides.

"A lifetime for a fourteen-and-a-half-year-old is different than a lifetime for a thirty-five-year-old person," Wald said. "I realize that. But fifteen years—that puts a price of something like a year and a half per murder, and that's a pretty cheap price."

Greenholtz, for his part, acknowledged Wald's concern, but countered with a reference to "numerous letters from all over the country, from people who are shocked that we have kept her as long as we have. That's the difference in people," he went on, with more than a hint of condescension. "Some people have far more compassion than others."

The board's decision, two days later, may have been a foregone conclusion, but Smith, the old state trooper, almost spoiled it, casting the lone vote in opposition to clemency. In recommending commutation to the pardons board, John Greenholtz repeated his own favorite line for the press, declaring that punishment in every case "should have an end," or else the prison system would become "useless," a "slow, expensive, inhuman method of execution."

Days after that two-to-one vote, Caril caught another break when Harold Smith resigned from the parole board, and the panel was expanded to include five members. Greenholtz and Ed Rowley would remain; the three new members were Eugene Neal and Timothy Blankenship, both professional parole officers, and Rev. Marshall Tate, a black minister from Omaha. It was, from all appearances, a panel predisposed to grant her freedom, if the pardons board would only play along.

That august body met to consider Caril's case, in closed session, on September 25, 1973. Governor Exon and Secretary of State Allen Beermann voted to consider Caril's application, while Attorney General Clarence Meyer was opposed. The motion carried, and a public hearing on the question was scheduled for October 30, in Lincoln.

Things were looking up for Caril Ann. Besides the mostly favorable transcript from the last parole board hearing, she received high marks from Jackie Crawford, the superintendent at York, and from Dr. William Long, of the Nebraska Psychiatric Institute in Omaha. There was a glitch, however, and it threatened to derail her chances for release.

Specifically, in August, Caril Ann had testified that she had never previously filed an application for commutation of sentence. Now, while reviewing her file, the members of the pardons board turned up an application she had signed in March of 1969. That meant that she had lied to the parole board, under oath—a fact that had to be explained away, somehow, before the state could set her free.

Four members of the new parole board (Neal was absent) met at York on Friday, October 5, to question Caril and see if they could resolve the problem. Greenholtz showed her the previous application and asked if she had, in fact, filled it out.

"Well," she told him, "I don't remember making one out, but I guess I had to have made one out. This part is in my handwriting," she added, indicating three answers to various questions. The rest, Caril alleged, had been written by somebody else. Perhaps a former warden had been kind enough to fill the application out, without her knowledge. The more recent application, Caril Ann pointed out, was typewritten. She had no doubts about working on *that* one. Jim McArthur had been there to help her, making sure she got it right.

More troubling than the mere existence of the four year old application, though, were its contents, some of which not only contradicted Caril Ann's current application, but flew in the face of facts proved at her murder trial.

Granted, *some* of the answers were consistent, Rev. Tate pointed out. "All the way down till we get to number thirteen, where the question is asked you, 'Did you use a gun in the commission of your crime?' In 1969 you said, 'Yes.' And in the latter application you answered, 'I personally did not. He did.' Now, would you clarify that to the board, please?"

It was a tricky question, since Caril *had* been pointing a loaded gun at Carol King and Bob Jensen the night they were kidnapped, but she did her best to rewrite history. "In sixty-nine," she said, "at the time I wrote the 'yes,' it must have meant that there was a gun used in it, but I did not use it."

"So you are saying that you just didn't qualify who had the gun," Tate suggested, "but you were merely acknowledging there was a gun used?"

"There was a gun used, yes."

"And that gun was, in fact, loaded?"

"Yes."

At that point, Tim Blankenship interrupted the questioning. "I think what we should do, Mr. Tate," he said, "I think we should actually revert back to number eleven—'Name any witness against you . . . you thought was unfair.' In 1969 no comment was made, and yet in September of '73, according to your answer here, you contend that Charles Starkweather was an unfair witness against you. Why do you think there would have been that change of mind during that period of time?"

"Well," Caril replied, missing the point, "because it was due to Charles Starkweather that I'm here now. He was a totally biased witness against me."

Blankenship tried again. "The question at stake," he said, "is why didn't you share that information on this application in 1969?"

"Because," Caril said, "actually, it didn't occur to me."

If that incredible response startled any member of the board, there is no indication of it in the record. Blankenship continued: "Number twelve, what main statement you thought wrong. In 1969, again we see that this was not answered. In 1973 we see it's answered, 'His characterization of me as a willing accomplice. Not true.' Can you give us an explanation of why you took time to answer it in 1973, and you did not in 1969?"

"Well," Caril said, "because in the 1973 one, the one now that we are referring to before the board, I know it's not a retrying of my guilt or innocence. But this time here—this time in '69—I didn't have much of a chance to feel as my own individual and make—and say what I really feel. Okay . . . I feel more liberated in '73 than I did in '69."

Of course, by 1969 Caril Ann had already been jailed for a decade and was well along in her alleged rehabilitation, but Greenholtz saw what she was getting at.

"Well, let me interject something here for everybody," the chairman said. "In 1969 you were not assisted in any manner with this. Is that what you have been telling us? Right?"

342

That wasn't what Caril said, at all, but she was nothing if not eager to please. "Right," she echoed.

"And in this one, you were?"

"Right."

"In other words," Greenholtz said, "your attorney more or less put words in your mouth?"

"No," Caril answered, hedging. "I don't think he exactly put words in my mouth. He more or less *clarified* the feelings that I really felt, in a legal way."

Greenholtz hastened to assure his fellow board members that he wasn't finding fault with Caril. She had done her best, under the circumstances, and any discrepancies between her two applications—much less the lie about 1973's being her first—were trivial at best. Still, Rev. Tate was not completely satisfied.

"Caril," he said, "could we focus our attention one more time on paragraph fifteen? And by my own observation here, I see only one discrepancy. . . . In 1969, on the second part of your statement, you said, 'By the time I had come to my senses I was so deeply involved that there was no way . . . to escape from the horrible situation.' Then, the very first statement that you have on your 1973 paragraph in relation to number fifteen, you say, 'I had attempted to terminate my friendship with Charles Starkweather, which apparently made him very angry.' Now, somehow in my own mind, I think that may have been a discrepancy that the pardons board probably read and looked at, and to me, maybe that would need clarification by virtue of this meeting."

Caril had long since given up on shooting from the lip. *"What exactly do you want said?"* she asked the minister.

"Well," Tate replied, "in one you say, 'I came to my senses, but there was no way to escape from this horrible situation.' And in other words, it sounds like to me you are saying you were there, you were *involved,* and you found yourself without any reason—rather, *effort*—to try to escape. And over here you say you had attempted to terminate the friendship. I'm curious. What do you mean by 'attempted to terminate the friendship'?"

"When I told him that Sunday before all this happened," Caril answered. "When I asked him to leave and never come back."

"This is what you—"

"This is what set him off," she interrupted Tate. "I was not dating him when this actually happened."

"So, if you could add anything to that particular sentence," Tate went on helpfully, "it *may have read,* 'I attempted to terminate my friendship with Charles Starkweather before all of this started, which apparently made him very angry.' And over here you are talking about how all of this developed. You were just there. You were caught up in it."

That sounded good to Caril. "I was caught up in it," she agreed. "There was no way you—"

"All right," Tate cut her off, before she could put another foot in her mouth. "See, those are the two details, paragraphs—these are the only things that I see that are real conflicting."

The remainder of Caril Ann's interrogation veered back to safer ground, Tate and Greenholtz quizzing her about her membership in the Nazarene Church, her definition of a "reborn" Christian, and her interaction with fellow inmates at York. It was only toward the end that Caril came close to blowing it, remarking that she had "accomplished the art of survival" in her dealings with the prison staff, learning to "accept and do many things that maybe you wouldn't otherwise do" in order to avoid trouble.

"Is it suggestive," Blankenship inquired, "that you applied any of those past talents toward this board on October 5, 1973?"

Ninette Beaver, though not present, reports that "Caril's eyes flashed" as she replied to Blankenship. "Are you implying," she asked, "that I'm conning the board?"

"What I'm making comment to," he said, "I'm asking you for declarative statements, and that is, that if you've been indoctrinated for this period of time to lie, to use any means to survive and/or open a door, have you used any of those traits on this board today?"

Blankenship could have answered his own question from that morning's transcript, but he waited for Caril Ann's response.

"I'm not conning the board," she assured him, "and that is why I say that, if the record doesn't speak for itself, then there is nothing more I can say."

It was too close for comfort, as far as John Greenholtz was concerned. "Why don't we let Miss Fugate go?" he urged his fellow board members. "We've got all the information we need."

Rev. Tate, before he left, seemed bent on mending fences. "We appreciate your openness," he told Caril, "and I'm sorry that, if in any way, this seemed to be an inquisition all over again. But I think basically we are here to deal with inconsistencies. As the parole board, being the investigative agency of the pardons board, it is our responsibility to report back to them when there is something they do not understand. I think basically the things that they did not understand, you've made them quite clear to us—along with samples of your handwriting and these comments—and I think it's safe to say the big thing I saw in paragraph fifteen was a 'before crime' kind of relationship you tried to terminate, and involvement 'after the crime' that was kind of futile to terminate."

"That's right, Caril," Ed Rowley agreed.

"That's very well put," chairman Greenholtz chimed in, "and that's exactly the way I feel about it."

Even Blankenship was mollified. "Caril," he said, as the board members rose to depart, "have a nice day."

The Board of Pardons held its public hearing on October 30 as scheduled, fifteen years to the day from the commencement of Caril Ann's murder trial in Lincoln. The prisoner was not invited, but she didn't need to be. Of forty persons present, only one—a total stranger—rose to speak on Caril's behalf. Warren King presented the board with thirteen petitions opposing clemency, a total of some 195 signatures, while his mother and Pauline Jensen read prepared statements to the board.

All in vain.

Governor Exon had no doubt of Caril Ann's guilt, he told the relatives of murdered victims; that had been decided in a fair trial, years before. The board's job was to weigh the "consideration of experts who have worked with her that she should be given a chance at parole, now or in the future." Before the public meeting ended, Attorney General Meyer reminded the crowd that there were no established legal rules for granting or refusing commutation. It was, he said, "a highly personal thing, solely committed to our judgment."

That said, the three politicians spent another two hours in private, hammering out what reporters would dub "the Fugate compromise." It was within their power to fix Caril Ann's sentence at twenty-five years, thereby making her eligible for immediate release, but that seemed risky, under the circumstances. Rather, by a vote of two to one—with Clarence Meyer opposing any form of clemency—the board fixed Caril's new sentence at thirty to fifty years, a term which made her eligible for release in May of 1976.

Charlie Starkweather had gone to his death still obsessed with his "image," the notion of his place in history. "[When] I go to the chair," he once told James Reinhardt, "I'll be no more dead than the people I killed. They was buried and their relatives grieved. Only my mother would grieve for me. But millions will read about me, I guess, and talk about, don't you think?"

And he was right, of course, but he would never see his egotistical prediction realized.

In 1974, Starkweather's case was dramatized—some said romanticized—in *Badlands,* the cinematic tale of a teenage garbageman named Kit (portrayed by Martin Sheen) and his vacuous girlfriend Holly (Sissy Spacek), who kill her disapproving father (Warren Oates) and run amok in 1950s South Dakota. The change of scene did nothing to disguise the story's roots, presenting Kit and Holly as two mindless renegades who murder out of boredom, when they're not out dancing to tinny sounds of "Love Is Strange." A cult film with distinctly limited appeal, *Badlands* was widely panned by critics, one of whom described it as possessing "all the fascination of prying into a cavity with a bent hairpin."

Charlie would have loved it, all the same, and while he never made it as a reader, he would certainly have been amused to find himself appearing—as a red-haired quick-draw artist called "The Kid"—in Stephen King's epic novel *The Stand.* He comes to a bad end, of course, devoured by wolves in the wake of a global plague, but Charlie would have understood.

Shit happens.

One aspect of his notoriety would certainly have pleased him more than any other, given Charlie's love for rock 'n' roll. To date, he has been mentioned by two famous singers in bestselling songs. One spot, in Billy Joel's "We Didn't Start the Fire," is admittedly skimpy—"Starkweather homicide" rhymed with "children of thalidomide"—but the other, Bruce Springsteen's "Nebraska," was Charlie all the way, inspired by a reading of Ninette Beaver's brief for the Fugate defense.

Starkweather had been dead for thirty-four years before he made it to TV, portrayed by Tim Roth in ABC's miniseries *Murder in the Heartland.* Fairuza Balk was cast as Caril Ann, with Brian Dennehy as her defender, John McArthur, squaring off against Randy Quaid in the role of prosecutor Elmer Scheele. There were some problems with the network censors, going in, but director Robert Markowitz was able to preserve his vision more or less intact. It wasn't quite the kind of "shooting movie" Charlie would have liked—he did not come off looking like a hero of the rebel set—but it was *being remembered* that counted, more than the quality or content of those memories.

And it would be the final insult of his wasted life that Charlie was denied enjoyment of his notoriety on film and audio cassette. He had been looking forward to that aspect of the end.

"Then," he told Reinhardt, "I could go with my dreams fulfilled. Only my story will live."

Caril Ann Fugate was paroled to Michigan on June 20, 1976, after seventeen years and seven months of confinement at York. The move was a strategic one: a job was waiting for her, at an unnamed hospital, and it was calculated that her exile from Nebraska would make Caril's release more palatable, all around. Prison officials in her home state generally agreed with one official who told *Newsweek*, "She's earned it; society has gotten its pound of flesh." Surviving relatives of those who died in 1958, for their part, were predictably upset. "I don't see how that's justice," one complained, remaining carefully anonymous. "It's all to make life better for the murderer."

Caril Ann, at thirty-two, presented the appearance of a subject who would rather skip the controversy. "All I want to do," she told the press, "is settle down, get married, have a couple of kids, wash the socks, burn the toast."

That dream was not to be, but Caril had freedom coming, anyway, if she could only wait it out. Her friend John Greenholtz was still in charge of the parole board five years later, when Caril Ann was formally discharged in September 1981. For all intents and purposes, she was free as a bird, but Caril showed no signs of abandoning her modest life in Michigan.

"I think she had some disappointments in the free world," said Lucille Splinter, assistant superintendent at York, adding that Caril Ann "broke all ties" when she departed from Nebraska.

"You have to admire her," Splinter told the press. "I think she came through [as] a caring, thinking person. When she left, she said she didn't want any publicity, and she stuck to it."

That was about to change, though, as Caril Ann pursued her single-minded goal of trying to persuade a largely hostile world that she was innocent of any wrongdoing in 1958. The first step was to schedule an appearance on the controversial TV program *Lie Detector*, hosted by celebrity attorney F. Lee Bailey. *Lie Detector* drew its audience from those who would, a decade later, make "trash talk" a staple of the air waves, putting guests who ranged from porn star Linda Lovelace to convicted killer James Earl Ray on camera, to plead their innocence and sit for polygraph examinations, with the test results announced before the credits rolled.

It was a gamble, at the very least, since leading experts in the field agree that polygraph exams maintain an average 25 percent margin of error—the chief reason their results are inadmissible as legal evidence in most states—but Caril Ann was willing to risk it. After her segment was taped, in February 1983, Caril told the press that she was "very pleased with the way it came out." And, indeed, the program broadcast nationwide appeared to buttress her longstanding claim of innocence. On camera, she was asked three questions: Did Charlie Starkweather threaten to kill her family? Did Caril believe his threat? While on the road with Charlie, did she know her relatives were dead?

Caril Ann said "yes" to the first two questions, and "no" to the last. Ed Gelb, past president of the American Polygraph Association and F. Lee Bailey's resident expert, reported that "in two areas" he thought she was telling the truth. After the broadcast, Caril Ann told reporters she felt "vindicated," finally released from the "iron grip" of notoriety.

Or, maybe not.

As Nebraska Attorney General Paul Douglas pointed out, back in Lincoln, the polygraph results were equivocal at best, subject to personal interpretation by the operator, and the questions had been strictly limited, avoiding any mention of the murder that sent Caril to prison. "They didn't ask if she killed anybody," Douglas complained, "if she had helped [Starkweather] commit the crime, if she had a chance to get away. They didn't ask her a lot of the pertinent questions."

A poll of Nebraskans, conducted by SRI Research Center of Lincoln, a month after the *Lie Detector* broadcast, showed 51 percent of those questioned agreeing with Douglas; 22 percent believed Caril's account, while another 27 percent remained on the fence. Caril Ann was no doubt disappointed, but the world, she told reporters, was "entitled to believe what [it] wants."

Another six years and eight months elapsed before she changed her mind. The vehicle, in November 1989, was *A Current Affair,* the flagship of syndicated tabloid television. Weeping for the cameras, Caril told her interviewer that she felt she had been cheated out of life. The only thing left that could make her happy, she went on, was "to have one person in Nebraska who always believed with no doubt that I was guilty, understand what transpired and say to me, 'I might have been wrong.'" Nine months later, she was still looking, mailing two-hundred-odd copies of her trial transcript to randomly selected Lincoln residents. She had taken the unusual (and expensive) step, Caril said, "so that the people of Nebraska would know" that her "first confession [*sic*] was the true confession."

Back in Lincoln, retired police chief Joe Carroll had a different take on Caril's latest publicity campaign. "Those false tears didn't impress me," he said. "I don't think she'd qualify as an actress."

Notes

Prologue: Teenage Waste Land

p. 2: Truman Capote's comment on Jack Kerouac is quoted by William Manchester in *The Glory and the Dream* (New York: Bantam, 1974), page 727.

p. 3: Robert Lindner is quoted by Graham McCann in *Rebel Males: Clift, Brando and Dean* (New Brunswick: Rutgers University Press, 1991), page 146.

p. 4: Frank Sadilek's Hollywood pilgrimage is described by Yves Lavigne in *Hell's Angels: Taking Care of Business* (Toronto: Deneau & Wayne, 1987), page 29.

pp. 4–5: Dean's biography, with the remarks by Clift and Brando, is taken from Graham McCann's *Rebel Males*, pages 126–33.

p. 5: Dean's sex life and autopsy are described in McCann's *Rebel Males*, pages 152–53. Andy Warhol's description of Dean is quoted by McCann on page 125; Lee Strasberg and Elia Kazan are quoted by McCann on page 26; Dean discusses his parents on page 143; his drug abuse and violence toward women are described by McCann on pages 27 and 154; Leon

Rosenman is quoted by McCann on page 157; Dean describes his own fascination with speed on page 27 of *Rebel Males*.

pp. 5–6: Dean's ambivalent remarks on death are quoted by McCann in *Rebel Males,* pages 27, 155 and 162.

p. 6: The comment about Dean's "great career move" is cited by McCann on page 162 of *Rebel Males;* Elvis Presley is quoted by McCann on page 163; Bob Dylan's fascination with Dean is described by McCann on page 7.

pp. 6–7: Carroll Edward Cole described his obsession with Dean in personal interviews and correspondence with the author, prior to his 1985 execution in Nevada. His story is told in *Silent Rage* (New York: Dell, 1994).

p. 7: Starkweather's sister is quoted by Randall Riese in *The Unabridged James Dean: His Life and Legacy from A to Z* (New York: Wings Books, 1991), page 504. Sal Mineo's observation on Dean is quoted by McCann in *Rebel Males,* page 26.

p. 7: François Truffaut is quoted by McCann on page 141.

p. 8: The cases of Howard Unruh and William Cook are described by Carl Sifakis in *The Encyclopedia of American Crime* (New York: Facts on File, 1982), pages 170 and 733.

1 The Charnel House

p. 10: All dialogue presented in the text is drawn from public records, court transcripts, interviews, or published accounts of the case. Where contradictory transcripts exist, I have used my own best judgment to resolve any discrepancies through logic, in accordance with documented facts.

p. 16: While the police saw no need to contact the family's doctor, Bob Von Busch made a call and discovered that the doctor had not seen the Bartletts recently. Detective Harold G. Robinson, an expert in police procedures imported from California to investigate charges of negligence in the case, agreed that "under ideal circumstances of experience and training," the patrolmen should have done what common sense led Bob to do. That said, he dismissed public criticism of Soukup and Kahler, noting that Caril Ann's behavior gave no cause for further investigation at the time. Robinson also explained why the

Lincoln police took Caril Ann's word over Bob's. As detailed in his report: "Your investigator had an opportunity to check the files of the Lincoln Police Department with respect to police matters handled in the past relating to the family and relatives of Robert Von Busch. Your investigator was impressed with the number of instances where police attention had been requested on matters arising out of domestic difficulties. Although police officers are admonished not to evaluate the seriousness of an assignment prior to inquiry, it is the writer's conviction that the police officials had an awareness of the number of incidents involving domestic difficulties requiring police action which had occurred in the Von Busch family previously." Bob's response to the charge: "It's ridiculous, just another example of the way the police do things around here. They got me mixed up with Sonny Von Busch and his family. My side of the family never went to the police about anything—and we were never in trouble with the police, either."

p. 20: Pansy Street would later say that she was far from satisfied with the investigation at her daughter's home. Detective Robinson had this to say about the police search on January 27th: "In examining the interior of the dwelling it is standard procedure for an investigator to look for articles or furniture out of place, upset, damaged or strewn around as an indication that they had been ransacked or that some act of violence had taken place. Even acknowledging that some future disarray undoubtedly took place incidental to the search and photographing of the interior of 924 Belmont by police authorities, your investigator asserts that it would be difficult indeed even at this time to resolve the question of whether violence had occurred therein. It is also noted in this connection that according to information given your investigator Charlie and Caril 'cleaned up' the house after removing the bodies of the victims." Robinson further disagreed with Pansy Street's contention that she "knew something was wrong" at the Bartlett home on January 27. On the contrary, he reported that Mrs. Street had been "perfectly satisfied that everything was normal." Police had not searched the outbuildings behind the house, Robinson said, because Mrs. Street never asked them to do so.

NOTES

2 Little Red

pp. 24–25: The Starkweather family history is gleaned from William Allen's *Starkweather: The Story of a Mass Murderer* (Boston: Houghton Mifflin, 1976), page 17.

p. 25: Comments from the Starkweathers' neighbors are quoted by James Melvin Reinhardt in *The Murderous Trail of Charles Starkweather* (Springfield: Charles C. Thomas, 1960), page 9.

p. 26: Reinhardt is quoted in his biography of Starkweather, page 37. Starkweather's reminiscence of childhood is quoted by Reinhardt on page 24; the description of his sister's injury is quoted on page 25.

p. 27: Charlie's memories of childhood were published before his death, in *Parade* magazine, and afterward by James Reinhardt in book form. The "enchanted forest" comments are drawn from Reinhardt, page 52.

p. 27: The debate over compulsory education is described by James Olson in *A History of Nebraska,* page 351. Charlie's description of the walk to school is quoted from Reinhardt, page 26; the account of his first public speaking experience is taken from Reinhardt, page 42. In this and all subsequent passages quoted from Charlie's autobiography, I have corrected much of his "creative" spelling and punctuation in the interest of legibility.

p. 28: Charlie's memories of the public-speaking incident are quoted by Reinhardt, pages 42–43.

p. 29: Starkweather's feelings in the playhouse are quoted by Reinhardt, pages 43–44. As previously noted, Charlie's grammar has been sanitized to make it comprehensible. Some his writing, as with the original version of this passage's reference to "harhequinade, stripped from that of munner life leaving only naked being-hate," defies translation.

p. 30: Charlie's memory of the playground incident is quoted by Reinhardt, on page 45.

p. 31: Starkweather's self-description of his craving for revenge is quoted from Reinhardt's *Murderous Trail,* page 46. His contradictory account of being "a little mad" in school is recorded by Reinhardt, without comment, on page 29.

p. 33: Charlie's jailhouse descriptions of his "black moods" and schoolyard brawls are quoted by Reinhardt on pages 41 and 42.

p. 34: Charlie's memories of school life after kindergarten are quoted by Reinhardt on pages 30 and 31.

pp. 35–36: James Reinhardt offers the psychoanalysis of Starkweather on page 57 of his *Murderous Trail*.

p. 36: The remarks of Charlie's grade-school principal and teachers are presented by Reinhardt on pages 10 and 46.

p. 37: Charlie's observations on his father and firearms are quoted by Reinhardt on pages 39, 49 and 63.

p. 37: Starkweather's comments on the hunting ethos are cited by Reinhardt on pages 16, 40 and 50.

3 Death Dreams

pp. 39–40: Charlie's recitation of the after-school incident is presented in Reinhardt's *Murderous Trail*, pages 94–95.

p. 40: Starkweather's affinity for art is examined by Jeff O'Donnell in *Starkweather: A Story of Mass Murder on the Great Plains* (Lincoln: J & L Lee Co., 1993), page 100. Two of Charlie's paintings were reprinted in *Life* magazine's issue of February 10, 1958.

p. 42: Bob Von Busch's memories of Charlie are quoted by William Allen in *Starkweather*, pages 22–23.

p. 42: Charlie's junior-high romance is described in James Reinhardt's *Murderous Trail*, pages 7–8. Starkweather's observation on his teenage dates is quoted by Reinhardt on page 23.

p. 43: Charlie's memory of the girl who upset his "death deal" is recorded by Reinhardt on page 48, along with his rationale for avoiding "nice places."

pp. 43–44: Bob Von Busch's memories of adventures with Charlie are quoted by William Allen, on page 23.

p. 44: Charlie described his hot-rod period to James Reinhardt, who quotes his comments on pages 34–35 of *Murderous Trail*.

pp. 44–45: The recollections of Charlie's classmates, counselor, and teachers are quoted by Reinhardt on pages 10, 16, and 48.

pp. 45–46: Descriptions of Charlie's various fights are

drawn from Reinhardt, pages 6–7, and from Glenn Desmond's *Charlie and Caril,* page 98.

p. 46: The observations of Charlie's neighbors are quoted by Reinhardt on pages 8–9; the excerpt from Starkweather's prison memoirs was published in *Parade* magazine, and later in Reinhardt's *Murderous Trail,* page 23.

p. 47: Charlie's commentary on life is quoted by Reinhardt on pages 22–23; the description of Starkweather from his classmate is cited by Reinhardt on page 73.

p. 48: Charlie's memories of working at the Western Newspaper Union are quoted by Reinhardt on page 48. John Hedge's description of Charlie on the job is quoted by William Allen on page 27.

p. 48: A significant number of serial killers have suffered traumatic—sometimes repeated—head injuries in childhood or adolescence, before they began hunting humans. No positive link has been proved between such trauma and subsequent acts of episodic violence, but the "coincidence" is still intriguing, reflected in the lives of such ruthless murderers as Earle Nelson, Henry Lee Lucas, Charles Manson, Gary Heidnik, William Heirens, and Bobby Joe Long. In several cases, violent mood swings, fits of depression, and chronic headaches have been associated with blows to the head which rendered the subject unconscious.

p. 49: Bob Von Busch's comparison of Charlie and James Dean is quoted by William Allen, on page 24 of *Starkweather.*

pp. 49–50: The anonymous drinker's description of Charlie is quoted by Reinhardt, on page 91.

pp. 50–51: Charlie's protestation of innocence is quoted in Reinhardt's *Murderous Trail,* pages 47–48.

p. 51: Charlie's discussion of dreams and nightmares is discussed at length by Reinhardt. These quotations are drawn from pages 65 and 81.

pp. 51–53: Charlie's ruminations on death are quoted by Reinhardt on pages 32–35 and 81.

p. 52: Starkweather's rationale for "necessary" homicide is quoted by Reinhardt on pages 56 and 100.

p. 53: Charlie's thoughts on love and isolation are quoted by Reinhardt, on pages 58 and 96.

4 Something Worth Killing For

p. 54: Allen quotes Bob Von Busch on page 25 of *Starkweather*. Charlie's early assessment of Caril Ann is quoted by Reinhardt on page 77 of his *Murderous Trail*.

p. 54: Charlie's descriptions of Caril Ann's impact on his life are quoted by Reinhardt on page 69.

p. 56: Caril's natural father, William Fugate, had a criminal record that included charges of assault, public intoxication, voyeurism, and contributing to the delinquency of a minor.

pp. 58–60: Starkweather's impressions of Caril, their relationship, and their plan for the world are quoted by Reinhardt on pages 74–76.

p. 61: Guy Starkweather's description of his final argument with Charlie is quoted by William Allen, on page 28.

p. 62: Robert McClung's testimony is quoted by Allen on pages 30 and 31 of *Starkweather*. Charlie's assessment of the garbage trade is quoted by Reinhardt on pages 54, 60–61, and 74.

p. 63: Starkweather's vision of the future is quoted on page 60 of James Reinhardt's *Murderous Trail*.

p. 65: Marion Bartlett's reaction to Starkweather's marriage proposals are quoted by Glenn Desmond on page 51 of *Charlie and Caril*. Charlie's thoughts on marriage and children are quoted by Reinhardt on pages 67 and 77 of his *Murderous Trail*.

pp. 65–67: Charlie's violent fantasies and plans for "something big" are quoted at length by Reinhardt on pages 51, 76, and 83–84.

p. 67: Starkweather's vision of the future is quoted by Reinhardt on page 53. His thoughts on Caril Ann and the "end of the road" are quoted by Reinhardt on pages 66, 76, and 100.

5 First Blood

p. 70: Colvert's conversations with his wife are quoted by Glenn Desmond in *Charles and Caril*, pages 18–19 and 29–30.

p. 74: Charlie's dialogue with Caril Ann is reconstructed by Desmond, on pages 24–25.

p. 78: Charlie's implication of Caril Ann in the filling station plot is quoted by Reinhardt on pages 108–9.

p. 78: Reinhardt quotes Charlie's contradictory statements about Colvert's murder on pages 79–80 and 109.

p. 81: A minor but enduring controversy surrounds Charlie's take from the gas station robbery. James Reinhardt states that Charlie's "reward was one hundred and sixty-five dollars." William Allen and Jeff O'Donnell place the total at $108, with O'Donnell breaking it down by specific bills, Allen adding that "later the station manager would estimate $160." In fact, since the money was never recovered and Charlie was vague on the details, no precise accounting is possible.

p. 85: The excerpt from Harold Robinson's report is quoted by Reinhardt on page 123 of his *Murderous Trail*. Ironically, Charlie's gloves were an unnecessary precaution in the Colvert slaying, since no Nebraska Starkweather had ever been arrested, and their fingerprints were not on file.

p. 86: Police were widely criticized for failing to trace Charlie Starkweather on the basis of McClung's description. Harold Robinson's report brusquely disposed of that criticism.

"Concerning the report that a description of Charles Starkweather and his car had been given to the authorities, your investigator reports as follows: A former employee of the Crest Filling Station was interviewed in the County Attorney's office on December 16. He identified a number of the employees and previous employees of the gas station, and gave information concerning persons who had loitered around the station. Included therein was his statement that a 20- to 21-year-old redhead who drove a 1949 Ford two-door sedan used to stop in the station at night. The attendant who had been relieved by Colvert on the night of the murder was similarly interviewed on December 17, but he did not make any reference to the 20- to 21-year-old redhead.

"The file indicates that the manager of the Crest station was interviewed on December 17. All the frequenters of the station were reviewed, and the manager was specifically asked concerning the identity of a 20 to 21 year old red head. He stated that he had no information concerning such an individual, and believed that the person referred to was Dale Gardner, also called 'Pinky.' It was suggested that this response by the manager of the station somewhat clouded the need for concentrating on a further identification of the 20 to 21 year old red head."

Robinson does not explain why authorities waited two weeks before questioning the Crest station's employees. His report blamed various employees at the station for failing to report that Starkweather sometimes slept on the premises, and that he had "evidenced an interest in the counting of the cash at the change of shifts at 11 P.M." Even so, he concluded that the crime was too "bizarre" for swift solution. His report continues:

"At the outset of an investigation, in the absence of any tangible clues, it is necessary to set up certain presumptions and attempt to develop or reject them by further investigation. The bizarre circumstances of this crime brought to light after the apprehension of Starkweather would indicate that it would be virtually impossible to set up any presumptions which would match the circumstances under which the crime was committed. To wit: A person known to employees at the station, entering the station with a red hunting cap, a bandana over his face, and attempting to hold up an illuminated station on a well traveled highway with a shotgun."

In Robinson's opinion, the crime was "amateurish," but Charlie had "apparently absorbed from his comic-book and detective-story reading a knowledge of criminal activities which instilled a sense of cunning." Thus, he was empowered to baffle manhunters and remain at large until his final murder spree, leaving Robinson to conclude that "the investigation of the Colvert slaying by law enforcement agencies was not inadequate in any material respect."

pp. 86–87: Mrs. Kamp's description of Charlie is quoted by Reinhardt, on page 107. Her comments on the police interview and second sighting, with the police response, are recorded by William Allen, on page 39 of *Starkweather*.

p. 87: Sheriff Karnopp's observation was recorded in an interview with William Allen, quoted on page 40 of *Starkweather*.

6 Hang Time

p. 90: Jeff O'Donnell, in *Starkweather,* reports as fact that Caril Ann accompanied Charlie on his run to dispose of the shotgun, but there seems to be no record of Charlie ever placing her at the scene. He *did* claim to have told her all about the robbery and murder, after the fact, but Caril Ann tells a different story, denying any knowledge of the crime before her parents died. In Charlie's version, he initially blamed someone else for shooting Colvert, but explained that Caril "wasn't fooled. She saw right through that. She knew me like a book." Several coin wrappers from the robbery were later found in the Bartlett home, after Charlie and Caril Ann had fled, but their significance remains unclear, in terms of Caril Ann's guilty knowledge. O'Donnell "recreates" a conversation, during which Charlie confesses the murder to Caril and hands her the wrappers; William Allen, meanwhile, is content to write that Charlie "put a box of empty coin wrappers in Caril's room" shortly after the holdup. Sheriff Karnopp later suggested, based on the wrappers, that Marion and Velda Bartlett had knowledge of the murder, "holding it over his head" to make Charlie break up with Caril, but the theory seems fragile, at best, since he continued seeing Caril Ann for another seven weeks, with no complaint to the police.

pp. 93–94: Charlie's remarks on the Colvert murder and his obsession with Caril Ann are quoted by Reinhardt on pages 77–78 of his *Murderous Trail.* The comment on his fast-draw practice comes from page 42.

p. 96: Starkweather's comments on impending death are quoted by Reinhardt, on page 74.

7 A Kind of Thrill

pp. 98–99: Charlie's confrontation with Marion Bartlett is described by Glenn Desmond, on pages 52–53 of *Charles and Caril.*

p. 100: Starkweather's brief encounter with Barbara Von Busch is related in Jeff O'Donnell's *Starkweather,* page 19.

p. 101: Charlie's assessment of Betty Jean Bartlett is quoted by William Anderson, on pages 47–48.

pp. 103–04: Virginia Robson's afternoon encounter with Marion Bartlett is described by Jeff O'Donnell, on page 23.

p. 105: Glenn Desmond, in *Charles and Caril* (page 53) ignores Charlie's problem with the car and describes him driving off to fetch Caril Ann from school. The "recreated" scene helps strengthen Desmond's description of Caril as an active participant in the slaughter of her family, but there is no evidence to support its occurrence.

pp. 105–07: Charlie's description of the Bartlett massacre is quoted by William Allen, on pages 50–51.

pp. 108–09: Starkweather's letter to police is quoted by William Allen, on page 54.

p. 110: Charlie's remarks about Caril Ann and the aftermath of her family's murder are quoted by William Allen, on page 55 of *Starkweather*.

p. 111: To date, no one has ventured to explain what Charlie and Caril Ann did for toilet facilities over the next six days, while the outhouse was occupied by corpses. The oversight would seem to be a glaring discrepancy in Caril's "ignorant hostage" scenario.

p. 111: Police later speculated that Charlie used the door as a litter for transporting Marion's body, and in the absence of drag marks on the frozen ground, they further hypothesized that Caril Ann must have helped him carry the corpse. Charlie denied it, and while author Glenn Desmond described Caril's participation as established fact, there is no evidence of her involvement in moving her stepfather's body.

8 The Honeymooners

pp. 114–15: Caril Ann's encounter with Bonnie Gardner is described by Jeff O'Donnell, on page 29 of *Starkweather*.

pp. 116–17: Charlie's thoughts on murder and the "end of the road" are quoted in Reinhardt's *Murderous Trail*, on pages 35, 78, and 107.

p. 117: Charlie's description of the "hostage" ruse is quoted by William Allen, on page 59.

pp. 118–20: Excerpts from the jailhouse statements of Charlie and Caril to Dale Fahrnbruch are quoted by William Allen, on pages 59–62 of *Starkweather*.

p. 123: Robinson's description of Caril Ann is quoted by Reinhardt, on page 128 of his *Murderous Trail*.

p. 124: Investigator Robinson off-loaded some of the blame for Charlie's murder spree on Guy Starkweather, for his failure to report the damaged .22. Robinson's report states that "serious consideration should attach to the possibility [that a] forthright action in bringing the gun to police headquarters on Sunday, January 26th, would have averted the events which were discovered [*sic*] on January 27th." In fact, however, the "events" found on Monday were simply three corpses, of victims murdered six days *earlier*. Nothing Guy or Rodney could have done on Sunday would have turned the clock back on those murders, though it might conceivably have saved six other lives.

p. 124: Charlie's comment to Fahrnbruch is quoted by William Allen, on page 73.

p. 125: Years after the fact, Chief Joe Carroll was still defending his department's slow start on the Starkweather manhunt, noting with some justification that his officers were hampered by a lack of full disclosure from Guy Starkweather, Bob Von Busch, and others. "Once we knew who our man was," Carroll told William Allen, "it was then a matter of putting certain routine procedures into motion. The hard cases are the ones where you have no clues, no motive, no suspect. My biggest worry wasn't Starkweather, it was what the community might do to itself before we caught him." Otherwise, Carroll stood by what he told reporters in the aftermath of the grisly find on Belmont Avenue: "At no time until the discovery of the bodies was there any indication of foul play. We investigate thousands of domestic complaints a month, and this one appeared to be nothing out of the ordinary. We had no legal right to make a forcible entry into the house and no evidence urging us to do so. It is easy to look back now and see what could have been done, but we had no knowledge at the time of anything in the nature of a crime. I fail to see any grounds for criticism of the handling of this investigation."

9 Dead People Don't Talk

p. 127: Various sources also refer to Dale Smallcomb as "Halcomb" or "Holcomb." Author Jeff O'Donnell, in *Stark-*

weather, manages to use all three names within the space of two pages.

p. 129: The official police chronology of events on January 27, 1958, has Charlie and Caril pulling into Tate's Conoco station at 1:30 P.M., then reaching August Meyer's farm by 1:45. The first time listed is almost certainly a typo, since fifteen minutes is clearly inadequate for repairing a tire, cooking four hamburgers, and driving the six or seven miles to Charlie's final destination. All things considered, author Jeff O'Donnell is probably closer to the truth when he describes Charlie and Caril reaching Tate's "a little after 12:30."

pp. 130–32: Various sources recount Charlie's visit to Tate's Conoco station on January 27. The most detailed account of his conversations with Homer Tate and Marv Krueger is offered by Jeff O'Donnell, on pages 44–46 of *Starkweather.* Juanita Bell's observations of Charlie and Caril are quoted by William Allen, on pages 75–76.

p. 132: Caril Ann's reaction to the inferior hamburgers is reported identically by William Allen (on page 76) and Jeff O'Donnell (on page 47).

p. 133: Charlie's memory of Caril's wish to kill August Meyer is quoted by Jeff O'Donnell on page 48. Caril's version of the conversation is reported by William Allen on page 77.

pp. 135–36: Conflicting descriptions of the Meyer shooting are quoted by William Allen, on pages 78–79 of *Starkweather.*

pp. 137–38: Caril's description of Charlie searching the Meyer house is quoted by William Allen, on page 80.

pp. 138–39: The encounter with Howard Genuchi is described by Jeff O'Donnell, on pages 56–57 of *Starkweather.*

p. 141: Caril's explanation of the Kansas road map purchase is quoted by William Allen, on page 83. Charlie's description of Caril Ann's supernatural fear is presented on page 84 of the same work.

p. 142: Author Glenn Desmond, in *Charles and Caril,* rearranges the events of January 27 for "dramatic effect." In his version, Charlie's sixth and seventh victims—teenagers Robert Jensen and Carol King—are killed *before* August Meyer, after which Charlie and Caril spend the night in Meyer's house. The purpose for this deviation from established fact is unclear, since no evidence supports the fictional version.

10 The Cave

p. 144: The poem from Robert Jensen's sales receipts is quoted by William Allen, on page 85 of *Starkweather*.

p. 146: There is a persistent problem with times in the Starkweather case. The official police chronology reports that Charlie and Caril got stuck in August Meyer's driveway for the last time at 5:40 P.M. on January 27, and that they "got in Jensen car" at 7:45. There is no explanation for the gap of two hours and five minutes, which clearly conflicts with the description of events from the two surviving principals. Author Jeff O'Donnell further complicates matters by having Jensen and King abducted at 8:30 P.M.

pp. 146–49: Charlie's version of the Jensen-King abduction is reported almost identically by William Allen (pages 87–90) and Jeff O'Donnell (pages 63–67) in their books, both titled *Starkweather*.

pp. 151–52: Excerpts from Charlie's statement to Dale Fahrnbruch are quoted by William Allen, on pages 92–93 of *Starkweather*. Charlie's comment to James Reinhardt is cited on page 110 of Reinhardt's *Murderous Trail*.

p. 153: Everett Broening is quoted by William Allen, on page 93.

p. 154: Charlie's description of the argument with Caril is quoted by William Allen, on pages 93–94. Caril Ann predictably denied Starkweather's version of events, maintaining her role as the more-or-less innocent hostage. Author Jeff O'Donnell, meanwhile, on page 72 of *Starkweather*, describes Caril holding Charlie at gunpoint in the car, bossing him around in no uncertain terms, until he finally agrees to "do it your way." Even Charlie's final version of events stopped short of giving Caril Ann that much power, indicating that O'Donnell may have "improved" the scene for dramatic effect.

11 Mad Dog

pp. 158–59: Merle Boldt's discovery of Charlie's abandoned car is described by Jeff O'Donnell, on pages 80–81 of *Starkweather*. Author Glenn Desmond, in *Charles and Caril* (page 66), credits unidentified "farmers" with finding both the car and August Meyer's body, but his dramatic recreation of events may safely be dismissed, since it conflicts with the reports of sixty-odd witnesses.

pp. 163–64: Bob Von Busch's description of the abortive rendezvous with Charlie is quoted by William Allen on pages 102–03 of *Starkweather*.

12 "I Knowed It Couldn't Last Long"

p. 168: Bob Von Busch told author William Allen that Charlie knew Lillian Fencl, and that the maid had asked him in for supper more than once, when the Wards were not at home. Allen was properly skeptical of the report, which contradicts Starkweather's statements to police, but the story resurfaced as "fact" seventeen years later, in Jeff O'Donnell's *Starkweather*. There, on pages 76–77, O'Donnell "recreates" a conversation between Charlie and Caril, Starkweather boasting of his several visits to the mansion. He also claims to know that Lillian Fencl is "kind of deaf," a statement that flies in the face of his subsequent actions and description of events to the authorities.

p. 168: Glenn Desmond writes a scene in *Charles and Caril,* on pages 116–17, depicting Clara Ward and Lillian Fencl together in the kitchen, sipping coffee and chatting when Charlie arrives. Their "recreated" conversation has a ring of authenticity, until we remember that Fencl was nearly stone deaf. Desmond's sketch also ignores repeated statements from the only living witness—Charlie Starkweather—to the effect that Mrs. Ward "came down" once he was already inside the house holding the maid at gunpoint. There is no good reason to believe that Charlie lied on that point, or that Desmond's version is correct. Jeff O'Donnell is equally shaky in his speculation (on page 77 of *Starkweather*) that Fencl "thought she recognized [Charlie] as one of the boys who had worked the garbage route before."

p. 170: In fact, the Skyline Dairy driver did not notice Jensen's car. When he was questioned later, by police, the milkman had no memory of any vehicle in Ward's drive-way. He kept his mind on business and saw nothing out of place.

pp. 171–73: Charlie's statement to Dale Fahrnbruch and Caril Ann's courtroom testimony are quoted by William Allen, on pages 104–7 of *Starkweather*.

pp. 173–74: Excerpts from Charlie's statement to Elmer Scheele are quoted by William Allen, on pages 99–100. Despite the fact that Charlie found another .22-caliber rifle at the Wards' home, no evidence exists that Clara ever fired the gun. There were no "extra" bullet holes around the premises—nor, according to Charlie's own statement, did Caril Ann hear a shot before he came downstairs.

pp. 174–76: Charlie's description of Lauer Ward's death and his departure from Ward's home are quoted by William Allen, on pages 108–09 of *Starkweather*.

pp. 177–80: Caril Ann's statement to Dale Fahrnbruch is quoted by William Allen, on pages 110–12. Dr. Zeman's assessment of the murder weapon used on the Wards and Lillian Fencl is quoted by Allen, on page 109.

p. 181: Nebraska authorities were widely criticized for their failure to apprehend Charlie and Caril before the Ward massacre. Harold Robinson rose to their defense in his report, writing: "In the opinion of your investigator, and considering the confusion which of necessity attended a rapid [*sic*] developing series of shocking crimes, it is my opinion that the law enforcement agencies participating in the investigation subsequent to 4:30 P.M. January 27th, did a remarkable job in coping with a situation which greatly exceeded the available manpower, and taxed the experience and training of the available personnel to the utmost."

13 Shoot to Kill

pp. 188–89: The excerpt from Rev. Raible's sermon is quoted by William Allen, on page 118 of *Starkweather*.

14 Trapdoor

pp. 190–91: Charlie's statement to Fahrnbruch is quoted by William Allen, on page 120.

p. 195: Charlie's "trapdoor" statement, which provides

this chapter's title, is quoted by James Reinhardt, on page 100 of his *Murderous Trail*.

p. 197: Starkweather's description of the Collison murder is quoted by William Allen, on page 123.

p. 197: In *Caril,* their sympathetic biography of Caril Fugate, authors Ninette Beaver, B. K. Ripley, and Patrick Trese state that Caril Ann was crying as Joe Sprinkle approached Merle Collison's Buick. That fact is not reflected in quotations from his statements to the press, but even if true, it proves nothing about Caril's complicity in ten homicides.

p. 198: Joe Sprinkle's description of his fight with Charlie Starkweather is quoted by William Allen, on page 124, and by Jeff O'Donnell, on pages 105–06.

p. 200: Caril Ann's admissions to Romer and Baldry are quoted by author Jeff O'Donnell, on pages 107–08 of *Starkweather.*

p. 201: Sheriff Heflin's assessment of his own marksmanship is quoted by William Allen, on page 125.

p. 203: Charlie's comments to Heflin and Ainslie are reported with trivial variations in numerous sources. I have quoted here from William Allen's *Starkweather,* page 127, as a generally reliable source.

15 Buried Alive

pp. 204–05: Deputy Romer's comments to the press are quoted by William Allen, on page 127.

p. 205: Charlie's boast to the authorities is taken from page 128 of William Allen's *Starkweather.*

p. 206: Sheriff Karnopp's observation on the Lincoln vigilantes is quoted by author Jeff O'Donnell, on page 112.

p. 206: Lt. Henninger's memory of the confrontation with Sheriff Heflin is quoted by William Allen, on page 129.

p. 207: Charlie's memories of his first night in jail are quoted in James Reinhardt's *Murderous Trail,* on pages 105–06.

p. 209: Starkweather's facetious remark about the gas chamber is quoted by William Allen, on page 131.

p. 210: Sheriff Karnopp's opinion on Charlie's escape plan is quoted on page 131 of William Allen's *Starkweather.*

p. 211: The exchange between Charlie and Sheriff Karnopp is quoted with minor variations by several sources, including William Allen (on pages 131–32) and Jeff O'Donnell (on page 114).

pp. 211–12: Gertrude Karnopp's conversation with Caril is quoted by William Allen on pages 133–34.

pp. 213–16: Excerpts from Charlie's confession of February 1, 1958 are quoted in *Caril,* on pages 95–106.

p. 216: A transcript of Caril Ann's February 2 interrogation is preserved as an appendix to Jeff O'Donnell's *Starkweather,* on pages 167–79.

pp. 221–22: Excerpts from Harold Robinson's report are quoted by O'Donnell, on pages 163–65.

p. 223: Starkweather's letter to Pansy Street is reproduced by O'Donnell, on page 182.

pp. 224–25: Selections from Charlie's statement of February 27 are quoted in *Caril,* on pages 106–11.

pp. 225–26: Charlie's letter to Elmer Scheele is presented intact by author Jeff O'Donnell, on page 180.

p. 226: The excerpt from Charlie's second letter to Scheele is quoted by William Allen, on page 141.

pp. 227–28: Helen Starkweather's letter to the *Lincoln Journal* is reprinted by O'Donnell, on page 181.

p. 228: Charlie's comment on prison and death, which provides this chapter with its title, is quoted by James Reinhardt on page 51 of his *Murderous Trail.*

16 "Nobody Remembers a Crazy Man"

pp. 229–30: Excerpts from the *World Herald* editorial are quoted by William Allen, on page 137 of *Starkweather.*

p. 230: Judge Spencer's remark to the lawyers is quoted by Allen, on page 139.

p. 230: Clem Gaughan's observation is quoted on page 130 of William Allen's *Starkweather.*

p. 232: Charlie's comment on Elmer Scheele is quoted from page 63 of Reinhardt's *Murderous Trail.*

p. 232: The psychological assessment of Charlie is quoted by Reinhardt, on page 11. Clem Gaughan's announcement of the insanity plea is quoted on page 140 of Allen's *Starkweather.*

p. 233: Charlie's remarks on insanity and the desire to "burn" are quoted by Reinhardt, on pages 32 and 72. John O'Hearne's diagnosis of Charlie is quoted by William Allen, on page 160.

p. 236: Charlie's fear of being portrayed as insane is quoted by Reinhardt, on page 32.

pp. 236–38: Excerpts from Charlie's conversations with Reinhardt are drawn from Reinhardt's *Murderous Trail,* pages 13, 19–20, 80, 82, 92, 104–05, and 107–08.

p. 239: Reinhardt's conclusions on Charlie are gleaned from pages 31, 53, and 108 of his book on the case. Charlie's description of his dream gone sour is quoted by Reinhardt on page 90.

p. 240: The appeal court's assessment of Charlie is quoted by author Jeff O'Donnell, on page 157 of *Starkweather.*

17 Self-Defense

p. 243ff.: Except where noted otherwise, all dialogue quoted in this chapter is drawn from the transcripts of Charlie's murder trial.

pp. 247–48: John McArthur's comment to the press is quoted on page 123 of Jeff O'Donnell's *Starkweather.*

p. 252: Guy Starkweather's congratulations of Elmer Scheele is quoted by William Allen, on page 145.

p. 256: Charlie's clash with the Iowa photographer is described, with variations, by both William Allen (page 137) and Glenn Desmond (page 147).

p. 272: Guy Starkweather's remarks to the press are quoted by William Allen, on page 156, and by James Reinhardt, on page v.

18 "I Don't Care If She Lives or Dies"

pp. 274–75: Excerpts from Caril Ann's press conference, along with Ninette Beaver's impressions, are quoted by authors Beaver, Ripley and Trese in *Caril,* pages 128–29.

p. 275ff.: Except as noted otherwise, the dialogue from Caril Ann's trial is quoted from court transcripts.

p. 295: Beaver's observation is recorded on page 151 of *Caril.*

19 A Handful of Sand

pp. 312–13: Charlie's correspondence with his family is quoted by various authors, including William Allen, on pages 166–67 of *Starkweather*.

p. 312: Starkweather's observations on prison life are quoted by Reinhardt, on pages 110–11.

p. 313: Marjorie Marlette's remarks on Starkweather are quoted by William Allen, pages 10–11.

p. 314: Dialogue from Charlie's April 1959 clemency hearing is quoted from the transcript of that proceeding.

p. 316ff.: Dialogue from Caril Ann's May 1959 hearing on McArthur's motion for a new trial is quoted from the official transcript.

pp. 319–20: Caril Ann's correspondence with the White House is quoted by various authors, including Beaver et al., on page 216 of *Caril*.

pp. 322–23: The text of Charlie's final interview is reproduced in an appendix to Jeff O'Donnell's *Starkweather*, pages 184–86.

p. 323: Charlie's response to Warner Smith is described, with variations, by William Allen (page 175) and Jeff O'Donnell (page 154). His comments to Mike Shimerda and his mother on June 24 are quoted by Allen, on page 175.

Epilogue: "Only My Story Will Live"

pp. 329–30: Excerpts from Caril's February 1967 testimony are quoted by authors Beaver, Ripley, and Trese, on page 239 of *Caril*.

p. 331ff.: Quotations from various interviews in the NBC documentary "Growing Up in Prison" are reprinted in *Caril*, on pages 256–67.

p. 334ff.: Testimony from Caril Ann's parole hearing is quoted in various published sources, including Glenn Desmond's *Charles and Caril* (pages 162–64) and the sympathetic biography *Caril*, pp. 290–301.

p. 344: Beaver's description of Caril Ann's "flashing" eyes is quoted from *Caril*, page 310.

pp. 345–46: Excerpts from the October 1973 pardon board hearing are quoted from *Caril*, page 314.

pp. 346 and 348: Charlie Starkweather's craving for publicity is documented with quotations in Reinhardt's *Murderous Trail,* on pages 90–94.

p. 348: Quotations regarding Caril Ann's 1976 parole are drawn from *Newsweek* (June 21, 1976), page 50.

p. 348: Lucille Splinter is quoted from a UPI interview, published on September 28, 1981.

p. 349: Comments relative to Caril Ann's appearance on *Lie Detector* are drawn from the *New York Times* (February 20, 1983) and UPI interviews published on February 21–22, 1983. The results of the SRI Research poll were published by UPI on March 27, 1983.

pp. 349–50: Caril Ann's continuing campaign for vindication, including her comments on *A Current Affair,* is covered in a UPI wire story of November 3, 1989, and in the Omaha *World Herald* (September 14, 1990). Joe Carroll's response is quoted in a UPI interview published on November 7, 1989.

NEW YORK TIMES BESTSELLING
AUTHOR OF *RAGING HEART*

SHEILA WELLER

SAINT
OF
CIRCUMSTANCE

THE UNTOLD STORY BEHIND
THE ALEX KELLY RAPE CASE:
GROWING UP RICH AND OUT OF CONTROL

In this explosive book, Sheila Weller reveals the
untold story of rapist Alex Kelly—exposing a
community of wealth, privilege, and closely
guarded secrets.

**Available in Hardcover
from Pocket Books**

POCKET
B O O K S